KILLING
MR. HYDE

by
MICHAEL LASSMAN

ISBN: 978-1-942451-02-0
eBook: 978-1-942451-12-9

Published by
Yorkshire Publishing
6271 E. 120th Court
Suite 200
Tulsa, Ok 74137
www.yorkshirepublishing.com

Text Design: Lisa Simpson

CONTENTS

Author's Note

Some of the names in this book have been changed to protect the anonymity of those discussed and some details of history have been omitted to protect the "not so innocent", especially myself.

Time, long periods of incoherency and despondency have blurred some of my memories and I also realize that perceptions of history are sometimes recollected based on how we subconsciously need to piece together the past. The stories in this book are to the best of my knowledge true, but I stand to be corrected.

Dedication

For Lori, Steven, Caroline, and my friend Lord. Thank you for your patience, unconditional love, and support. I hope I'm better than I used to be in your eyes.

PREFACE

Don't allow the opening pages of this book to frighten you away, and try not to roll your eyes in exhausted annoyance, wrongly assuming that I'm simply another "Bible thumping" pastoral zealot, hell bent (heck bent, I mean!) on forcing more boring, confusing, and wordy Bible verses on you. Refrain, at least for a few more chapters, from speculating that this book is probably just another diatribe full of religious and spiritual rhetoric that will have absolutely no meaning or bearing on your life whatsoever. I know you want something different! I did too!

I've read dozens of religious, spiritual, and self-help books. Some of them were very good, but most did not translate into life-changing habits for me. I'd finish them, say, "that was nice, or good, maybe thought-provoking or insightful," and then I'd go about my life still saddled with the same poor spirit I'd had for years and feeling no closer to God, no different. "Can someone PLEASE give me some kind of practical application that I can actually use to make my life better? Can someone draw me a 'road map for dummies' on how to better live my life? How about show me a few ways where I can improve my life and its impact? Could you make that God of mine something real and interactive, not just conceptual, confusing, or a million miles away? While you're at it, can you throw in some tangible benefits like happiness, joy, and feelings of freedom? Don't tell me the meaning of life with esoteric, generic, lofty words from a higher spiritual plane; show me what the meaning of MY life is! Teach me how to identify, in concrete terms, just what my purpose in this life is, and give me a step-by-step guide on how to pursue it! I hear Christians talk about communicating with God, but I don't get it. I don't believe them. Is it really possible to communicate with God? Is it really possible to hear what he's saying to me?"

These are all questions I used to ask. The answers seemed too far out of reach for me, too confusing, incomprehensible, and to be honest, like unattainable ideals I was certain I'd never find and really didn't care to waste time trying.

I wasn't looking for God. He was looking for me. And He found me.

He's trying to find you too! You just have to be willing to let Him! Willingness is a process, however, and an assignment that takes some difficult work. It's difficult, because allowing God to find you is a game that requires you to feel pain, frustration, sadness, hopelessness, and a whole lot of ego deflation before advancing toward the objective. In the final analysis, however, the happiness, joy, peace, love, and freedom you receive will dwarf the small amount of fire you'll have to walk through to get it. You see, God doesn't make the terms too hard for those who honestly seek Him.

This book chronicles the exact process I went through that allowed me to have this life-changing spiritual awakening. It will illustrate exactly how I recovered from a hopeless state of alcoholism, the path God allowed me to go down, and the experiences He allowed me to have that He knew would drive me back into His arms.

This book isn't about alcoholism or addiction. That was just my journey back to God. It's about any adversity God may choose to put in your life as a means to draw you back to Him. It could be divorce, chronic unemployment, the death of someone close to you, or haunting sexual, physical, or emotional abuse. Maybe it's cancer, another sickness, trouble with the law, jail time, loneliness, depression, mistakes from your past, financial ruin, a seemingly hopeless marriage, or problem children. You see, God will do "whatever" He needs to do in your life to bring you back into the safety and middle of His herd. For most of us, myself included, those methods usually involve a significant amount of pain, because pain motivates change. Fences built to keep sheep in God's pasture aren't made of leafy greens. They are coursing with electricity, lined with barbed wire, and are designed to cause pain when one attempts to leave the confines of God's meadow.

So if you're outside that fence right now, tired of hurting yourself or hurting others, and if you really want to change your life, then keep reading. If you're desperate to be happy, joyous, and free, don't put this book down. If you want to learn how to really, I mean really, communicate with God, then this book might just promise that. If you've never found God or lost Him somewhere along the way, these pages can show you just how to find or reunite with Him. My experiences may show you how to develop a very personal relationship with God, to see exactly what God's purpose and plan for YOUR life might be, and give you a step-by-step road map of just how to navigate that journey! All you have to be is "open" and "willing" to stop "fighting!" Be ready to surrender to everyone and everything you are battling and be open to whatever God begins to ask of you. Frightening, I know! I was willing to do neither. My mind was closed and I wanted to fight everything and everyone that crossed my path in life. It wasn't easy, but that "electric fence" worked!

The purpose of this book can be summed up in a paragraph or two with the following analogy. It's the first thought that God put into my mind before He asked me to write this book. It describes my relationship with God before my awakening and transformation and it goes like this . . .

Imagine the days before cell phones when calls were transmitted over long, convoluted, and disjointed telephone wires. I'd place a "landline" call to God and He would pick up. I sensed He was always on the other end but was forever cutting in and out. There was a lot of static on the line. I could sometimes make out a phrase or two, but most of the time I'd either catch a cryptic word here or there or couldn't hear anything He was saying at all. I was pretty sure God had the same problem. He couldn't hear, with any clarity, what I was saying or asking, because there was just too much interference on the line. We had a bad connection every time I called Him or He tried to call me. I didn't know if my prayers were getting through to Him, and I certainly couldn't ascertain what He was trying to say to me. Communication was broken, if not completely nonexistent.

All that "static on the line" represented the things that were blocking me from being able to communicate with God: my pride, ego, self-will, self-sufficiency, selfishness, resentments, fear, shame, and guilt were all causing two-way transmission problems. My unwillingness to surrender to God, closed-mindedness, and lack of discipline in life, as well as my refusal to help others, were also things keeping me from being able to communicate with God.

Does that sound about how you'd describe your communication efforts with God? Vague at best, unclear, uncertain, frustrating, and ineffective? That was mine, so I just stopped calling until my life became desperate and broken enough to want to begin to remove that static, one segment at a time. As I did, the communication began to improve, and God's voice became clearer to me. He could hear more of what I was praying and I more of His direction. What started out as a process I nearly gave up on became easier and went faster as those lines began to open up and a relationship began to form.

What is the "static" on your line to God? What's blocking you from effectively communicating with God and from developing a personal relationship with Him? In my case, I didn't know, and you may not either, but God showed me and He helped me remove it, and by reading on, this book may help you find and remove what's blocking you from God! So hang tight!

Why did I write this book? Because the last time I called God, He told me to do something to help others find what was given so freely to me. I didn't want to open my life up to you. It's an embarrassing, humiliating, painful, and frightening prospect. But God has asked me to do it. This book is all part of God's plan and purpose for my life. God says He has given us EVERYTHING we need to serve His purpose with our lives, and that includes our experiences. He says that NOTHING is wasted and that everything that has happened in our lives, overlaid with the gifts and talents God has given each one of us as individuals, needs to be used to make us most effective in executing our mission in life.

As you join me on this journey, you'll find this book littered with very personal, but true, stories. Some are serious, some sad and tragic, some, at times, unbelievable and funny, but in the end you'll see a triumphant victory over a seemingly hopeless situation. You'll see pain, sadness, evil, weakness, and desperation converted into healing, restoration, strength, and happiness.

I paid an expensive price for a lot of those experiences, as did those close to me, but Christ paid the most expensive price for all of us. Jesus didn't hide out in the wilderness, nor did He avoid God's children throughout His life, then quietly and anonymously sneak off into a cave and allow Himself to be crucified. Who would that have helped? No one! He opened up His life and His death so that others could see the path to eternal life. Christ's responsibility, given to Him by His Father, was to show the world His mission in life.

And I have that same responsibility. I can hide out behind my computer screen, in the office, or at home. I can avoid people, keep the "good news" of my conversion to myself, and seal away my life and experiences, the death of my old self, and the resurrection of a new me, and no one would ever know. That, unfortunately, would be a sad use of my life, a monumental shame, a disservice to God, and a colossal disappointment to all I faced as I walk through the pearly gates someday. I can't live with that. So with God's help I am obligated to share my life, my death, and my resurrection with you in humbling detail. My life's misery has become a part of my ministry that illustrates a story that may help you find or reconnect with the same God who saved my life.

You see, I was what they call a "lost sheep" in the Bible. Sounds kind of sad, yet sweet at the same time, doesn't it? But don't let that picture of a gentle Jesus cuddling a cute little lamb fool you. God will do whatever He has to do to reach us, to find us when we're lost. He will use any means necessary to bring us back, and His ways are not always gentle. In fact, they're rather anything but gentle. God sought me out and he found me all right. He returned me to his flock, but it wasn't in the pleasant kind of way most of us visualize—a soft-spoken shepherd combing the rolling fields of green grass searching for a silly little sheep. He wasn't a bemused "tender of the flock" playing hide-and-seek on a warm sunny day, looking for a charming lost lamb, oblivious to his plight, chewing on fresh flowers and drinking from cool, clear, bubbling streams. It was cold, dark, rainy, and anything but pleasant. I was hurting myself, hurting everyone I came into contact with, and doing everything I could to hide from my Shepherd. I didn't want Him to find me. But He did, and my life was changed as I discovered how to have a relationship with God where I could actually communicate with Him, hear Him. I found how to identify just what my purpose in this life is, just what God's plan for me was. And along the way I found a happiness I didn't think existed, joy in everything I do, and a personal freedom that can be hard to explain, but easy to reach! And because of the transformation in my life, I'm confident that this book can help you attain that same wisdom, purpose, and joy. I'm hoping I can share, exchange, and transfer all of that to you. Well . . . I can't do it. God can do it through me and He has not only asked me to do it, He's promised to show me exactly what to write and how to best convey it to you! So as you read my story, don't look for the differences, look for the similarities. My life and experiences are unique, but my problems are universal.

My quest for happiness, meaning, and purpose is probably similar to yours. Look at my process and try to make it applicable to your life, and hopefully, unlike all the other "life-changing" books that you've finished reading (or quit reading by chapter three), this one might just actually resonate!

I'm not religious or a Bible scholar. As a matter of fact, I have the equivalent of a third grade education when it comes to the Bible. I still have to use the table of contents to find the books in the Bible and, more often than not, I find the "children's versions" easier to understand than Mr. King James. (I really like the pictures!) When it comes to the Bible, the most interesting and perplexing thing to me is how those super thin pages are so durable! They never tear! Have you ever seen a Bible with torn pages? Neither have I! (Maybe that's because no one ever reads them!) For this book, however, I will generally refer to the Bible my mother gave to my wife the day we got married some twenty-seven years ago. The same Bible my wife eventually threw out, along with me, the day she'd finally had enough! I guess Mom had enough foresight to know that the poor, unsuspecting, and unfortunate woman who became my wife might just need it along the way. It turns out she was right.

I'll be starting with this first Bible quote in a few moments for two reasons: The first is that I've learned to always bring God into everything I do. I have learned to invite Him in with a prayer, a quiet invitation, or with a focus on His word. The second reason is that God communicates with me today, and He is the one who asked me to write this book. It wasn't always that way though, as you'll see by reading just a little bit further. I really don't know why, but when He tells me to do something today, I just do it. I do, typically, make the mistake of asking Him why. Or where is this going God? But just like Jack Nicholson says in *A Few Good Men,* God snaps back, "You can't handle the reason." He's probably right. If God unfolded the whole plan behind this book to me and everything that followed its publishing, I'm sure I'd "freak out" and not do it, or figure out a way to screw it up. So God gives me just one instruction at a time and I've learned to "Just do it."

When the message came to me to write this book, I said "Okay God, I'm not an author, an English major, or even a good typist, but if you tell me to, then I will." Once that decision was made, I then waited for the next message. Someone explained God's instructions to me like this. When God speaks to you and tries to give you direction in life, it's like walking in the dark with a dimly lit lantern. You can only see a few feet in front of you and you're only sure of your next step or two. If you try to figure out what's up ahead, you just get lost, confused, and disillusioned. It's just too dark and you'll never be able to see what lies out there in the blackness, what lies in your future. Probably a lot of frightening things, that if known, would keep you from pushing on through this thing we call life. There are probably many wonderful surprises as well, some of those even coming from a few of the frightening moments we're sure to encounter along the way. In any case, doing nothing, not trudging forward into the unknown is a sad prospect for a life. You might be able to avoid some of the struggles, obstacles, and pain that lie ahead, but you'll also miss out on all the joy, the happiness, and the victories that result from overcoming adversity! Plus . . . you never know who you might run into in the dark!

So I asked, "What's the first step God?" and He said, "Start." That instruction came directly through the pastor at LifeChurch! It was a Wednesday when God told me to write this book. That Sunday I went to a LifeChurch service and Pastor Craig Groeschel, as if he were looking directly at me, said, "Maybe God has been calling you to write a book and the only message he wants you to hear is 'Start!'" So I did! I plopped down at my computer, typed out the title of this book, and then just sat there staring at a mostly blank page patting myself on the back for "Starting!" Not much of a start, but a positive action nonetheless. So I sat there staring, chuckling to myself about my momentous beginning and thought, "Okay, now what?" Well since James Earl Jones's voice didn't fill my office with the next bit of inspiration, I had to think to myself for a minute. "Okay Mike, how does God speak to people?" Well occasionally He does speak to people directly, like with Moses and Abraham, but it's rare. More often than not, I find that God speaks to me in three other ways. The first way is through my own thoughts. Usually there is only one person in my head, and that's the person God directs most of the time and wants me to hear. But today there isn't much going on up there, so I go to option two. God speaks to me through other people. I got up from my computer, went to talk to my brother and his wife, and then ran down to Starbucks and creeped out some poor little barista with too many questions and WAY too much interest in everything she said. Nothing. So I went to my last option, which should have been my first, and pulled out my Bible. The Bible IS God's word, so whatever you read is always God speaking to you. As I opened it up something unexpected happened. There was a small piece of notebook paper inside. On it, written in my fifteen-year-old daughter's handwriting was "Lamentations 3: 1-33." I went to the table of contents because, who in the heck knows where Lamentations is? I read the passage and it described in detail exactly where I was in life less than a year ago. I knew then that this was where God wanted to begin telling this story. Every paragraph, every sentence in this book, might have been typed by me and revised by some editor, but the message is directly from God. Why he wanted me to write it and what "life" it takes on is anyone's guess; all I knew was that I was supposed to write it. I have a notion that the pages of this book were meant for someone else, probably you, since you're reading it, but I can't say for certain. All I know is that God uses us in all kinds of ways to serve His purpose, and HIS purpose is ALWAYS to bring unbelievers into the fold and to make current believers more useful in serving the purpose He has assigned to them. So I'll go out on a limb and say we wrote this book to help others, but who knows? It might just end up in the scrap heap behind my house, much like the human scrap heap I ended up facedown on just a year ago.

The verses said, "I am the man who has seen the afflictions that come from the rod of God's wrath. He has brought me into deepest darkness, shutting out all light. He has turned against me. Day and night His hand is heavy on me. He has made me old and broken my bones. He has built forts against me and surrounded me with anguish and distress. He buried me in dark places, like those long dead. He has walled me in; I cannot escape; He has fastened me with heavy chains. And though I cry and shout, He will NOT hear my prayers! He has shut me into a place of high, smooth walls, He has filled my path with detours. He lurks like a bear, like a lion, waiting to attack me. He has dragged me into the underbrush and torn me with His claws, and left me bleeding and desolate. He has bent his bow and aimed it squarely at me, and sent His arrows deep within my heart. My own people laugh at me; all day long they sing their ribald songs. He has filled me with bitterness, and given me a cup of deepest sorrows to drink. He has made me eat gravel and broken my teeth; He has rolled me in ashes and dirt. O Lord, all peace and all prosperity have long since gone, for You have taken them away. I have forgotten what enjoyment is. All hope is gone; my strength has turned to water, for the Lord has left me. Oh, remember the bitterness and suffering You have dealt to me! For I can never forget those awful years; always my soul will live in utter shame."

I bet you're thinking to yourself, "Wow, I can't wait to get to know this kind of God; he's definitely someone I want in my corner!" This may sound strange to you, but that's exactly the kind of God I needed! One that would do "anything necessary" to rescue me from myself! May you come to find God a little easier than I did!

CHAPTER 1

DESPAIR

I awoke fully clothed, facedown on the living room floor of my apartment. My head was perfectly centered in a large pool of bloodstained ivory carpet. I rolled over on my hands and knees, then up to my feet and staggered to the bathroom to check my face in the mirror. I vaguely noticed that the sliding shower doors in the guest bathroom had been completely knocked off their tracks and were lying precariously against the back wall of the shower. I don't recall how that happened. I looked in the mirror and saw nothing. No cuts, no bruises, no scrapes or scratches, no dried up bloody nose. Just carpet imprinted bloodstains on the side of my face that had been pressed against the floor for who knows how long. As the drawn face stared back at me, I studied the black shadows under my eyes and how they contrasted with my unruly brown and gray hair that looked more like dried out straw, no doubt brought on by dehydration from the alcohol. A five-day patchy salt-and-pepper beard highlighted my glossy bloodshot eyes, and I wasn't sure I recognized the image reflecting me. I couldn't tell you what time it was, or even what day for that matter. To this day, I have no idea where that two-foot bloodstain on the carpet came from. The sad thing about the mysterious bloody spot and fallen shower doors was that I really didn't give it another thought. The dominant thought in my head was, "Where is that bottle of vodka?" The preliminary "shakes" were beginning, and without a few quick shots they would soon turn to uncontrollable tremors. I found the bottle on the kitchen counter about a third full. Without missing a step, I grabbed the bottle and took a big swig, but before the antidote hit the back of my throat, I vomited it back up along with a stomach full of bile. This was a common problem and usually a violent reminder that in order to get myself to a point where I could drink again, I'd have to ease into those first couple of shots before my stomach would begin to relax and allow me to take it down with ease and volume. I tried again, this time with a smaller sip, then another, and another. After six or seven small shots, my insides had relaxed enough, the trembling stopped, and I was able to begin to take some larger gulps.

Thirty minutes later, after setting myself straight and finishing what was left of the bottle, my senses (or at least what I called "my senses" those days) began to come back. I made a cursory review of my apartment and checked the date and time, both being of paramount importance. It was not Sunday, which was good, because hard liquor isn't sold on Sundays in Oklahoma, and it was not before 10:00 a.m. or after 8:00 p.m., liquor store opening and closing times.

I then checked my phone to see who called or texted me, or more concerning to me, whom I might have called or texted, which was always a frightening prospect, because there is no telling what I might do or say in a blackout. Several missed calls from friends, family, and employees, but unlike some days, no horror-filled texts. Fortunately I hadn't terrorized anyone via my cell phone the night before.

As I began picking up a few things around the apartment trying to piece together the evening in my head, I started contemplating a shower. A trip to the liquor store would be required to make it through the day and that night. Not much of a thought beyond that. As I picked up, I noticed the dining room table buried in work checkbooks, invoices, bills, and half-written illegible checks. Atop it all was a loaded 9mm automatic Smith and Wesson handgun.

I stopped and stared at it for a moment. I'd always told myself suicide was not an option, and I tried to block that notion from my mind, but as the bits and pieces of the evening before resurfaced in my memory, I recalled putting the gun to my head just to see what it would feel like, never intending to follow through. I even recalled dropping the clip, checking the chamber, and pulling the trigger, just to hear and feel the "click" and cold steel against my temple. It wasn't the first time I'd done that. I'd say the actual thought of going through with it wasn't an option, but I'm not so sure of it. In any case, it was a dangerous proposition, since not only did I rarely remember what I'd done in a blackout, I certainly had no control over it.

I hadn't been to work in a week and my business was a colossal mess. There were past due invoices, unshipped items, bank reports due, taxes not paid, and volumes of unreturned messages overfilling my office voice mail account. My twenty-four-year marriage was over, my kids wouldn't speak to me, and my family was beside themselves trying to figure out what to do with me. For the most part, they had all exhausted themselves with failed attempt after failed attempt, detox after detox, and treatment center after treatment center to help me get sober. They had pretty much given up. So had I.

I tilted up what was left in my vodka bottle and washed down a Xanax before turning on the shower. I had a small window of time I could spend out in public, and it was time. Drunk enough to function fairly well, but not drunk enough to draw much attention to myself. Besides, I was only going down to the liquor store and then right back to my apartment to drink myself into oblivion again. I'd long since stopped caring what the guy at the liquor store thought about me. I used to rotate which liquor stores I went to so the same employees wouldn't see me every day, but rather once a week. I had a little routine where I'd wander around the store, ask a few refined questions about this merlot or that chardonnay, then pick one for show, grab a twelve-pack of some fancy imported beer I pretended would be for my sophisticated friends, and finish with a large bottle of vodka. After a while I realized the clerks had seen enough guys like me that they knew I was a raging alcoholic and frankly didn't give a damn. So I stopped the show, swallowed what little pride I had left and just went straight for the vodka. I guess waiting outside the liquor store twenty minutes before opening time was giveaway enough. The pride might have been gone, but the shame wasn't. No matter how hard I tried, I recall never being able to look the cashier in the eye. It wasn't because I was embarrassed or afraid of him, it was more the horror of seeing my own reflection in his eyes, in his pity for me. I knew who I was, I just didn't like the painful reminder of seeing the person I hated the most in someone else's eyes.

I left with my bottle, had the cap off, and took a long slow pull on it before I even left the parking lot in my "drunk truck." I called it my "drunk truck" because my primary vehicle had an interlock system installed in it from a DUI I'd gotten a year earlier. I might as well have just thrown the keys to my primary vehicle away. Since having the device installed, I can count on one hand how many times I was below the limit which was required to start it. Realizing that I had to be places and that I also had to have alcohol in my system at all times made it necessary for me to buy an old "beater" pickup under the guise of it being a "work truck." Not to mention, it was less likely anyone would recognize me in that old truck. It was time to get home. What I'd bought, I thought, should be more than enough to get me through the day, the night, and have enough left over in the morning to take care of the morning terrors. I was always wrong about that.

I tried to send out a few jolly texts in an attempt to fool family, friends, and employees that all was well, or that I was busy with this or that. Then I'd cozy into my easy chair and two hours later was out again.

This time I woke up and it was dark outside. I reached for my bottle and it was way past the "low fuel" line, and I knew I'd never make it through the night, let alone the next morning. Rationing was not an option, so I chugged the remainder, shook the cobwebs out of my head, brushed my teeth, and left the apartment for a convenience store a few blocks away. Too drunk to drive, I decided to walk. It was about a ten-minute jaunt down Denver Avenue, which crossed over a busy highway, and then two more blocks south. I would get a case of 3.2 beer that would get me through the rest of the night, when I woke up around 4 a.m. beginning to withdraw, and then enough to keep me stable until 10 a.m. the next morning when the liquor stores re-opened.

I clanged through the apartment's courtyard gate and out onto Denver Street, sensing an unsettling aura on this unusually quiet night. I always took my 9mm handgun, because the southwest side of downtown Tulsa wasn't the safest part of town. As I crossed the overpass on foot, I looked down at the cars racing by on the highway below, and a fleeting thought of jumping crossed my mind but quickly faded as I approached the other side. Another block and I was inside the convenience store, had my arms around a case of Natural Light, a sandwich, and a can of Skoal. I always used a credit card, because I found that the trembling of my hands often made it difficult and embarrassing to dig for cash and accept change. As I walked out the side door and back down to the street I had to duck into the alley to slam a couple of beers before heading home. Waiting wasn't an option due to the "shakes," so I tore back the cardboard packaging, popped the top on the first one, and took it down in one drink. The second quickly followed, and I tossed both empty cans into the bushes nearby. If you had seen me, you'd have thought, "what a bum," but I didn't think that at all. I had no idea who I was.

As I reached the overpass again, I paused and looked across to make sure it was clear. I didn't like getting trapped on the bridge when a bum (I guess another bum), vagrant, homeless man, or some hoodlum was also passing. All clear. I began walking, case (minus two) in hand, feeling a sense of ease just having the booze tucked under my arm and a little in my stomach. At the midpoint of the bridge I looked up, and out of nowhere appeared a middle-aged black man wearing a hoodie. I was immediately startled, because I'd checked that bridge and there was absolutely no one near it. I had no idea where he came from, but there he was, twenty paces in front of me and walking directly toward me. It was too late to cross to the other side without making it look obvious that I was avoiding him. I patted my pocket to make sure the 9mm was still there and walked with a little more authority, with my head up as we drew closer together. I glanced quickly up into his eyes. They were bloodshot and seemed to have a yellowish glow to them. He glided eerily toward me, and something told me this wasn't going to be an effortless walk by. As we approached each other, everything seemed to shift to slow motion. He locked in on my eyes and without missing a passing step uttered the words, "I see death." It didn't feel as if he were talking to me but rather reporting my status or condition to himself, or more so to some unknown person he appeared to be in contact with. My heart skipped a beat and I kept walking, half sober now and half in shock. I turned around after I was eight or nine steps past to make sure he was still moving in the opposite direction. He was gone! I knew that was impossible since the overpass bridge was another fifty yards across, and unless he jumped in that few seconds, he just disappeared. You might think I'm crazy or that I was delusional from the booze, but it was clear as day to me. He was Satan or one of his minions, and I knew it.

I hurriedly walked back to my apartment, and while ascending the three flights of concrete stairs, tripped on the way up and fell face-first into the concrete steps, scattering beer cans down toward the last landing. Man that hurt! Blood began pouring from my nose and the newly created gash on my forehead. I quickly scooped up my now dented and shaken beer cans, hustled back to my apartment, locked both locks, wiped my face, sat back down in my chair and downed three more beers before I was finally able to calm down again. An hour later I was out.

You might think this was "the bottom" for me, but it wasn't. The worst was yet to come. I knew it, but couldn't—or worse, wouldn't—do anything about it.

It was hard to imagine how I'd fallen into this hopeless state of disrepair. I'd come from a perfectly stable, loving, and normal middle-class family. I suffered no childhood trauma and was a privileged kid that had everything I needed and most of what I wanted. I was a well-adjusted, popular teen who performed well in school and even better in high school athletics. I was fortunate enough to graduate from a major university and had a wildly successful career in the energy business, even spending time on Wall Street with the prestigious Goldman Sachs. I'd started and managed several successful businesses, from coffee franchises to overstock outdoor gear. I had a beautiful wife of twenty-four years, two incredible and talented children, a big house, a bigger 401k, and a highly regarded reputation in community, social, and religious circles in my city. It was a perfect life to someone looking in from the outside. A disaster from someone on the inside, looking out.

In a few short years, all that was gone. The career, the businesses, the wife and kids, the money, and the reputation had been lost. I was now in a downtown Tulsa apartment, alone with my bottle. I was watching what was left of my business and finances implode. Communication with my children had been severed, and the served divorce papers were lying on the coffee table under a scattered mess of beer cans and spit cups. I couldn't stay sober long enough to pay my bills, manage my business, or even respond to the divorce summons. Most of the family and friends who had tried to help me earlier had pretty much given up on me, and even if they hadn't, I wasn't willing to let them help me. It's laughable to say, but even in the condition I was in, I had too much pride, or maybe too much shame, to accept help from anyone offering.

I could sense the walls of a disintegrating life closing in on me, but I just couldn't, or wouldn't do anything about it. I had no plan and no wish for recovery. All I knew was that I couldn't survive without alcohol. The primal and innate drivers of the normal man—food, protection, and love—had all been usurped by an insane need for alcohol. Feeding the addiction was more important than my wife, my children, my family, my reputation, my finances, and even my personal protection.

I was in a complete and hopeless state of despair, utterly demoralized, broken beyond repair, delusional and actually insane, even though I didn't think so at the time. I guess the only real plan I had was to do whatever it took to satisfy my addiction and hope that someone else would come and save me. I was certainly incapable of saving myself, and my cries to God had fallen on what I thought were deaf ears. The only problem with that plan was that no one else could save me. The irony and the tragedy of it all was that the two people who could return me from the gates of insanity and death were the last two I ever thought to call on. Myself and God. I wasn't willing, and I assumed He wasn't ready.

So the nightmare would continue. . . .

CHAPTER 2

CHILDHOOD

In retrospect, it's really amazing to me how much events from our childhood can shape our lives. I'm convinced that the greatest need for psychology, the time in your life where some psychological guidance would be most effective, would have to be in your early developmental years. The problem is that human nature never takes a preventative approach to anything. We wait until we're "all screwed up," until our lives have become unbelievably complicated and complex, and then we seek help. Then it takes years of help and layers of unhealthy behaviors to unwind, only to find that the root of our troubles happened with what appeared to be insignificant childhood events. But they weren't insignificant at the time!

The other problem is that most kids just aren't that emotionally mature, introspective, or insightful enough at those ages. They can't comprehend their feelings, certainly can't verbalize them, and aren't developed enough to understand their emotions, the realities of life, or how to solve their pressing emotional crises. It's one of life's tragic ironies I suppose. Maybe it's the responsibility of the parent, but even that's an unfair burden to saddle on our caretakers, who are doing their best just to manage their own lives, provide for their children, and stay focused on the immediate needs of the family. Food, clothing, shelter, protection, and schooling all seem to overshadow psychological care for our children. Even if parents wanted to address the cognitive needs of their children, kids would be required to communicate what was going on in their little complex and undeveloped minds. The reality is that most simply aren't capable of that. In any case the preadolescent child is not well understood, and his or her psychological balance is given very little serious consideration.

When a boy finds himself on the losing end of a schoolyard scrape, his Dad may respond with phrases like: "Boys will be boys." "You're gonna get into fights." "You gotta learn how to defend yourself, kid." "Fight like a man." "Come here, let me show you a few schoolyard scrapping techniques." "What'd the other boy look like?" "You'll be all right." They may be all right physically, but how about emotionally?

As parents, we often focus on the wrong thing! We look at the surface, the situation, the fight in this case, but do we ever consider the emotional and psychological issues behind it? There are real emotions inside our children, like fear, anger, anxiety, self-consciousness, guilt, embarrassment, humiliation, and a whole host of other psychological viruses that most children just don't know how to process. These are the childhood scars that begin to shape lives. These are the events that form personalities and can define our future neuroses as well as spiritual and emotional maladies later in life.

Let me give you an example. When I was five years old and in kindergarten, my ears were the same size as they are today (but with less hair on them). So as a boy with a five-year-old head and body and ears the size of a grown man, I looked "goofy." My first week in kindergarten, and while on the playground, I was minding my own business playing on the jungle gym when some snot-nosed kid started calling me "Dumbo" because of my ears. Before long, a small contention of other children were chanting the same name. "Dumbo, Dumbo, Dumbo. . ." I was completely embarrassed and humiliated. I couldn't wait for recess to be over so I could run home and hide. That night after I'd said goodnight to my mom and dad, I pulled out a roll of duct tape and taped my ears back to the side of head, hoping they would begin to affix themselves alongside my noggin and not stick out as much. I didn't want anyone to make fun of me anymore. It was a very big deal to me. It may sound silly or petty, but their words and their actions (and that duct tape) really hurt!

In one day, at the age of five, and over a five-minute period, I became afraid of people! They made me nervous. I was scared of them, mortified that they would publicly embarrass and humiliate me! I began trying to position my head so no one could get a straight on view of my ears and see how much they stuck out. I began to hate recess, to avoid the mean kids, and to overcompensate in other areas to deflect attention from my ears. I prayed for cold days when I could wear stocking caps. Pretty ridiculous, huh?

Five years old and five minutes of teasing in 1969 began instilling in me a lifetime fear of others, irrational insecurity, high anxiety, and unhealthy and negatively compounding coping mechanisms that have lasted a lifetime! It may sound exaggerated, but it's true!

Looking back with a more mature and experienced mind, I can see how preposterous that entire scene was. My ears are normal sized now that my body has grown into them, and I never looked as goofy as Dumbo. For the five people that made fun of me, there were fifty that thought I was great. Everyone was different. Everyone had their own physical and outward flaws. Nobody was perfect. I had many other great qualities, but as children we often don't make that connection. We learn that we're different, weird, ugly, fat, stupid, or poor, and it's glaringly obvious to everyone. It defines us. At least in our own little minds!

That seed of emotional hurt began to blossom into a monster that would one day cut me to pieces through one of the most harmful coping mechanism there is—alcohol.

What about you? Can you think back to something that now seems it should have been incredibly insignificant in your childhood, but that has shaped a large part of who you are today? Some embarrassing moment or hurtful comment from a schoolmate, teacher, coach, or parent? Maybe it was something more serious? Child abuse, divorce, sexual abuse, or some horrendous family secret? Whatever it was (and I'm sure it was something), I'm going to speculate that its origins have played a large part in shaping and defining your life and your personality today. Think about it . . .

I was sadly reminded of this recently while attending a Kansas State versus Oklahoma college football game. (Go Cats! We won 31-30.) At halftime, I headed down from the stands and into the tunnel to join the other 450 boys crowded in the men's room and was patiently waiting my turn to shoulder up next to someone I didn't know to relieve myself. As I waited in this extremely crowded restroom, I heard the angry shouts of a man. I looked left, and there in the middle of the men's room an irate father was screaming at his eight-year-old son, squeezing the life out of the poor kid's right arm, and then he suddenly started beating this boy on the butt and the back of his legs. The young OU fan was crying, looked mortified, humiliated, embarrassed, and frightened as he was publicly abused in front of a huge crowd of mostly shocked other males. I was sickened. Partly because I'm not a believer in corporal or physical punishment, but mostly because it's appalling to see parents who publicly reprimand their children. I don't really know what was going on, but I'm thinking that the boy didn't want to expose himself at the long trough-style urinal just inches away from men on either side of him and was arguing to use the private stalls whose lines were three times as long. I'm guessing his "old man" wasn't willing to wait that long, was tired of his son's protestations about the urinal, and was a little cranky because his Sooners were losing. I took care of my own business and left, but couldn't help but think about the permanent scar that had just been inflicted on that poor boy. Here he was, on this absolutely beautiful, sunny Saturday, at the big game with his dad. What a special experience, the kind of day every kid looks forward to and looks back upon with fond memories. Unfortunately, not this boy. He will forever remember that awful day, where he was embarrassed, humiliated, and beaten in front of his male peers. Every time he sees an OU football game, his memory may go to that awful place, the shame, the embarrassment, the disappointing remorse of upsetting his father. Right then and there in that three-minute period, the boy was dealt an emotional and spiritual wound that could last a lifetime. On the face of it, it might not seem like much. Kid's being a pain, his dad gets frustrated, yells at him and pops him on the backside a few times, but I guarantee you, that kid is carrying around that hurt today.

The physical pain of the moment is dwarfed by the psychological damage that incident will most likely cause as it infiltrates the boy's developing spirit.

Anyway, back to me and off my preachy soapbox . . . Fast forward a couple of years, and after I'd learned enough unhealthy behaviors of my own to co-exist with others, I received a second dose of humiliation. Two of the schools bullies approached me one day in the school cafeteria and point blank asked me if I thought I could "beat up" Troy Pipkin, another boy in my grade. I had no beef with Troy; he was just another kid in my class. I certainly didn't want to fight anyone. I'd never been in a fight before, never even with a sibling, and had no idea how to defend myself, let alone strike any kind of offensive! But being in fear of these two bullies calling me a "sissy," or worse, making a lunchroom spectacle of me, I said "Yeah, I could beat him up!"

As was their mode of operation, they immediately went to Troy and told him I was telling everyone I could knock the crap out of him. They chided him into saying that he could beat me up, and with the grade school skills of a Donnie King, a fight after school was scheduled, followed by their relentless promotional efforts that attracted several dozen kids looking for some entertainment after the 3:00 bell! I was stuck! When the bell rang, there was no getting out of the fight! The word was out, and worse yet, the news had spread to the female population!

Two separate contentions of excited kids started for the park across from Lakeside Elementary. Mine consisted of me and one friend who was so frightened he couldn't speak all the way over to the park. The other included Troy and about twenty-five others, all slapping him on the back, getting him fired up, and inciting his anger by telling him that I told everyone he was a "wuss" and I could beat the heck out of him! I suppose most everyone in the larger group had figured out which side would win in advance, and they had all thrown their allegiance toward Troy.

As we reached the park, the traditional fight circle formed and we both stood in the center. Troy said, "Did you call me a 'wuss' and say you wanted to fight me?" I don't recall offering a response before a right hook popped me in the jaw. To see it again today, it probably looked and felt like getting hit by a Styrofoam water noodle swung by your grandma, but back then it was enough to knock me down and make me begin to cry. The circle erupted in laughter, began calling me names, and then rushed Troy with congratulatory slaps on the back and chants of good cheer. I slowly got up and headed toward my house several blocks away, still crying, with my friend following a few steps behind me. Halfway home, I asked him not to tell my parents. I cleaned up my red and tearstained face and went straight into my room. I was mortified, humiliated, frightened, and ashamed. It was further confirmation in my own mind that people were scary and unpredictable, and I didn't want to be around big groups of people without some kind of protection or escape plan in place.

After a while, that fear of others spawned a new and unhealthy behavior of desperately "seeking acceptance of others." My mother was the kind of parent who heaped mountains of unrealistic praise upon me, fueling that acceptance fire. She was continually letting me know that I was the smartest kid in school, the best athlete, the most popular, the best looking, and it was just a given in her eyes that I would excel at anything and everything. I believed most of it, because

I wanted to. Her affirmations comforted me and gave me a sense of confidence I was unable to generate on my own. They built up an unsure and fragile ego, and fed a delusion that was more appealing than reality. At the same time, however, those praises established an expectation, a self-imposed responsibility, that drove my need to excel in every area of my life in order to not only validate my mom's affirmations, but most importantly, also not to disappoint her.

She was just being a good mom, who loved her son and was trying to do what any good mom would do—instill confidence in her children. But like anything else, too much of a good thing is not always best. Installation of confidence is great, but it really needs to be mixed with a few doses of humility and, more importantly, reality. Was I really going to become president of the United States? (I certainly had the ears for it; sorry, Barack.) Or an eight-year-old genius? Were the Lakers already scouting me in my canvas "All Stars" and knee-high double striped socks? Of course not, but I wasn't so sure of it all. I certainly believed much of what I heard from her, and at a minimum, I allowed it to set an expectation of me that I was destined to fall short of!

This is why I'm not a supporter of "everyone gets a trophy, a medal, or a ribbon; everyone gets equal playing time, everyone wins, no one gets their feelings hurt," and so on. You get the picture. That's just not reality! Someone does lose. Someone does sit on the bench, everything is "not" fair and equal, and someone does get their feelings hurt in life. It's better to learn that when the stakes in life are lower than when it's too late as an adult and the consequences get more serious.

The flip side of this coin is exactly what parents should be teaching their kids these days. That is, we're all different. We're all uniquely and perfectly designed by God. We all have special, but different, talents and we all can't be the best in everything, but we can be the best at something! I'm not blaming my parents at all. I made the exact same mistake with my own son. I wanted him to be a "sports" kid, a popular kid, a highly social kid, an involved in every activity kind of kid. Sports, popularity (as I defined it), and extracurricular activities of my interest were important to me, but not to my son. He was crazy smart, intellectual, spatial, creative, introspective, and slightly introverted. He was happy playing alone, crafting Lego marvels, building science projects, watching political satire, and reading books on physics! But that didn't stop me from buying him baseballs, footballs, golf clubs, and motorcycles (all of which were essentially untouched by him). His lack of interest didn't stop me from dragging him to sporting events, trying to make him watch the NFL on Sundays, and continually trying to divert his attention from the academic to the mainstream! What was I telling this poor boy? I'm not happy with who you are? Really? Talk about terrible parenting! I finally figured that all out later, but what must my son have thought? My father isn't proud of me, I'll never be good enough? NO! I was absolutely proud of him, but that wasn't the message being transmitted. It was no different than the same message sent by my mother: "I'm trying to tell you you're something you're not."

My father, on the other hand, wasn't the type to heap praise and affirmation on anyone, but kept a quiet vigil, and in my mind at least, an unspoken mandate to win, to be the best, and to be successful. He used to tell me, "You can brag when you're the best, but until then don't get too cocky." I interpreted that as, "I expect you to be the best." He never came out and said he demanded greatness, but I still put that goal in my own mind. Meeting and exceeding mom's affirmations and making dad proud were the two real driving forces behind my existence. I was willing to do anything to achieve it, and "not short of sin!"

There also came this notion, this coping mechanism originating from my fear of others, that if I could somehow "win" their acceptance by any means necessary, they wouldn't want to challenge me or potentially hurt me emotionally or physically. It became extremely important for me not to be made fun of in school, not to be humiliated in front of others, not to be "called out" by the teacher or the coach, not to let others down, and not to give people a reason to think poorly of me.

I thought the answer was to become someone who was praised for their accomplishments, such as intelligence, athletic abilities, and position in the world. It's meaningless to call someone "stupid" if they are making all As. It's hard to call someone a "wuss" if they are the star quarterback on the football team or score twenty points a game on the basketball court. It's difficult to make fun of someone who wears "the right clothes," hangs out with "the right people," or does things that get noticed. It all became an elaborate "deflection" scheme to keep people from making fun of me, to avoid being embarrassed or humiliated, which were all fears that stemmed from my earliest significant childhood experiences on the playground and in the after-school fight.

Much later in life, I found out that "acceptance" was the answer. What I didn't realize back then was that acceptance means accepting others for who they are, accepting situations as they present themselves, and most importantly, accepting myself for who I am and for who God intended for me to be. But as an adolescent, it meant doing whatever I could do to get others to accept me. And so began a decade's-long journey of doing what I thought I had to do to be accepted. It was all driven by my fear of others.

By the time I was ten, my "how to function in life" operations manual was beginning to take shape. You already know that I'd developed an unhealthy fear of others, that I was willing to go to any lengths to avoid embarrassment and humiliation, that I was a people pleaser who couldn't accept failure, and that I'd perfected the "art of deflection" by appearing to excel in as many areas of my life that mattered to others in order to divert their attention from my own flaws.

What soon became evident, which I wish I could have figured out at the time, is that I wasn't the smartest kid in class. I wasn't the best athlete in school, I wasn't going to be the next Brad Pitt, and I wasn't the most popular guy this side of the Mississippi! That was a problem. If I couldn't be the best, not only would I let my parents down, but I'd lose my greatest defense mechanism, deflection. And if I couldn't deflect, people would begin to humiliate and embarrass me again. That was not an option and posed a real dilemma. If you're not the best, how do you become the best? That was easy. You lie, you cheat, you steal, you derail your competition, and you present a false image! Talk about more unhealthy layers! But that's what I did.

Don't get me wrong, it wasn't like I was in a perpetual state of deception, corruption, and sin. I only resorted to those tactics when they served my purpose. Most of the time I was a pretty good kid, a pretty normal kid I guess, and most of my existence was of good. But everyone knows that once an apple develops a rotten spot, the rest of the apple quickly deteriorates unless the decaying spot is cut out and removed. I wasn't ready to cut that spot out until much later in life, and the core of my life became rotten very quickly!

In the fifth grade a new progressive reading program was implemented in our school system. Each grade was given a series of small books that increased in difficulty. Step one books had large print, simple words, and required minimal comprehension. Step two was a bit more difficult, and by the time you reached step ten, it felt like you were reading *The Hobbit*! There was a buzz around the school and with the parents over this new progressive program, and it was clear to me that I not only needed to advance quickly through the book progression, but I also needed to do it more quickly than anyone else. Back then, it was the "honor system." When you finished one book, you notified the teacher, and she congratulated you as all the other kids looked on in either envy or in deflated self-loathing. I actually read the first couple of books and finished fairly quickly, but noticed a few of my classmates were keeping up with me and even burning through them faster than I was, so I began to develop a speed reading technique which was actually closer to "skimming and skipping pages." The pace I kept started out a half a book ahead of the other "so-called great readers" and eventually stretched into a book and a half lead. As one boy inched closer to me, I took it upon myself to tell the teacher he was cheating. The nerve! He was reprimanded and sent back down the chute just like in my favorite childhood board game! So there you have it. When necessary, I cheated to win, even sabotaged a friend to win, but I won, and no one could make fun of me for being stupid! Mission accomplished. What I didn't realize was that through this process feelings of guilt, shame, and paranoia began to develop within me and my self-image was beginning to deteriorate. None of it seems like a big deal when you're reading fifth grade *Nancy Drew* books, but it becomes a very big deal when you're managing millions of dollars on Wall Street! But that all comes much later; don't worry, we'll get there!

The same modus operandi continued on through the years. Lying to avoid punishment or being reprimanded, cheating to win and stay on top, undermining competitors, cutting corners whenever and wherever possible, and presenting and promoting a false image of who I really was, while portraying an image of who I thought others wanted me to be. It actually worked pretty well, and I don't ever recall being caught or found out. If I was, I always had a convenient excuse or a great story to cover it all up. But those same spiritual maladies I'd begun to incubate were beginning to grow. The guilt, the shame, the remorse, the paranoia, and the anxiety were growing like a cancer.

Another vivid memory of mine happened three years later when I was thirteen. The all-city two-day golf tournament was upon us. I had entered and needed to win. There was a player who was clearly a better golfer than I, and I'd made my mind up before the first tee shot that it would be necessary to cheat if I expected to win. I discussed this strategy with my two playing partners and roped them into the ruse. I would kick one here, not count one there, give myself a putt or two, and use the pencil if it became necessary. (Normal behavior for most of the golfers I play with today!)

After the first day, I "miraculously" shot a three-over-par round and had an eleven-stroke lead over the boy that should have been winning. Not bad for a thirteen-year-old! The whole thing was so unbelievable, and my cheating was obvious to everyone, including the tournament directors, parents, and the players. No one had to confront me. I knew it and was incredibly ashamed of myself, embarrassed by my actions, and extremely self-conscious about the incident. I didn't stick around to have sodas with the boys and headed out as quickly as possible, praying somehow this would end well. That night, my mother praised my efforts, congratulated me profusely, and confirmed her belief that I was such a great golfer. Dad commented that "I'd really have to blow up not to win this one!"

Well, it didn't end well. The next day, the tournament organizers assigned an adult to shadow me and only me around the entire course. The hushed whispers and the silent scornful looks of family gallery were enough to make me want to hit my ball into the woods and never come out. I finished the day twenty-six-over-par and won the tournament by one stroke! As the crowd gathered for the trophy presentation, I laid as low as possible and didn't say a word. When they announced my name as the first-place winner and handed me the largest trophy I'd ever received, the crowd fell silent. I don't recall a hint of applause, congratulatory slaps on the back, or even any smiles. As the second-place trophy was awarded to the better golfer and the one who should have won, the crowd erupted in applause and gathered around the boy who rightly deserved the first-place trophy. I slunk away from the golf club and over to a nearby park in hopes no one would confront me before my ride home appeared.

Later that day I made the mistake of going to the city pool where I was accosted by a handful of the school's most popular girls. They immediately began to verbally attack me. "You cheated. Steve really should have won. You're a cheater!" As fear and anxiety welled up inside of me, I responded with a "No I didn't," but it was too late. My cohorts in the scheme and playing partners had already betrayed me, and there wasn't anything I could do but slink away again and hide out until it all hopefully blew over.

There it was again, public humiliation, embarrassment, and other people trying to hurt me. It was more confirmation that solidified my fear of others. But hadn't I brought this on myself? Am I not the one whose actions brought disdain, trouble, and heartache? Obviously yes! Just like the fight from a few years earlier. Was I not the one who said, "Yes, I can beat him up"? Of course I was, but I didn't see it like that or all other similar episodes that followed until much later in life. People were simply responding and retaliating from "toes I'd stepped on" by getting the ball rolling with my actions! I just couldn't figure out how to manage my life. I didn't feel comfortable in my own skin. On the inside I was an introvert who just wanted to live in a basement and avoid people, but to the world I felt as if I had to play the popular extrovert. That dual personality was the cause of much angst, and it became an exhausting role to have to play throughout life.

None of it made sense to me back then. I didn't understand what was happening to me. Why things were always going wrong. All I knew was that I was filled with a great amount of fear, anxiety, guilt, shame, self-consciousness, and low self-worth. All I craved was a solution. A way to make those feelings disappear, to go away. But I had no idea how to make that happen until later that summer when I found a "solution" that would eventually destroy me later in life.

CHAPTER 3

I FOUND THE SOLUTION!

His name was Chris Toburen, and he was my hero. Chris was three years my senior and the son of one of my father's law partners. Under normal circumstances, I never would have gotten to know Chris due to our age difference, but as it turned out, his dad, Nelson, and my dad were avid canoers. About three or four times a year the four of us would head east to "float," as they called it, down some river in Arkansas or Missouri.

Chris was a "star" football player on the high school team who had the skills and the aspirations to play Division I college football, which later he did at Kansas University. While there, he was named "All Big Eight Defensive Player of the Year" and probably could have gone pro, but decided to join the Marines instead to fulfill his dream of flying military helicopters. Either path would have made his father proud, but I imagine in hindsight, Nelson would rather have seen his only son opt for the NFL instead of the USMC. Nelson had played with the Green Bay Packers back in the '60s before an awkwardly approached tackle of Johnny Unitas broke Nelson's neck and ended his career. He recovered and in a morbid kind of way would likely rather have seen his son end up with the same career-ending injury than what later befell him.

Chris was tall, strong, and full of great energy, a wild and fierce middle linebacker in both high school and college. He was the coolest guy I ever knew and I utterly idolized him in every way. I liked the way he walked, the way he talked, the relationship he had with his father, his attitude, his energy, his clothes, what he ate, and most likely the kind of underwear he wore if I'd have ever seen them! There was no one like Chris in our small town, and for an impressionable thirteen-year-old boy, he was "all that" to me!

Beyond just his "larger than life" physique and personality was even something more special to me, and what endeared me the most to him. For some reason Chris chose to treat me like his best buddy on those canoe trips. I'm sure around school and in his social circles back home our relationship would have been much different, but during those times it was just the two of us. I was just "one of the boys," and he regarded me as such. Chris probably thought I was just a little punk, but for whatever reason, he made the exception for me the second our trucks, canoes, and gear hit the highway every summer. I stood up a little straighter when he was around, puffed my chest out, and spent most of my time trying to impress him with whatever athletic or redneck river skills I may have had. He laughed and joined in as he assumed and accepted his well-received mentor role over me. He knew he had an eager student to mold, and he wasted no time enlightening me as I studiously attempted to emulate his every move.

There were a thousand lessons to learn on every trip, and I soaked up as much as one possibly could. On one trip, as we walked across a dam during a pit stop along the river, Chris looked over at me and said, "Why are you walking like that?" Somewhere a few months earlier, I'd convinced myself that walking with a little "hitch/strut" in my step was cool, and being certain he would approve and be impressed, I exaggerated it even more when he was around. Apparently I'd overestimated the "coolness" of the walk and Chris let me know. "Don't walk like that; you look like a dork. Just walk normal." So I walked normal. A few yards later with my index finger halfway up my nose, Chris would say, "Hey, it's cool if you've got to pick your nose, there's nothing wrong with that, just use a Kleenex." I never picked my nose again.

Throughout the seasons and the frequent float trips, Chris taught me all kinds of great life lessons and I couldn't get enough. I was a sponge and mimicked his every move, his every action, his every word, and took to heart every piece of advice he was willing to give me. He sang ridiculous songs like, "Old Man River was a mean old man, he washed his face in a frying pan, combed his hair with a wagon wheel, and died with a toothache in his heel. Get out the way of old man Tucker, he's too late to eat his supper. Supper's over and breakfast is a cookin', old man Tucker just a stands there lookin'." I have no idea what that song was about, but I memorized every word and can obviously still remember it today. In addition to prattling off foolish songs that used to make his dad angry because he'd always begin them just prior to a heavy rapid run that required some level of focus and attention, he would stand up in the canoe and scream "Braveheart-like" battle cries with no warning or seeming impetus.

His dad would tell him to sit down and shut up, but instead, Chris would rock the boat as hard as he could in an attempt to topple his old man over into the river. I laughed and loved it, fixating on his every move and gesture. Those were some of the greatest days of my life and memories I still call on today when I'm feeling down. We invented all kinds of river games along the way, challenged every rope swing we saw, and there wasn't a cliff he wasn't willing to jump off, with me following shortly behind. I felt like a real man, with a real friend. I "belonged" all because this big old loveable kid decided to show me grace and friendship!

Part of the logistics of every canoe trip required a "shuttling" of the trucks. When we first arrived at the mouth of the river, or the origin of our journey, we would unload the canoes and all the supplies for the day. Once everything had been dispensed, our fathers would each drive their respective trucks to the mapped out terminus of our journey (usually some 45 minutes away). They would leave one truck downstream and drive back together in the other truck to our point of entry where Chris and I waited, usually raiding the cooler for cold fried chicken, or throwing rocks at empty pop cans. When our "float" was finished at the end of the day, we'd reverse the procedure. Both dads would get in the truck parked at the end of our journey, drive back to get the other truck, then return so we could load everything up and head home. Chris and I would again wait, guard our equipment and possessions, while figuring out what kind of game we could invent. Nelson and dad usually returned about an hour later.

The afternoon that changed my life and helped me discover that "solution" I'd been searching for to ease the spiritual maladies I'd been fighting came during one of these "waiting for the shuttle" sessions.

Chris and I were playing a newly invented game called "Beer Tab Olympics." The object was to search the ground for those old style beer tabs that completely pulled off the can. You'd break the ring off the curved little petal-shaped tab, insert it into the notch from the ring, pull it back, and let it fly. The ring would whiz off like a mini flying saucer and travel anywhere from a few feet to ten or fifteen yards depending on your technique and skill. The goal was to see who could launch one the farthest. As we sat on the coolers, launching beer rings and talking, I noticed Chris reaching into one of the coolers and pulling out a beer. He popped the top, took a big swig, let out a big "aaaahhhhh," and then looked over at me. "Want one?" A feeling of excitement and exhilaration came over me. Never having had a beer before or any alcohol for that matter, and not wanting to be a "wuss," I said, "Sure." He reached in, grabbed one and handed it to me. "Don't tell your dad," he warned. "I won't," I replied.

It was a surreal moment in time and a confusing mix of emotions. I was frightened and nervous, felt guilty and paranoid as I held that cold and wet can in my hand. There was something awkward and uncomfortable about the self-visual of a thirteen-year-old holding a beer, sitting on top of a cooler. "Would I like it? What's going to happen to me when I drink it? Am I crossing the line here? What if I can't handle it and Chris laughs at me?" It was no different, however, than climbing that bluff above the river, edging out to the end of the rock, looking down at the water fifty feet below, and watching Chris leap into the unknown with a whoop and a holler all the way down, emerging from the river with a victorious scream. He walked through the fear, and I couldn't chicken out. I had to do the same. Chris had never let me down before, and I wanted that victorious feeling of accomplishment as well, be it cliff or Coors.

So I popped the top and took a big gulp! The thickness of the barley ignited my senses and the carbonation burned my nasal passage as my eyes began to water ever slightly. I wasn't overly fond of the taste—it was no NuGrape soda—but there was no turning back, and I was in mid-air on my way to that exhilarating splash into the untamed river below. I'd never felt more accepted in my entire life. Here was this seventeen-year-old superstar, my friend, and we were sealing our bond over a cold beer. I remember the moment so vividly. As I drank that beer, swimming in euphoria, I knew from that first rush of alcohol to my brain that this magic potion was not only the remedy for my emotional maladies, but also a symbol of acceptance. It was a rite of passage into manhood, friendship, and the common bond between men who would forever revere each other. The allure was indescribably powerful.

After finishing my first beer, I asked for another. Chris obliged, but said no on the third. It didn't matter. I was in heaven and everything was right with the world.

Right there, on that late summer afternoon, sitting on a cooler in the woods along a gravel access road next to my hero, I learned that the secret to all my problems, all my insecurities, and all my irrational fears, was alcohol. I had found the ever-elusive solution. Turns out I'd be right about that for many years to come.

Later that fall in my eighth grade year, alcohol confirmed its special powers when a friend of mine suggested we get his older brother to buy us some beer and have a little party. At the time, my father owned some land on the south side of town, close by, but secluded. I offered the property as a beer party site and the ill-gotten plan was quickly underway. For the first time in my life, I was the confident one, the aggressor, the instigator, and the one with the seeming upper hand and confidence. As I invited friend after friend to the event, I put them in the uncomfortable position of having to accept or deny the challenge. I got to be "the cool one" who was having a highly illegal and risky party. Just being able to invite people awarded me with a newfound respect and awe from my fellows that almost guaranteed I'd never be thought less of or made fun of again. To those who accepted, a new bond was forged. To those who declined, I had the opportunity to feel superior to them, to shame them, and to make them feel the "outsider," or "less than." The tables were turning for me.

On the afternoon of the party, a dozen of us set off on foot toward the land site some two miles from where big brother delivered us the three twelve-packs of Budweiser beer. As we approached the homemade fire pit surrounded by a half dozen bales of hay, we all took a seat and my friend began passing out beers. A quick bit of math showed that with thirty-six beers and twelve boys, each of us was entitled to, or saddled with, however you wanted to view it, three beers. Wanting to lead the charge, I accepted the first one, popped the top, took a big swig, and followed it with the "ahhhhhh" that I'd learned from Chris. I then watched my fellow compadres to see who and how they followed. Some of the boys popped their tops and took little sips, others delayed the process, popping the top and just holding the forbidden beverage for a minute or two. Before most of the guys had taken their first drink, I had downed my first and was theatrically making it known I was ready for another. Two beers in, I began to take notice of my posse. Some were still cautiously sipping, others still hadn't taken a drink, and a few pretended to drink, but were covertly pouring out what they could when no one was looking. Three beers in, I'd finished my allotment and wanted another, victoriously announcing, "Three down boys! Who wants to share one of theirs with me?" To my surprise, almost everyone quickly offered their extras to me, and I quickly polished off numbers four, five, and six. It became clear to me right then and there that I was once again different than everyone else. No one was drinking like I was. In fact, no one seemed to be enjoying this little adventure at all, but I was drunk, filled with euphoric confidence and a sense of superiority over my friends. When the beer was gone, either sipped away, poured out, or chugged by me, we headed out and walked a mile or so to a nearby ball field where we decided to sit down and rest. I fell asleep, or what later became known as "passing out," and woke up feeling a little groggy but on top of the world. I'd walked into uncharted territory a scared and geeky preadolescent, and walked out a new man, brimming with confidence, and in my mind, adored, feared, and respected by my peers for a daring ability to outdrink them all. Chalk another one up for this life changing elixir!

A few days later the word was "out" and I became an instant celebrity at school. The risk-taking "bad boy" reputation suited me well. People were treating me differently, some with respect, others with awe, and a few with fear. The way the girls looked at me had also changed. I wasn't "Dumbo" any longer. I wasn't the weak kid who got beat up anymore. I was mysterious and cool! Even the older bullies in school saw me through a new pair of glasses. They no longer picked on me or tried to embarrass me. But they still scared me, and even more so when they asked me to come with them after school one day.

"So you like to party, do you Lassman?" "Sure," I answered. "Well let's go! You ever smoked pot before?" Oh crap! This is not the path I wanted to go down! But what was I to do? I'd made a new name for myself, was on the verge of "being cool" and accepted by the band of bad boys that I feared the most. One decision away from being back in the "picked on wuss" category or one decision away from being accepted by the outsiders! Well, I wasn't going back. It was too painful, and one little puff or two on a joint wasn't going to kill me. So I went. One more little step in a wrong direction that felt so right! I was hooked. Not on pot and not "yet" on booze, but rather on what they were able to do for me, which was gaining the acceptance of others.

As I eased on into high school, my drinking patterns settled into a predictable little routine. The pot smoking, however, never caught on. I didn't like it. It always burned my throat, and I don't think I ever got "high." Marijuana never made me feel different. It never made me forget who I was, or turned me into someone I'd rather be. Maybe I didn't "inhale," and if not inhaling exonerated a former president, surely it exonerates me! In retrospect, if one of them had to stick, I wished "the pot," as my grandpa used to call it, would have stuck and I wouldn't have liked drinking. Something tells me that wouldn't have ruined my life the way alcohol eventually did.

The drinking, unfortunately, DID catch on, and if not for high school sports could have gotten out of hand very quickly. Between football, cross-country, basketball, and the golf team I stayed very busy after school and most weekends. My need to impress, to please, kept me very focused on succeeding in all those areas, including my schoolwork. The only free night I typically had was Saturday, and it was always reserved for drinking.

It was a different time back in the late '70s and early '80s. Growing up in a small town back in those days was even more different. Underage drinking was typically overlooked, more accepted, and certainly under-penalized. The DUI (called a DWI back then) wasn't a prevalent arrest. Open containers hardly raised a cop's eyebrow, and the only liquor stores and bars that carded, or required an I.D., were the ones that would soon be out of business. I used to own a jacket that had the local college logo on it. It's the one I wore into a liquor store down on east Fourth Street that was owned by a ninety-year-old woman who classified everyone under forty as a kid. To her, everyone looked young, and if you were wearing a Pittsburg State jacket, you must be in college and therefore old enough to buy booze. So every Saturday night, we'd visit Eunice's liquor store and I'd buy a twelve-pack of "Little Kings" malt liquor and split them with my best friend. Six bottles of 6 percent beer was enough to do the trick every Saturday night. We had the best times, driving up and down Broadway Street doing all the stupid things teenagers do. Every once in a while we'd get pulled over by the local police. They knew we were drunk and usually had beer bottles on the floor or in the cup holders. It was always the same story. "What are you boys up to tonight? Can I see your licenses? Oh, you're Garry Lassman's boy. You all better get on home." There were no consequences to underage drinking and driving back in my hometown, so we drank and drove. Later in life I found out other cops weren't so lenient!

During the summer months, the drinking always increased some, but never to the point of being out of control. It's just what kids do I thought, or maybe it's just what I did. I honestly can't remember getting into too much trouble while drinking back in those days. Trouble was limited to things like climbing the water tower to spray-paint our names on it, driving like idiots, staying out past our loose curfews, or finding someone or something to vandalize.

But I needed it. It just wasn't fun going out without being drunk. I was too socially awkward to feel comfortable around others without it. A drink or two gave me courage, the right words to say, and a sense of belonging. It changed me for the better, I thought. Gave me confidence, provided laughter, fun, excitement and made me feel "a part of" just like my hero, Chris, did back in those canoeing days.

As those "float trip" days became less and less frequent, and Chris was busy finishing high school, being recruited by Division I schools, and preparing to go off to college, my feelings of insecurity became more and more prevalent. I was losing that feeling of fitting in, and being a part of that came from spending time with Chris. He eventually left for college, and I never saw him again. I longed for the opportunity to recreate what we'd had, but it was gone. Life changes, and they say nothing good lasts forever. I was depressed, sad, and missing my friend and all the good feelings that just being around him afforded me.

I searched for many years trying to recreate those summer memories and special days I had with Chris. The canoe trips were gone and my idol, mentor, and sense of being accepted had disappeared as well. The only thing that remained was the beer. If it worked with him, it would work with someone else. So I kept drinking, trying to bring back that elusive time in my life, and desperately seeking the acceptance I craved. I never found it again.

Chris went on to play four stellar seasons of football at Kansas University. He won the prestigious title of "Big Eight Player of the Year" and graduated and pursed his dream of joining the Marines and learning to fly military helicopters. I graduated from high school with good grades and a chest full of medals, trophies, and letter jacket pins for athletic and academic achievements and was off to college as well.

One weekend, on a visit back home from college, I walked into my parents' house and greeted my mom and dad. Before I even had a chance to sit down, dad handed me a copy of the Pittsburg *Morning Sun* newspaper, and right there on the front page was a picture of Chris under a caption that read, "Local hero dies in helicopter accident." It said he was flying a training mission in the mountains at night, and his team was relying on their instrumentation to guide the chopper. A mistake was made, and the chopper crashed into the side of a mountain. All four marines on board were killed, including Chris.

I was dumbfounded. My parents left the house shortly thereafter to run an errand, and I sat down on the sofa and cried the first real emotional tears of my life. My friend, my inspiration, my mentor and hero was gone. The person I looked up to the most in the world was dead. There was regret over never telling him how much I respected him, remorse for not thanking him for being so kind and nurturing to me. I wondered what I would do without a role model. The pain was too great, and I wanted to make it go away. I felt so alone, so naked, so frightened and unsure of myself. If the world could take my hero and a "superman" like Chris, what was it going to do to me? It was too much to deal with, so I resorted to the only thing I knew that would make the pain subside, allow me to hide, and make everything better—alcohol.

CHAPTER 4

LOVE HURTS

Ask anyone who their "first love" was and they could probably rattle that person's name off without hesitation. Falling in love for the first time is a life experience indelibly imprinted upon our hearts. That first love experience establishes an emotional place card with that person's name forever burned upon our souls. The question for most is, "Can you ever let it go?" Can you find the value and lessons in the experience, grieve and accept the finality of the relationship, and move on without being burdened with the heartache, pains, and regrets that come from a first real breakup? I don't know the actual odds, but I'm guessing it's one in a million people who actually marry their first love today. Kind of makes me wonder if the way society has developed didn't mess up God's original plan for marriage. Back in Biblical times everyone seemed to get married when they were like fifteen. They found their first love and married her (then usually married five or six more). I imagine back in those days the odds of marrying your first love were about one out of one! Today, most in our society would say, "No, that's crazy! You can't get married at fifteen. You have to enjoy your high school years, go to college, find a job, and establish yourself before you even begin to think about marriage." So we do. The first love comes and goes, sometimes branding a wound into our souls, making us think from time to time, "If only?"

The loss of that first love brings as much, if not more, pain than the joy it brought us when it first happened. Getting over it can be hard, and the scars it leaves, the closure of it all is another one of those lasting emotional maladies that, if not resolved, contributes to unhealthy and negative emotions that constantly yearn for relief. Some find relief by falling in love again, some with the passing of time, some with friend therapy, and some, like myself, with the bottle.

My first love was a girl named Kala. It was love at first sight, at least for me. I met Kala the summer between our sixth- and seventh-grade years. Sixth grade was the end of grade school and seventh was the beginning of Lakeside Junior High, which as fate would have it, consolidated our respective grade schools and brought Kala and me together. Well, actually, not at first. That pre-junior high summer, Kala and three other girls had prearranged a little "dance party" at her parents' house under the auspices of forwarding the friendly integration of both school and gender. Unbeknownst to me, the girls had premeditated a little more than just a good-faith mixer. The group had been analyzing the soon to be combined boy population, and each had chosen their favorite crush and invited us four unsuspecting boys over for a Friday night filled with food, soft drinks, and dance. I knew how to do two of those activities! The moment I walked into the suburban rec room turned disco, I fell in love with Kala. Unfortunately, I wasn't her "crush pick," and I soon found out who I belonged to! Feeling duped and a little more than awkward on the dance floor, I did my best to go with the flow and show as much interest as an extremely distracted adolescent brain could muster toward my pre-assigned partner. Throughout the entire dance-a-thon, which consisted of only two slow songs that we actually attempted to dance to, Kala was rarely out of my sight while a plan to make her mine was developing.

Incessant daydreams of Kala continued through the entire seventh- and eighth-grade years, and into the summer between the eighth and ninth. (Back in those days, ninth grade was still considered junior high.) Despite my best efforts or how hard I tried, and no matter how strong my desperate, love struck telepathic signals buzzed with high frequency, I couldn't illicit a single bit of romantic interest from Kala. Looking back, I imagine the pathetic aura that oozed from every fiber of my being was probably a little creepy and most likely a turnoff to her. What I did illicit, however, was a new negative emotion—jealousy. Kala always had a boyfriend. She went through them like Q-tips during an ear wax epidemic. It used to eat me alive watching her walking the halls with a new boy, hearing they were going "steady," watching her laugh and adore the lucky duck who should have been me. It was terribly painful and an emotion I just wanted to go away, but saw no way to relieve.

Fate, however, was waiting patiently, and all it took was a broken ankle, a pair of crutches, and a dramatic football injury to finally bring us together. I was #41 and the starting running back for the undefeated Lakeside Junior High Wildcats. Seven flawless games into the season, I heard the call, "Swing left, quick pitch." That was mine! On the second hut, I exploded from my stance and headed left, pitch on its way. Ball in hand I looped left toward the sideline, waiting for my hole to open so I could cut back against the grain and run victoriously toward the end zone. In a split second, there it was! A hard cut right, then up the field. He's at the 30, the 25, the 20, the 15, the 10, then BANG, a blind shot from the free safety that took me down at the 5, followed by what seemed like a ten man pile on! I don't remember what happened after that, because I think I passed out briefly. When the pile cleared, I came to and felt this unbelievable pain around my right ankle. I rolled over on my back with the referee hovering over me. He said, "Son, put your shoe back on and get up." I looked down and said, "My shoe's already on!" His face went ghost white and I lost consciousness again. I had snapped my tibia and fibula, and my ankle was at a perfect 90 degree angle from the rest of my right leg. It was almost identical to the break Joe Theismann had in 1985 during a *Monday Night Football* game after being tackled by Lawrence Taylor, if you remember that. If not, Google it; it'll make your stomach turn. I still can't watch it to this day. Time out was called, and the medics were called in. I say medics, but I think they were a couple of guys from concessions who had taken a first-aid class. Whatever their training, they weren't equipped to handle this kind of an injury. As it turns out, neither was the football stadium. Someone had wisely called an ambulance, which arrived promptly only to find that the emergency vehicle gates to the stadium were padlocked and no one knew who had the keys. Four janitors, 187 keys, and 45 minutes later, the emergency vehicle was in, and I was loaded up and on my way to the hospital. I should have been in unbearable pain, but I wasn't. While lying there on the field, with half a leg dangling from my body, I was administered one of the best drugs known to mankind—Love! While lying on the ground surrounded by players, coaches, and my dad, the most beautiful knock-kneed cheerleader in a purple skirt and painted purple face popped her head into the crowd. Our eyes met, and through her pained and compassionate stare, there was something else in her eyes that didn't have anything to do with feeling sorry for me!

Okay, okay! If it took a broken leg to win her heart, then so be it! I had no pride when it came to Kala. My own best efforts were of no avail, and I'd take it any way I could get it. That "look" had been long awaited, and that compound fracture became the best injury I ever suffered! One hour later, in a hospital bed, gown, and with a soothing morphine drip, my world was right. Semiconscious, I watched as the doctor used great personal force to snap the leg back in place, doing his best to align the severed bones so the wonder of the human body could fuse them back together with the help of time and a full leg plaster cast!

Back at school a few days later, I was an instant celebrity. I was a hero to the fellas and a vulnerable wounded warrior to the dames, all who seemed to have assumed the role of my very own Clara Barton. Maybe it was my bravery, my resolve to fight through the pain, or my new "coolness" that after two-and-a-half years I finally attracted Kala, but that's doubtful. It was probably more a case of instant fame and a newfound attraction from a host of other fifteen-year-old bleeding hearts. I like to call it the "last dress" theory. There are half a dozen ugly floral dresses hanging on the rack. Week after week they hang there, and occasionally someone with bad taste buys one; another dress leaves the rack as a gag gift, another for a costume party, and still another to someone who's color-blind, but doesn't know it. Finally, after weeks and months, there is one lone floral dress remaining. Thousands of women have walked by it, turned up their noses, and quietly gagged. Then, all of sudden, a woman, a reasonably cute woman, picks up the dress, holds it up against her body, gets that look that says, "I think I'm going to buy this." An in-store telepathic pandemic erupts as internal female sirens begin blaring from all parts of the store and they all begin moving zombie-like toward the dress just like in a scene from *The Walking Dead*. Verbal positioning begins. "Oh, that dress is so ugly." "Cheap material, not your color." Then the backbiting begins, and before long, a fierce battle breaks out for the last dress! That was me. I was the last dress and was okay with that.

The next school year my mind was in a perpetual state of euphoric bliss. I had a new popularity never experienced before, my leg was healing and would be ready for basketball season, and I had the woman of my dreams. Many evenings were spent at Kala's house, fumbling all over myself, starry-eyed, melting from every kiss she deemed me worthy of and was lucky enough to get. Some nights, Kala would come to the gym with me and rebound while I practiced my shot and rehabilitated my leg. When I got home from Kala's house, I'd call her and we'd talk for hours on the phone. The next day at school, she would wear my letter sweater and we'd hold hands on our way to class. When the season started, I was on the court scoring baskets while she proudly cheered from the sidelines. Life was perfect, and I was head over heels in love. When they talk about "blind love," I know exactly what they mean. She had me whipped! The word blind, however, eventually became the operative word. I didn't see the breakup coming before it ran me over like a freight train. One evening I arrived at her house, she opened the door with tears in her eyes, and it was over. I can't even remember the reasons she gave me. I was in utter and complete shock. My entire world had just come crashing in upon me. Her words left this vulnerable ninth grader a bumbling, crying mess, sick to my stomach, and with what felt like an irreparable hole in my heart.

The emotional hurricane that ensued became what was one of the most painful times of my life. I was spinning in a sea of heartache, self-consciousness, self-pity, anxiety, anger, insecurity, jealousy, fear, and my self-esteem was about as low as it could get without wanting to kill myself. Why doesn't she love me anymore? What did I do? What's wrong with me? I must be unattractive just like the kids in kindergarten used to tell me by calling me "Dumbo." I'm not smart enough, funny enough, or popular enough. I had put all my emotional stability in one basket—hers—and now that fragile mistake was crushed into a million pieces and I had no idea how to put myself back together. Talk about the spiritual malady! I didn't have God in my life at that time, and my spiritual resources were nonexistent. I was a real mess. Days were spent trying to figure out how to win her back; nights were sleepless, filled with a continuous flow of sorrowful thoughts, painful longings, and depths of self-pity. Jealousy and quiet rage consumed me as she moved on with her life and with other boys. I could think of nothing else for years! Years! I'm not kidding. The harder I tried to win her back, the further I drove her away. Whatever I did was exactly the wrong thing. I was pathetic. I knew it, she knew it, and everyone else knew it.

It was around this time in my life that I started drinking more heavily (it's not your fault, Kala!). The emotional pain and discomfort I was living with every day was easily numbed away after a few beers. Those Friday and Saturday nights, with six or seven beers under my belt, became a welcome reprieve from the heartache that seemed impossible to shake. My solution was discovered, just as it had been after the loss of my friend, Chris Toburen, and as it had been with my friends sitting around the campfire at dad's farm. And it worked, temporarily. The problem was that when it wore off, the same emotional nightmares returned, and I'd be looking for the next opportunity to drink it away. What started out as once a week became twice a week, and even more often during the long summer nights.

With the help of booze, time, and a series of girlfriends who wish they never would have met me, the pain slowly started to fade. Maybe fade isn't the right word. The pain was being sufficiently covered up with unhealthy behaviors might be a better way to describe it. I survived, but left a trail of unhappy, confused, and hurt girls in my wake, and had begun to develop a concerning drinking habit.

I didn't fall in love again until my sophomore year in college because it was too hard to allow it. Kala was still the only one in my heart and I couldn't let go. I couldn't move on. No one ever matched up and, even if they did, a burning notion revolved in my mind that one day Kala and I would be reunited and we would get back that love and that happy time in our lives. Until then, I would medicate the pain with alcohol, a drug from time to time, or an unhealthy relationship. Then, during my sophomore year in college, it happened again. I was smitten with a new junior college transfer. Her name was Jennifer, and the exact same saga happened again. I fell head over heels and had found what seemed to fill my broken heart and empty soul. I spent a year completely enamored with the woman I was sure would become my wife. Wrong! Gut punch number two in the love arena! She broke up with me, then slept with my best friend. I was devastated, but this time around my emotional hurt was easily solved. I got a job at a bar, worked and drank just about every night, and stayed in a state of continuous inebriation, which really helped me get through it. I woke up a year later, the summer between my junior and senior year in college, when I met my now ex-wife. Determined not to screw up this love, I waded in a little slower, a little more cautiously, and a real relationship formed.

Lori was the love of my life, and I could write an entire book on that relationship and twenty-four-year marriage, and maybe I will. Maybe we will. I've been thinking about asking her if she would co-author a book called, *I Married an Alcoholic* or, better yet, *Threesome,* subtitled, *Husband, Wife, and Bottle,* where we would each give our undoubtedly conflicting insights on what that was like. Most likely I would write it from the perspective of a drowning man, trying desperately to hang on to the one person he thought could save him, and she would write more of a tragic horror story.

As I reflect back on my romantic relationships, I now see repeating and recurring patterns. The insanity of exhibiting the same behaviors in each relationship and getting the same devastating results made my love life feel like "Groundhog Day." I exhibited so many character defects and owe many amends, mostly to my ex-wife. It is a miracle we made it twenty-four years. I was selfish, prideful, dishonest, controlling, irresponsible, and below that an entire subcategory of negative adjectives! My drinking was the catalyst that finally ended our marriage, but it wasn't just the drinking. It was the continued wrong thinking and harmful actions that became an unhealthy by-product of the drink. Stupid decisions, hurt feelings, inattentiveness to her needs, emotional distance, and dishonesty were some of the less distasteful ones I can talk about in this book. If getting over Kala took six or seven beers a couple of times a week, and Jennifer took several months of drinking, Lori took a couple of years of serious alcoholic drinking before I could bring myself to the point of getting over her and on with my pathetic life. Things got bad, Chapter One kind of bad, for a long time.

My inability to understand how to have healthy love relationships, especially the one with Lori, left me so spiritually and emotionally sick that I thought I may never breathe another sober breath before what was beginning to look like a life that might end thirty years early. No one, especially Lori, was to blame for any of it. I was. Oh, I tried to blame them all. If they would just act like this, or be like that, everything would have turned out fine. They all drove me to drink; it's their fault! I went through long periods of blaming others, but deep down I knew I was at fault. The truth was as clear as the vodka bottle in my hand. I needed to fix myself, repair the damage I'd caused, and learn to love myself before anyone else could truly love me, or I could have a genuine capacity to love another. I just didn't know how. By the time my marriage was over, I was physically sick and addicted, but was unaware of just how spiritually and emotionally ill I had become. I certainly didn't know how to even begin unwinding my complicated mess. It was easier to drink it away. Finding the solution, one drink at a time, was my answer to everything. It was taking the easy way out, another one of my character flaws.

Why the chapter on love? Well . . . love is one of the most powerful and most painful of emotions. It drives men and women to kill, to commit suicide, to stalk, to sabotage, and to venomously spatter hurts that do so much damage and create injury that oftentimes it can never be repaired. It is the core of the spiritual malady and the nucleus of so many psychological problems. The heart wants what the heart wants, and John Mayer sings it best when he says, "You love who you love, who you love." That love, however, doesn't always come back to you the way you want it to. The one you love doesn't always love you back. They may not love you as much as you love them either. The lucky couples love each other equally, but for most, the "love imbalance" found in many relationships usually becomes the impetus for problems down the road.

It seems to me, upon reflection, that lasting love is found not among couples who love each other so strongly, but more among couples where each partner loves himself or herself first and foremost. Lasting love comes from partnerships where each lover finds his or her self-worth, value, and capacity to love others from a sense of being loved by Christ. When both parties seek and receive their love from God and learn to love themselves, only then are they capable and in a position to love each other, or to love anyone for that matter. I don't recall where I saw it, but it must have been some sermon or seminar on relationships and I've never forgotten it. The speaker drew a big triangle on the white board. In the bottom left corner, he wrote "husband." In the bottom right corner, he wrote "wife." And at the top of the triangle, he wrote "God." Then he proceeded to explain that as the man and wife grew closer to God and moved up the triangle toward Christ, they grew closer to each other. A simple love lesson using geometry! That was a really powerful visual, but what was more powerful, as he explained more geometry, is that if the woman begins to grow closer to God, but the man stays stuck in the bottom left corner, they are still the same maximum distance away from each other. So the love relationship doesn't grow stronger unless both partners are moving toward God. He also explained with examples how couples he knew had grown very close to God, and hence close to each other, but then one of them began to fall away from God and back down the triangle. The result was that the marriage grew weaker as the distance from his or her partner began to widen.

The other important point of this chapter is to remind you that we all have to deal with the spiritual maladies generated from broken romantic relationships. They need to be addressed in the same manner as how we deal with all spiritual discomfort. My experiences in love left me with a broken heart, feelings of inadequacy, self-doubt, jealousy, anger, guilt, shame, frustration, resentment, sadness, and mountains of self-pity. Those emotional piranhas weren't dealt with early on in life, and that neglect created a host of negative, neurotic, unrealistic, and delusional behaviors that I carried into each subsequent relationship. With each new partner, I added another layer of unhealthy coping mechanisms, like passive-aggressive behavior, distrust, fear of people, defensive and protective mechanisms, emotional distance, and of course, more alcohol.

Being stuck in the past and weighed down under "pick-up sticks" of negative behaviors caused me to drink away the pain. If it was possible to go back, knowing what I know today, I would have leaned on the answer, Christ, and I would have asked Him to remove these painful emotions from me. I would have talked through my feelings with a friend or counselor, and I would have turned my thoughts to God and asked Him to show me someone I could help as a way to escape the distorted thoughts in my own head.

It's really a simple process and will be discussed in greater detail later in the book, but the best and most practical analogy I ever heard about this spiritual malady-curing formula came from a friend of mine. I have always had a lot of anxiety about walking into rooms full of people. Whether it's church, a fundraiser, a school play, a business seminar, a reception, or a cocktail party, my level of anxiety always explodes off the charts. As I explained these feelings to my friend (step one of the simple process), he said, "Just fire up a quick prayer to God to take away your anxiety [part 2 of the solution], walk into the room full of people, and look for the one person in the room who looks more uncomfortable than you are, and go over and strike up a conversation [part 3 of the solution]." It always works!

CHAPTER 5

WARNING SIGNS

Despite the fact that I wasn't emotionally or psychologically healthy enough to get married, Lori and I wed a year after graduating from college. It was the '80s, and back then that's just what you did. We both had been in and out of relationships throughout high school and college and had developed enough experience dating to think we knew what we wanted. We had new jobs, were entering more responsible phases in our lives, and could see a wonderful future together. The drinking hadn't spiraled out of control at this point in my life or was at least masked by our circumstances. Binge drinking was prevalent enough in college, and problem drinkers, like me, went largely undetected, even among ourselves. College kids like to party, and I was no exception. No longer having the "college kid" excuse, I supposed the drinking would slow down as we left the confines of irresponsibility and entered the job market. Having to work five or six days a week, ten hours a day, would surely mute some of the drinking patterns that were so acceptable in college, and they did to a certain extent. Muted is probably not the right word; I would say it was more like "readjusted." Instead of blowout binge drinking, the pattern became more of a solid drinking routine. Two or three weeknights, the boys from work would meet at 6:00 p.m. for a couple of beers (which usually meant four or five), then we'd part ways and I'd head home to Lori and have dinner, which always included a few glasses of wine and another beer or two. Friday nights were almost always the blowout drunk nights with the "dink" (duel income, no kids) couples. Saturdays were spent watching afternoon sports with a few beers, a nap, and were followed by a nice dinner for two complete with a bottle of wine or more. Sundays were reserved for nursing a weeks' worth of mild hangovers with several beers and some pro football; then I'd start all over again Monday morning. What used to be the irresponsible drinking in college had turned into more of a controlled and managed drunk. Again, it was just kind of what everyone did, so my drinking behaviors were hardly noticeable to anyone else, including myself. I don't recall a lot of problematic incidents around drinking that first several years of marriage. We were young and fun loving, just a part of the exciting newlywed scene. We had money for the first time in our lives, and our careers were motoring along nicely.

It wasn't long before my first job with Koch Industries was ready to transfer me from Wichita, Kansas, to Minneapolis, Minnesota, to the greatest paid work opportunity a budding alcoholic could wish for. Little did I know, that transfer would be the first of many unhappy scenes in our marriage. With the exception of some minor stresses and hurt feelings around a Catholic wedding, Lori and I hadn't had any real difficult relational issues up to this point. In hindsight, the whole Catholic wedding and all its sore spots should have been a signal that we both had a lot more to work out before getting married, but we chose, for the most part, to overlook them and proceed. I did not grow up Catholic and didn't particularly care for the Catholic doctrine, but wasn't a strong or faithful enough Christian at that time to argue much against it. Looking back, I can't believe I didn't give more thought and weight to what I was being asked to agree to. Signing a document, promising to raise my future children Catholic, and essentially committing to go to Catholic mass every Sunday hardly caused a "blip" on my religious radar screen. There was also the underlying notion, maybe even expectation, that soon I would personally convert to Catholicism, of which I had no intention. I think our biggest argument over the wedding ceremony revolved around requiring my non-Catholic groomsmen to kneel. I don't know why it was such a big deal, but some of them didn't want to do it, nor did I. Why I drew a line in the sand on that one and not on more important topics like converting, agreeing to raise the kids Catholic, or committing my Sundays to mass didn't make much sense, did it? I guess I was feeling a little "run over" throughout the wedding process, and when belittled and controlled, I got a little defensive in front of my friends and rebelled. I eventually capitulated and apologized because I loved Lori and wanted to marry her. I can say, and it was obvious from day one, that I had some pretty big resentments that stemmed from the Catholic way of life I felt I'd been pressed into, and believe me, I made it known for twenty years.

When I got the call that we were being transferred from Wichita to Minneapolis for my dream job, I was pretty excited. I immediately picked up the phone, called Lori, and said, "Pack your bags, baby, we're heading to Minneapolis in three weeks." Expecting to hear some excitement, some congratulatory praise and prideful affirmations, I was quiet taken aback instead to hear the tears and anger that followed. That's not how my mother would have reacted! The self-centered part of me couldn't understand what was happening. Sure Lori was back in the city she grew up in, surrounded by close family and friends. Sure she had a job she loved, a hip apartment we'd just finished decorating, and I hadn't bothered discussing the move with her before accepting the position, but to react like that? Can you imagine? Duh! First real "bad husband" mistake and first real resentment deposited in Lori's resentment bag that would eventually become so completely full she wouldn't be able to carry it any longer. I didn't see it. I assumed that she revolved around me and that what was good for me was good for her. I'm not sure I apologized, but rather went into my "sales" mode, spending an inordinate amount of time trying to convince her that this was a good thing. It was more money, career advancement, an exciting new city, a chance to buy our first home, and much more. She begrudgingly came to a place of acceptance, and after a few months in Minneapolis she did become excited about the move and all the fun and new experiences Minneapolis promised to provide. Like everything else in our marriage, we didn't really stop to take the time to deal with issues. My upbringing taught me to sweep troubles under the rug and try to forget about them, but the lingering emotional metabolites stayed present, and I carried around some guilt and some anger over what I viewed as Lori not appearing to be more supportive of my career. Money, fun, and drink kept most of those feelings suppressed for the both of us, and we pushed forward to a happy place once again.

Our year in Minneapolis ended up being a lot of fun. We bought a great little house, made some great friends, and spent most free hours learning about and taking advantage of all the wonderful things the Twin Cities had to offer. Minnesota and Wisconsin have a hearty appetite for drink, and my job title could have easily been "Manager of Alcohol Deployment." I had no computer, no file cabinets, no one to directly report to, and no sales quotas to meet. I was simply given a company car, an unlimited expense account, a storeroom full of promotional giveaways, and was told that my job was to drive around Minnesota and Wisconsin and buy every willing propane dealer I could find a chicken fried steak, get them drunk, and leave them with a basketful of company trinkets. I employed this strategy two or three nights a week with the utmost skill. When I wasn't on the road getting fat and drunk, finding reason to drink near the office wasn't too difficult. Our offices were right next door to the Schmidt Brewery, where every afternoon from 3:00 p.m. to 6:00 p.m. they gave quick little brewery tours followed by free beer in their "testing dungeon." Again, I don't recall any real trouble related to alcohol while we were in Minneapolis other than a wrecked company car and snowmobile, both blamed on bad weather, or so I said!

In February 1988, I was contacted about a possible move to Houston, Texas, to join Koch's natural gas marketing group. This time I was smarter about presenting it to Lori as a joint discussion and family decision. It wasn't hard to convince her to move from the great white north in February to a sunny and 70 degree Houston. It helped that she wasn't happy with her job, and a few weeks later we sold the house and made the move to Houston.

The period after relocation to Houston is when my drinking finally started catching up with me and where some of the first serious warning signs appeared that I "might" have a problem. The job in Houston was quite different from the one in Minneapolis. It required business-casual attire and a suit from time to time. I was in a more formal office and had some real business responsibilities. Lori and I bought a house in a northern suburb, joined the local country club, and quickly made many work and neighborhood friends. Heavy drinking was primarily relegated to Friday and Saturday nights with neighborhood friends, or for special events when they arose (which was all the time!). As always, there were a couple of beers with the boys after work, and believe it or not a six-pack for the carpool ride home, since open container was legal at that time in Texas. Golf and beer, not in that order, consumed the weekends, and no amount of yard work was done without an appropriate refreshment nearby.

Warning sign number one came after my first year in Houston. While having lunch at a downtown Mexican food restaurant with a couple of customers, we decided it would be a good idea to have a margarita with our meals. That was quickly followed by a second and several subsequent rounds. Soon we were seven or eight margaritas in before someone in our party said, "I've got a meeting at 3 o'clock, and we better have one more, then go [finally, a reasonable voice]." I managed to make it back to the office, but shortly after, the booze caught up with me and I found myself extremely drunk. I shut the door to my office, propped a chair under the knob, and passed out on the floor. An hour or two later, my boss finally forced the door open and asked me what the hell was going on. After hearing my explanation, he minimized the severity of the incident, laughed it off, and although I sensed he was a little disgusted, he told me to go home and not tell anyone about the luncheon lest it get back to the corporate office and I be reprimanded.

The following week I found myself shaking my own head in disgust at our next door neighbor, after deeming him a grotesque alcoholic. Nearly every weekend, we or one of our neighbors would throw an impromptu party. Everyone would bring food and drinks and we'd sit around talking, laughing, but mostly drinking. My next door neighbor would get sloshing drunk every time. Without alcohol, he was a complete introvert—shy, unsure of himself, and lacking any semblance of self-confidence. A few beers in him and he was as obnoxious and loud as they come. He staggered and slurred his words, was belligerent, and was lucky he lived only fifteen steps away. One evening, Lori and I hosted a party, and as usual, my neighbor got drunk as a skunk. Around midnight everyone left and we went to bed. The next morning, I came downstairs, looked out the window, and there he was, completely passed out on my deck bench being licked in the face by our overactive Dalmatian. I shook my head with condemnation and told Lori, "That guy's got a problem! He's a real alcoholic." Little did I know that he would later look like a teetotaler compared to me. For the time being, however, I liked having him around and was happy to use him as a reference point and deflection topic for my own drinking.

A second warning sign appeared in Houston several months later when a friend of mine from high school came down to visit. My wife was not a big fan of his, and he thought she was abrasive and wore the pants in our family. So to avoid having them spend too much time together, my friend and I went to a local bar in the midafternoon to drink and catch up. Several hours later, my phone rang. It was Lori. I had forgotten that we had committed to playing doubles tennis that evening, and I was late. We hurriedly finished our fifteenth beer, and I raced home to pick up my gear and get to the courts in time. Lori was pissed that I was drunk, and she let me have it, which further fueled my friend's opinion of her and made me feel belittled, weak, and angry. Being in the condition I was in, my hand-eye coordination was off a little as you can imagine, and my effectiveness on the court was a little less than impressive. I was playing against Lori and her friend's husband, while my friend sat on the bleachers drinking beers from a small cooler I'd brought and thoroughly enjoying the show. Lori is a fantastic tennis player and she was making mincemeat out of me, hitting every shot she could at me, behind him, in front of me, and past me before my severely impaired tennis skills could adjust. She was still angry, being very smug about picking on me during the game, and was handily embarrassing me in front of everyone. I'm not an angry person and I rarely get upset, but after I'd lost about our tenth game in a row, the humiliation took its toll and I picked up one of the balls, tossed it in the air, and smashed a line drive that hit Lori right in the face! Of all things! I couldn't get my racket on a ball all night, but the second I decided to physically lash out, I hit the shot of my life that imprinted a Spaulding logo on my wife's cheek. Tennis was over and it was a very uncomfortable ride home. I had lost control of my drinking, and now it was impossible to deny that my actions from it had had a direct impact on someone I loved very much.

A few years later, a chance encounter resulted in an opportunity to move to New York City and develop a natural gas trading division for the prestigious Goldman Sachs. It was the opportunity of a lifetime. Never in a million years would Goldman hire a very average student from a state college in Kansas, but as luck would have it, the natural gas futures contract was brand new and set to open in April 1990, and Goldman didn't have any Ivy Leaguers who knew the gas business. So through a rather odd coincidence, I was their first and only interview for the position. Several months earlier, an oil trader named Jim, who lived in my neighborhood, contacted my carpool partner and asked if he could catch a ride with us to work the following day as his car was going to be in the shop. We happily extended the invitation, and on the way downtown he turned and asked me what I did. I said, "I market Koch's natural gas production." He said, "Oh, that's great, let's pull over for some coffee and donuts." End of conversation and the last time I'd see Jim for six months. In the interim, Goldman had hired him to move to New York to trade their fuel oil portfolio. When the trading department decided they needed to be in natural gas, the managing partner asked the energy trading group if anyone knew anyone or had a contact in the natural gas business. No one raised their hand, not a soul. Finally, my donut-eating conversationalist spoke up and said, "I know a guy who works for Koch that markets natural gas." A meeting was set up with the intent of using me as a springboard for networking into the gas patch, but for some reason unknown to me, they actually liked me and invited Lori and me to New York City for an all-expense paid three-day weekend that included a casual interview. We jumped at the free trip but had little optimism for a job opportunity. A week later, Goldman requested a second interview and, a week after that I was up for a final interview and they offered me the job. I'll never forget it; the place was a buzzing madhouse of frenzied activity and excitement. Millions of dollars were being made and lost every day. I was captivated and very much wanted the job on the one hand, but on the other was feeling extremely under-qualified and not equipped to handle what I thought they were about to ask me to do. After a day full of revolving interviews, the head partner called me into his office. He took off his shoes, lay down on his couch, crossed his legs, and said, "Michael, tell me the most impressive thing about Kansas." I quickly replied, "That's easy, we have the world's largest ball of twine!" He laughed uncontrollably and I knew it wasn't at my quick-witted joke. He was laughing at me. He thought I was the biggest hayseed that ever graced the hallowed halls of Goldman Sachs, and I imagine he couldn't believe that this prestigious firm was about to offer me a job. He said, "Michael, we like you and would like to make you an offer. We would like to offer you a $100,000 annual salary." I just about peed my pants. My current salary was $32,000 a year at Koch. He then stopped (before I had a chance to pounce on the offer) and said, "No, let's make it $125,000. No . . . $150,000, plus we'll guarantee you a $150,000 bonus." $300,000 minimum! I was twenty-eight years old in 1990, had barely scratched out a 3.0 GPA from a Midwestern college in business administration, had a limited amount of natural gas experience, no accolades on my résumé, and absolutely no idea how to manage and trade complicated derivatives products, manage risk, or speculate in futures and other obscure complicated markets. Of course, I accepted.

This was an easy sale to Lori; the compensation offer alone would have been enough. She might have gone to Fargo, North Dakota, for those kinds of dollars. The fact that she would no longer be required to work was appealing, and the opportunity allowed Lori to pursue her passion for interior design. Our neighbors threw us a going-away party/early retirement party for Lori; she enrolled in the New York School of Interior Design, and a couple of country bumpkins from Kansas were automatically transformed into "city slickers." It was probably the most exciting time of our lives. No children yet, more money than we knew what to do with, and the most exciting city in the world. We left everything behind except the drinking and were off to begin a new chapter in our lives.

The Metro North train from our home in Connecticut to Grand Central, the subway to Wall Street, and a ten-minute walk to 85 Broad Street and I was "in the game." It was a wildly exciting time in the early days of the natural gas futures, derivative, and forward markets. Our business exploded, and we became one of the largest natural gas trading businesses in one short year. We made markets at over eighty different locations, traded forward markets out ten years, priced up all kinds of exotic options and swaps, and held massive high risk speculative positions on the books. Days were filled with enormous profits and losses, nights with Bombay martinis and $100 steaks. Goldman provided us with our own private car services that picked us up any time day or night, rolled our drunken bodies into the backseats, and delivered us safely home to the wives and children we rarely saw and were beginning to not know. Arrogance ran rampant, and I couldn't have had a bigger ego than at any other time in my life. I began yelling at brokers, cussing out poor service, snubbing anyone I felt was below me, and generally just being the world's biggest jerk.

A Wall Street job is probably one of the most high profile positions in the world and the dream of many aspiring businesspeople, but it has its costs. Over the years we were in New York, I found myself under a lot of stress and pressure to perform. Losing days caused much anxiety, and there was infighting on the trade floor, politics and positioning for bonuses, backbiting and sabotage, and that was all just before noon. After work, the Darwinian competitions continued at bars and restaurants to see who could party the hardest, be the craziest, and still make it to work the next day. There were many days I didn't make it back to Connecticut, and many mornings I was in no condition to show up. My boss said, "Party and drink as much as you want, but just answer the bell every morning." And I did. It wasn't uncommon for someone to throw up in their trash can on a daily basis. That earned you a badge of honor at Goldman. The other costs were relational. My wife rarely saw me. I was up at 5:30 every morning and oftentimes not back home until 7:30 p.m., or sometimes after 9:00 p.m. if I missed the train from Grand Central to Connecticut. Saturdays I was so worn out that all I wanted to do was lie around all day. It was worse after we had our first child. He was still asleep when my commute started and in bed, asleep, when I got home. I was too exhausted to be a good dad or husband on the weekends. At least that was my excuse. After a short time working on Wall Street, I had a nervous condition, had developed high anxiety, and my wild behavior was creating a whole host of emotional maladies that included guilt, self-consciousness, and fear. I don't think I would have lasted more than a year if I hadn't been medicating the spiritual maladies inside of me with alcohol. I was on a crash course, and it was just a matter of time before I hit the wall. I'm not going to give you all the gory details of that experience in this book, but believe me, there were a lot of them. I'm just going to tell you that it ended badly, and I crawled out of New York City a beaten man. I was embarrassed, ashamed, and probably lucky not to be in jail. What started out as an unbelievably exciting opportunity ended in a miserable and a nearly career-ending failure.

CHAPTER 6

A KNACK FOR THE WRONG FORK

Life's road has a series of forks, and I was certainly at one after resigning (before they fired me) from Goldman Sachs. With what transpired my last few weeks on Wall Street, I had pretty much resigned myself to the fact that my future in the energy business was over. When word of my portfolio's $40 million loss hit the street, getting hired at the lobby reception desk at any reasonable trading firm would be difficult for me. I wasn't sure what I was going to do. I certainly didn't have a plan, other than to put the house on the market, move back to the Midwest, and try a different line of work. I was wrong. Word got out all right, but not a peep about an out-of-control trader who'd just lost a whopping sum of money. Well, a whopping sum back in those days. Thanks to the likes of Nick Leeson, who lost $1.3 billion a year later trading for Barings Bank, my paltry $40 million loss looked a lot more like a rounding error. Later there would be others losing billions making rogue trading decisions, but the largest to date would come in 2005 when Yang Yanming lost

$9.52 billion for the China Great Wall Trust. He was sentenced to death, while I got to simply walk away with a deflated ego, some hurt pride, and a clinical case of self-consciousness.

Fortunately, I had underestimated the energy market's appetite for experienced traders, especially ones who had started and built one of the largest most complex natural gas portfolios in the industry. Having a new entry on my résumé that said, "Vice President of Natural Gas Trading–Goldman Sachs" didn't hurt either. Whether they were aware of my problems at Goldman or not, the job offers came flying in from Houston, Tulsa, Omaha, Connecticut, New York, Dallas, and more. It was shocking to me. I thought I was finished; quite the opposite, however. I was in more demand than at any other time in my career. The fork in the road narrowed down to a job in Omaha and an equally promising opportunity in Tulsa. Lori and I visited both, weighed the pros and cons, and were truly divided. They were both great opportunities. We had a great visit to Tulsa, loved the team, the city, and it was close to home. On our visit to Omaha, it was 20 below, the meetings were awkward, the penthouse hotel room we'd been renting flooded in the middle of the night, and the entire bathroom backed up with sewage. The impression was not good. We ignored the warning signs and chose Omaha. It was the wrong fork.

My acquired New York City bad attitude, overinflated ego, and "better than you" persona did not sit well with the Omahaians. I was given a spot on the trading floor, responsibility over managing the company's fixed price risk, and a "little" latitude to trade speculatively—100 futures contracts was my limit. To put that into perspective, I didn't have a limit at Goldman, and some of my positions exceeded 10,000 futures. Needless to say, it was difficult staying within my limits in Omaha. It seemed that my time and talents were being wasted, I didn't like being told what to do, and was frankly embarrassed about the short leash my boss had me on. It didn't take a week before I blew through my restrictions, was scolded, had to liquidate, and was publicly called out in front of a room full of snickering traders who were happy to see me put in my place. The second time it happened, my boss wasn't so nice; the third and fourth times, he began to issue job loss ultimatums. I had only worked there six months or so and really didn't want to get fired and have to move again, but I also couldn't stand operating in an environment that seemed below me, so I started pocketing trades. The term "pocketing" refers to buying or selling futures contracts or swaps and NOT entering them into the system where those in charge of risk control could oversee position limits. I'd make the trades I wanted, jot them down on a sheet of paper, stuff them in my desk drawer, and not enter them into the system. It was a major infraction and grounds for immediate termination at any trading company. Those kinds of behaviors eventually catch up to you as they did for me. When questioned and confronted, I admitted to it, fully expecting to get fired, but my boss seemed to want to come to an understanding and resolution. After some discussion, he finally asked me, "Mike, do you even want to work here?" I paused for a minute and simply said, "No, I don't." He said, "Okay, you're done then," and I walked out the door, filled with shame, anger, self-pity, and a whole lot of fear. The industry might come back after me again, but I couldn't face it any longer. At that time, I just didn't think I could work for anyone else after climbing to the top of the Goldman Sachs Mountain. It was like having dated Halle Berry or Angelina Jolie and then told your new girlfriend would have to come from eHomely.com. I may have been done, but my new strategy (or job) was to figure out how to hide. I had humiliated myself again. It was the same schoolyard, making fun of my Dumbo ears, laughing at me for getting beat up, or scornfully judging me for cheating in a golf tournament, except this time it was an industry full of business peers, who had just a year earlier adorned me with such respect and in such high regard. I couldn't deal with it, so I decided to get as far away from trading as possible and bought my way into the retail gourmet coffee business. That became a welcome reprieve for three years before my ego got the best of me again.

I really did love the coffee business at first. It was a fun change, but something was burning me up inside. I was suffering from feelings of failure, remorse, regret, and had a serious low self-esteem problem. These feelings were uncomfortable, so I medicated with alcohol rather than deal with and resolve them. I had an insatiable determination to redeem myself, my reputation, and to prove to all the imagined Mike Lassman naysayers that I was a success. That drive manifested itself into so many bad ideas, poor business decisions, and career moves, it's a miracle I'm not in a straitjacket in a padded room, drooling all over myself right now. I quickly expanded to a second coffee store before it was viable, and then added a holiday store shortly after. It was too much to manage, the business was barely profitable, and I was working seven days a week, fourteen hours a day on my way to another failure. To my surprise, someone approached me about buying the coffee business. A few months later, their generous offer took me out of a losing position and even put a few bucks in my pocket after the creditors were all paid off. I had lived to fight another day.

With a little money in the bank, I decided to open up my own personal commodities trading account, formed a little fund with family and friend's money, lost a big chunk of it, shut it down, and was bailed out once again with another Wall Street job offer. I was back, baby! Off to New York Lori and I went, only to quickly get in over my head once again, lose money, and get fired and tossed back out on the street with a now pregnant wife. Feelings of uselessness, demoralization, and self-pity radiated from every inch of my body, and I was in the dump again. Not to worry. A few weeks later and another great job offer came rolling in back in Tulsa. Still alive with another chance! This time I wised up a little and actually made it five years with this company and had a relatively successful stint while there. If cats have nine lives, I must have had nineteen. I just kept getting killed and somehow kept coming back to life.

We rode high for those five years and bought our first million dollar home against my wife's better judgment. Always the salesman, I assured her with my confident insistence that this was "just the beginning" of our financial good fortune. Little did I know, Enron and our industry were quickly unraveling, and so was I.

The collapse of Enron and the highly leveraged state of my company's balance sheet cost me that job, but at least I left on good terms and with a nice severance package. It was probably for the best anyway, because my drinking had become full-blown during my employment there. We were drinking every day after work or on some three-day golf junket every other week that included an insane amount of drunkenness. I often drank over lunch. Toward the end of my five-year stint, bottles of peppermint schnapps became one of the necessities in my briefcase, and I had begun drinking at the office on a regular basis. I also started hiding bottles of vodka in my garage freezer at home, and at least once a week it was safe to say that I would act exactly as my old neighbor, the alcoholic, used to behave. I had become him, but wasn't willing to admit it.

The warning signs were everywhere. I remember one cool fall evening, sitting outside, in front of the outdoor fireplace with my wife, drinking a nice cabernet when the harsh realization hit me. Turning to her I said, "I think I've got a drinking problem." She was empathic, but not surprised, and seemed genuinely concerned. She suggested, "Maybe you should just slow down a bit." I agreed, and we finished our bottle of wine plus another. The intent to "slow down" lasted about three days, and things continued to get much worse after that.

As the drinking worsened, the secretive and unusual behaviors continued. I was still hiding bottles all over the house, the garage, and the yard. I was filling water bottles up with vodka and stashing them in the back of the fridge. I was pre-drinking before going out to parties and events that would have plenty of opportunity to drink, and I was regularly drinking in the mornings, and oftentimes in the middle of the night.

Now back in the familiar territory of being unemployed and servicing a big mortgage, country club membership, private schools for the kids, and every ancillary expense that comes along with living the high life, I was dead again. The "cat," however, wasn't spent quite yet, and a very unique proposition came my way. A friend of mine in the energy business suggested I open up a futures services and clearing operation. Promising to guarantee its success, he would deliver me his company's business to get the operation off the ground. I was skeptical, and a five-alarm medley was sounding off in my soul. It sounded too good to be true. It was, but I accepted anyway. Another chance for redemption! I set up a company, rented some office space, got the appropriate licenses, and started clearing futures and options trades. I'd get up every morning at 5:00 a.m., drink about a third of a bottle of vodka to knock the cobwebs out of my head, take a quick look at the market fundamentals, do a quick study of the charts, and then slog together a "daily market update" that was e-mailed to all my customers. On more than one occasion I got a reply that said, "Seriously, were you drunk when you wrote this?" Yes.

Before long, my colleague's underlying reasoning for setting up this little clearing business became clear. It was simply just a cover for something much more interesting—personal profits! It was suggested that I open an account under my own name, deposit some funds into it, and sit tight while a series of unknown investors added to the fund's balance sheet. Those investors, I would later find out, were a consortium of industry traders and executives prohibited from trading their own accounts due to company policy, but they certainly could deposit money into a "blind" (wink, wink) trust that could. It was amazing how much free advice was given to me on which way the markets were going to move after that! We did well . . . for a while.

It was also about this time that the FBI began to pay me visits. That's right, the Federal Bureau of Investigation had me in their sights and had tracked me down. Ironically, their informal visits and investigations had nothing to do with this blind trading pool. The first time they visited, I was in my little two-man office, clearing futures and options and trading when my wife called in a panic from home and said there were two guys in black suits from the FBI at the front door and they wanted to talk to me. Imagine her surprise! I knew what it was about, so I asked her to send them down to the office and I would talk to them. When they arrived, I was well into a bottle of vodka that had been stashed in my desk drawer and was feeling pretty cocky. A mano a mano with the FBI—you couldn't dream this kind of stuff up! Just as Lori had described, they arrived wearing sunglasses, identical black suits, and were serious as a heart attack, just like they are portrayed in the movies. I invited them in, offered chairs and said, "How can I help you fellas?" It seems they'd been investigating an industry-wide price fixing scheme that encompassed a dozen trading firms and 100-plus traders, and my number was up! But then again, I knew what they were here to discuss, so I was prepared. It's a much longer story I'll talk about more in my upcoming Wall Street book, but the gist of it was that every month a commodities price setting publication reported one aggregate price for various locations based on verbal information received from a large polling of natural gas producers, marketers, traders, and utilities. That price, when posted, settled thousands of financial derivative trades that were tied to the number, so it was important the number came out high if you were long and low if you were short. Hundreds of millions of dollars settled against these unscientific postings.

I calmly did my best to explain to these seemingly confused FBI agents how the process worked, why it was flawed, and how producers always reported their highest prices, end users, their lowest, and marketers and traders reported prices based on their positions. Then I conveyed how partial information was reported, kind of like when I'd come home from the casino and only tell my wife about the hands of blackjack I won, but conveniently leave out the ones I lost. It wasn't lying, it just wasn't full disclosure. They seemed satisfied with my explanations and then asked me some very pointed questions, like "Did you ever knowingly report false trades or try to manipulate the index? Did you work with anyone who did? Do you know anyone in the industry that might have?" No sir, no sir, no sir.

They left an hour later after my slurred dissertation on the process and analysis of the situation, seemingly content, but came back the next day with follow-up questions, and then again a week later pressing me for information on other traders who worked for and with me. I never saw or heard from them again after that, and I just kind of blew it off with some nervous amusement. In hindsight, I should have been scared out of my mind, but the continuous state of inebriation I was in shielded me from the levity of the situation. All I could say was "Wow, the freakin' FBI!"

Had I understood the real gravity of the interrogation, or been sober, I might have been a little more respectful of the seriousness of their inquiries or even hired an attorney. As it turned out, a handful of my colleagues were charged and faced some jail time. Most got off with fines, but a couple of traders from the Houston area actually spent some time in jail for their parts in the alleged index fixing schemes. For my part, it seems that I dodged another bullet and used up yet another "cat" life.

It wouldn't be much longer before I needed to call on another "life." Shortly after setting up the secret trading fund, I started thinking to myself that I might just start putting some of this money to work in the commodities markets. So I did. The problem was, my drinking had gotten so out of control, I wasn't making rational deci-sions, and oftentimes forgot what positions I put on the day before. My routine became getting drunk by 5:15 every morning, passed out on the sofa in my office by 8:30, then back up again around 10:00 a.m. to start drinking some more. Several nights during that time were spent on the couch in my office. After one three-day bender, at least two days of it in a blackout, I woke up to a phone call from my broker saying the options position I'd sold short had moved seriously against me and I needed to post margin money or liquidate the position. I had to liquidate. I'd already lost most of the money in the fund and was going to exhaust the rest just trying to get out of the position. It was an awful day that got worse as I headed back to my million dollar, highly mortgaged house. When I arrived, my wife was standing in the kitchen, arms crossed, with a bottle of water on the table. "Is this yours?" Of course it was mine. Who else's could it possibly be? It seems she had a big tennis match, suited up, grabbed a bottle of water out of the fridge, and headed off for her doubles match. After the first couple of games, and on a break, she grabbed the bottle, took a large drink, and then sprayed straight vodka all over the court in front of her tennis partners. She was humiliated, and I had no good explana-tion other than to admit what I'd done. The reprimand straightened me up for a couple of days, and I made it to the weekend, fretting most of the week away wondering how I was going to resolve the fact that I had just lost a lot of important and frightening people's money.

That Saturday was our son's tenth birthday party, my parents had come to town to celebrate, and Lori had scheduled a joint birthday party for him and his buddy who was also turning ten. The plan was to go to the other boy's house at 7:00 p.m. for a swim party and then have all the boys back to our house for an outdoor campout in the backyard. My job Saturday was to mow and clean up the lawn, set up the tents, and prepare for the overnight party. With plenty of liquor stashed in the garage, I was happy to oblige and spent the entire day in the yard, preparing and getting drunk. By the time I finished up, everyone was ready to go to the pool party a few miles away. I was drunk and still needed to shower and pick up the pizza, so I sent them on ahead. I passed out and missed most of the pool party, but managed to deliver the pizza only after calling Lori and asking her to meet me out front, since I was in no condition to attend the party. She did her best to cover for me, as usual, and told everyone at the party I was sick and needed to go home and lie down. Everyone was more than a little suspicious, but I pulled myself together and did my best to fake it through the evening, once back at our house for the campout. Around midnight, I tried to sneak back into the house for another one of those "bottles of water," got caught red-handed by my wife, and was scolded about how irresponsible I had been and how everyone was let down by my behavior, especially my son. I felt horrible and was overtaken by waves of guilt and remorse. The next morning I shared with my parents for the first time that I was struggling with alcohol. They, along with Lori, staged somewhat of a mini intervention and wanted answers about my plans to stop. Rehab was discussed, but I scoffed and said I had my issue under control.

The matter was dropped, but a few days later at work, feeling the walls caving in on me, I got rip-roaring drunk again, left the office, and stumbled to my car located behind the office. My car was parked facing a very steep downhill slope that descended into a wooden fence and someone's back yard. I put the car in drive, then decided to get out and grab a bottle of whiskey I had stashed in the back. The car lunged forward, popped the parking block before I could leap back in, and careened down the steep hill, crashing through the wooden fence and into an elderly woman's backyard before I could regain control of it. With the car now at a complete stop, I paused for a moment to assess what had just happened, then turned around and looked back at my office building. The windows were filled with faces from other offices, and they were all just staring at me. I was mortified, quickly jumped back in the vehicle, locked the Jeep into four-wheel drive, backed it up the hill, over the parking block, and sped off back to the safety of my home. After arriving there, I went straight to bed and passed out.

The following day, the jig was up. My trading fund participants had been tipped off by a floor broker about the depletion of the account, and calls started coming in. Panicked, I quickly left the office, got drunk, and then told my wife, "I'm in trouble and I need to go to rehab." As disappointed as she was, she seemed glad I was finally willing to get some help. So the next morning I packed away a half dozen wine coolers and drove myself to Valley Hope Treatment Center 90 miles away and checked in. At that moment, I thought I had reached the lowest point in my life, but it wasn't. There would be lower, much lower, points. I had blown up a fund and lost much money for friends, colleagues, and my family. My spirit was beaten, and I was plagued with such guilt, shame, remorse, and fear. I needed rehab badly, but my willingness to go was just a convenient excuse to hide for thirty days until I figured out what to do about the colossal mess I'd made with my kids, my wife, my business, and my life.

Two or three days in detox with the proper meds gave me a much better perspective on things. It had been years since I'd gone three days without a drink. I fully embraced the thirty-day program with everything I had. I had the full support of my wife, my family, my friends, and my kids. I came out thirty days later a completely new man. It was the happiest and most optimistic I'd been in a long time. After returning home, my wife was loving, supportive, and forgiving. It was one of the happiest times in our marriage. We had been given an opportunity for a fresh start, and we embraced it with new resolve.

Although I was feeling physically and emotionally high, I did return to Tulsa facing quite a financial mess. About a half million dollars had to be repaid to the fund partners, a huge lifestyle "nut" needed covering, and I had no money in the bank and no job. I prayed a lot, and God provided the most unbelievable escape route. Selling a million dollar house in Tulsa doesn't happen overnight, and we figured it could take a year to sell it. We had no idea how we were going to be able to cover all the expenses. In the meantime, we just cut back everywhere we could. The country club had to go, the fancy car gone, cleaning lady gone. If it could be eliminated, we cut it, with the exception of our kid's private schools, only because Lori's parents were kind enough to continue to pay for the tuition.

Since I was now at home a lot, I spent most days trying to figure out how to pay back the investors, get a job, and sell the house. I had plenty of time to wander around and realized I'd scarcely seen more than four or five rooms of our home. I started taking care of projects around the house that I used to be too drunk or lazy to accomplish. One day, while in the basement of this enormous house, I came across a large store room filled from floor to ceiling with old magazines from the '30s, '40s, and '50s. *Harper's Bazaar, Glamour, Seventeen, The New Yorker,* and more. My original plan was to bag them up and throw them away, but some of them were very interesting and even "wall art worthy," so I jumped on eBay and looked up "Vintage magazines— *Glamour*" and learned they were selling for between $20 and $40 an issue. There must have been nearly a thousand magazines down there. I quickly threw my energies into taking pictures of the covers, listing them on eBay, and soon the dollars started rolling in. The newfound income was enough money to cover our monthly expenses. Before long our house sold for a profit, and with the gain and equity we had in the house we were able to pay off all the investors and had enough money left over to buy a smaller house. We were ecstatic! Life was good. I had cleaned up my debts, cleaned up myself, and my family had never been closer. Out of that recovery process, however, a new business idea was born!

CHAPTER 7

INSANITY!
SAME ACTIONS,
SAME RESULTS

EBay! The unexpected windfall made from selling vintage maga-zines happened about the time eBay, as a company, was about to explode. Stories of trash turned treasure, garage sale "finds" spun into gold, and frothy profits that turned housewives into profitable business owners had gripped the world. New eBay "drop stores" were beginning to dawn the landscape, and an unlikely new economic engine was quickly becoming Wall Street's newest darling. Auc-tionDrop, QuikDrop, ISoldIt, and others had popped up and were receiving millions of dollars of capital funding from private equity firms trying to capture a piece of this exciting new market. Why not me? So I grabbed the coattails of a burgeoning market, accepted a small investment from my father-in-law, and formed eMarket, LLC, Tulsa's first eBay drop store!

A fresh and unbridled excitement welled up inside of me at the prospect of being on the front end of what looked to be a wildly profitable trend. With my sobriety in check, restored relationships with my wife and children, and the full support of family and friends, I felt unstoppable and dove in headfirst. The press coverage eMarket received was unbelievable, and it didn't take long before we were a well-known and widely recognized concept in Tulsa. The company's entrepreneurial leader was no exception. That first year was a whirlwind, and I wish I had kept a daily journal. The stories I could have written about the people, their items, and the unbelievable interactions we had with the world's eBay buyers would have been a fascinating book in and of itself. We sold an old 1924 Chicago Derby trophy won by Oklahoma's "Black Gold" thoroughbred for $10,000 before we were contacted by descendants of the jockey, the trainer, and the owner, all claiming rights to it. A day later someone walked in with a rock from the Arkansas River and swore it had magical powers and was worth thousands on eBay. We, of course, got the potato chip whose burn marks looked like a picture of Jesus. It didn't sell, and I ate it. We listed a bulletproof vest one day, and the following morning found the Tulsa police department waiting in front of the store to retrieve it, as it appeared to have been stolen from them. We sold Elvis memorabilia, designer purses (oftentimes knockoffs, as it turned out), the first issue of *Playboy,* which fetched $2,500, and thousands of other items ranging from vintage fishing lures to RVs! The flow was incredible, but there was a serious flaw in the business model. First of all, for every 100 different items that came into the store, about three of them were worth listing. That meant spending a great deal of time up front with the customer and even more time sorting through and researching the possible value of each item. The second problem was that our customers all thought their "crap" was worth "way" more than it was, and our clients were always disappointed. Toss in our 30 percent commission plus eBay and PayPal fees, and virtually everyone that "dropped off" was disillusioned. Finally, the more stuff that came in, the more people we had to hire, and the more space we needed. Since every item was different, each one required time up front with the customer and independent research. Each piece had to be individually photographed, a unique description written, hundreds of questions answered from potential buyers, and finally it had to be specially packed for shipping. The bottom line is that there were no economies of scale, and it became evident within the first six months that this concept was not going to work. Did that warning signal stop me? No way. I opened a second location and eventually a third attached to a 10,000 square foot warehouse.

Around that same six month time period, as it became apparent the business might not succeed in its current form, my personal recovery efforts were beginning to take a backseat to everything else going on in my life. I was coming up on one year of sobriety and my dreaded fortieth birthday. I had stopped going to AA meetings and had become so focused on making eMarket a success that my spiritual and family life were fading away. I had fallen back into some old patterns of relying on myself, rather than God, doing whatever I had to do to win, and not reaching out for help. My family was in town for the big 4-0, and I wasn't in much of a mood to celebrate. I recalled my thirtieth birthday back in New York City when my wife secretly flew both our families to town and hit me with the greatest surprise birthday party I'd ever had. We laughed, danced, and drank the weekend away. It was quite a celebration, but ten years later, now staring at forty, I was filled with self-pity at not being able to celebrate the same kind of milestone. I was also in morbid reflection about my position in life, in regret about not being where I'd hoped to be financially or professionally, and I was depressed. I think I was actually having a mid-life crisis to be honest with you, and as I sat there listening to everyone sing Happy Birthday, sipping a diet Coke, and feeling self-conscious about the fact that everyone else wished they were drinking but couldn't because I was an alcoholic, had me crawling out of my skin.

Then a powerful notion hit me! A few weeks earlier, an eBay drop customer had dropped off about 100 collector bottles of bourbon. You know the colorful porcelain kind, sculpted into images of Uncle Sam, horses, dogs, historical characters, and things of that nature. They were all thirty or forty years old, many of them were empty, the corks were rotted out, but some of them still seemed to be in pretty good shape, and I knew a few of them might have some drinkable condition of bourbon in them. So I excused myself from the party, said I needed to run to the eMarket store for an hour or two to get some work done, and began sampling vintage bourbons. Most of them were rotten and awful, but I found a few I could choke down to get that relief I was looking for. Home an hour or so later, I made some evasive and quick small talk and excused myself to go to bed, undetected. The damage was done, however, and the start of another swirl down the toilet for me began. I managed to not come completely unglued at that point, but the seed had been planted in my mind that it was okay to drink again, if necessary. I just couldn't let anybody know about it.

Knowing the business model was failing, I came to the realization that some kind of adjustment had to be made. Since economies of scale was the key to success, it became apparent to me that we had to begin finding sale merchandise that could be replicated, which meant we needed to start buying multiple quantities of the same item. We needed to go into the overstock business. I decided to call the Coleman Company out of Wichita to see if they sold overstock goods. As luck would have it, they did, and I began buying small loads of outdoor and camping gear. I could buy 100 identical lanterns for instance, take one picture, write one description, and then schedule out the listings based on what the market would bear before the price started eroding. A new business model was born. It didn't take long before those small purchases became large purchases, and the semi-trucks of overstock goods started rolling in. We eventually phased out of the eBay drop business and became Just Camp, LLC. Although I was dead again with the eMarket concept, I was once again brought back to life, thanks to Coleman and a colleague who helped distribute their goods. After phasing out the eMarket stores and consolidating the entire enterprise into one large warehouse with a retail storefront, I had the platform in place to ignite my vision of growth. But it was never big enough or profitable enough for me, so it seemed logical to me to keep borrowing and expanding my way to greatness!

Things were looking better, sales were strong, profits were up, and my insatiable drive to become the largest outdoor gear seller on eBay was front and center. However, eBay was just the start. I created a similar business on Amazon and then our own proprietary online retail website called JustCamp.com. With the stress of managing what essentially boiled down to controlled chaos and finessing somewhat of a shell game using bank loans and good credit terms with vendors, I managed to keep the business afloat, but it was always teetering on the edge of insolvency because of serious cash flow problems. My ego, however, was sure it would all work itself out when I was finally able to liquidate what I'd calculated to be roughly a million dollars of inventory.

In retrospect, I was displaying the characteristics of the word "insanity" again, which meant I was doing the same things, but expecting to get different results this time. My foray into the eBay drop world was no different from my entrance into the gourmet coffee business. I was still searching for acceptance and a way to hide from my failed energy marketing and trading past, while at the same time trying to prove to everyone that I could be an overnight success. The parallels are so strikingly similar. I lunged in headfirst, worked seven days a week, fourteen hours a day, expanded to a second store before proving a first would work, and then quickly added a third and a 10,000 square foot warehouse. Borrow and spend, attract new investors and expand, promote, promote, and promote some more. The sense of impending doom and failure was reason enough for me to drink away these feelings that had once again consumed my spirit. And I did.

Things were not good at home. My wife excused the first several drunks and graciously wrote them off as "slips," but as they continued, so did her distance from me. I honestly don't remember much of those years. I can't recall if this was the start of a series of me having to leave our house, sobering up, and getting to come back, only to be sent packing again. All I remember from the early days of the warehouse are setting up a cot in my office and spending many a night there drinking myself to sleep. I vaguely remember having to live with my brother for a while, but mostly getting drunk and spending the night in the warehouse, oftentimes interrupted by a family member pounding on the front door and office windows trying to get me to unlock the door and let them in to help. I never did.

It wasn't long before my dad and my wife talked me into going to yet another rehab. I had convinced them that AA didn't work. Thirty-day twelve-step rehab programs weren't effective, and I couldn't afford to walk away from a business that I thought was solely dependent upon me. On some level I think they agreed and found a treatment center called Narconon that had an unorthodox approach to alcohol and drug addiction. It was a four-to-six-month program, but if you worked hard, you could graduate in three to four months. The best part is that they would allow you to bring a laptop and give you a few hours a day to manage a business, if you were lucky enough to have one. I agreed to go, but three weeks into it, my ego and stubbornness wouldn't allow me to run the business remotely, or focus on recovery, so I left. My wife was not happy, accepted my decision, but let me know I wasn't moving back into the house, so I went to live with a friend of mine. A few days later, I was drunk as a skunk and decided to drive myself back to Narconon. I dumped the entire business in Lori's lap to manage, alongside another helping friend, and checked back into the country club to try to get well. I used to always feel so sorry for myself having to go to rehab. I don't know why. Lori used to say, "I would give anything to go to rehab for four months. Check out of life, leave all my responsibilities behind, and just work on myself." I get that now. I didn't then.

Narconon is an interesting place, and maybe I'll write more about my experiences there along with the other four completed rehabs, my five rehab "check in and leave" a week or two later trips, my seven trips to detox, and my various hospital emergency stays someday, but not today. Narconon was not a Christian-based facility, but rather based on the teachings of scientologist L. Ron Hubbard. They used no drugs to help addicts and alcoholics detox (that was painful and dangerous), but rather a menu of health drinks, vitamins, mild exercise, and light massages. The second phase of treatment included thirty days in a dry sauna, six or seven hours a day that were intended to make you sweat out every last drug or alcohol metabolite your body had collected. It was then followed by a series of several "books" that essentially taught you how to address what they called an "emotional discomfort" that led you to seek instant relief by using drugs or alcohol. The whole program was an exercise in learning to control your own emotions, your environment, and the people around you, all with the goal of eliminating emotional discomfort. It was actually a pretty interesting program, and I learned a lot. The one thing I didn't learn was that Narconon, AA, any twelve-step program, another person, or even I couldn't relieve me of my alcoholism. Only God could and would if I were willing to seek Him. I wasn't.

I finished the program in three and half months, gave an emotional speech to the Narconon community, family, friends, my wife, and the kids at a graduation ceremony before heading back to Tulsa. My speech was intended to show Lori that I was better, a new and different man, sorry and ready to be the "man of her dreams" and father to our children. Actions, however, speak louder than words, and although my words were from the heart, my actions over the years never seemed to back up those words. Apologies and sweet promises to do better may work the first time or two, but after that, you're no better than the "boy who cried wolf." No one believed me because my history had shown my words were hollow and always broken. This time was apparently no different as Lori reminded me that I had complained to her shortly after the speech, saying, "It would have been nice if you had come up on stage and given me a heartfelt and forgiving hug or kiss. It's what the people wanted to see!" So much for sincerity. It was all just a show. I realized later that I hadn't changed, but had rather just given another self-serving elocution. "What's the use?" I wondered. It was sometimes a year later, sometimes a week later, but I always let them down and they all had learned the fine art of self-preservation and protection. Walls were up, and the only remedies for restored relationships were time and right action. This time was, once again, no different, and my passionate speech convinced my wife of nothing. She insisted I live in a rental house she'd purchased so I could focus on my recovery, give her and the kids time to heal the wounds my disease and I had inflicted upon them, and let time, sobriety, and trust dictate our reunion as a family. So I did.

I settled nicely into my new digs and was optimistic about the future. The business hadn't suffered much during my four month absence (hard to believe, I know! I guess maybe the world could survive without me), and I quickly re-inserted myself back into it and continued my quest of making it an international success. I was a little confused about my recovery going forward however, mainly because Narconon didn't really have much to offer in the way of continued care. Their view (or probably just the way I chose to interpret it) was that when you left the program, you were no longer an alcoholic or an addict. You still couldn't drink, but that negative title had been removed from you. They weren't advocates of AA meetings or support, which suited me just fine. Their only advice was to use the tools they had given you to manage your soul, your life, your environment, and the people around you. Fair enough. I knew their methods, had the books, and it was just a matter of practicing and mastering their techniques. I didn't.

I did stay sober for a couple of months. Things were going well at work, and I was in the process of purchasing a large four-story building downtown, expanding the size of our outdoor retail store to 20,000 square feet, and I had come up with an idea to build a 10,000 square foot indoor campground called "the Urban Campout." I had also contracted out the fourth floor of the building to a couple of cops who wanted to start up a photography co-op. My wife was also cautiously optimistic and hadn't given up on me yet. Our relationship was beginning to rekindle; in fact, it was kind of exciting at that time. We were seeing each other regularly, I was spending quality time with the kids, and things were looking up. Then in late December, Lori said, "It just not the same without you, and we think you should come home for Christmas." I was elated, but later found out I'd misinterpreted that statement. I immediately packed up the truck with all my belongings and moved back home. This was all I ever wanted. And I guess sometimes you just hear what you want to hear. Christmas was nice, but something seemed amiss, and after the first of the year, my wife told me that she didn't intend for me to move back in permanently, rather just come to stay a few weeks over the holidays. I was shocked, hurt, confused, and angry, all emotions that needed relieving of course. Rather than run me back off, we tried some kind of weird arrangement where we would live together as roommates, but she needed time and space away from me. I didn't get it, couldn't wrap my head around the arrangement, didn't understand how we could be married, live under the same roof, but act like friends. After two weeks, I wrote her a letter, complete with an ultimatum that it was impossible to live in this environment and if she didn't change her attitude toward working out our marriage and acting like married people, I was moving out. She didn't, so I rented the apartment downtown I talked about back in Chapter One, packed all my stuff back up again, and moved out. The kids must have been so confused. I was incredibly hurt, lost, and just couldn't understand. Layer on a healthy dose of guilt, resentment, and fear, and I was headed for inevitable disaster. I really thought I was better, had healed, was refocused on being the kind of husband and father a wife and kids would want, but I later realized that I was just bulldozing forward in all my selfishness, completely oblivious to what might be going on with them. Looking back, I made a mistake, and didn't even consider the fact that my wife was as sick as I was, the kids were suffering, and they all needed time and space to heal themselves before I came charging back into their lives. I just didn't see that at the time.

As it turns out, when my wife called my bluff, I think we both knew it was over. I wasn't coming back this time, and she wasn't letting me come back. She certainly knew it was over, and over the course of the next ten months, I did my best to cement that fact and decision in her mind. Although I wasn't ready to let her go, my actions over that period certainly didn't support that desire. I was drunk most of the time I lived in that apartment, but managed to function well enough to keep the business afloat, see the kids every once in a while, and put on a front for friends and family. I lashed out many times, usually in a blackout or when extremely drunk, and I spewed venom on her with texts, phone calls, and e-mails only to call or text back the following day apologizing profusely. Why do we hurt the ones we love most? I don't know, but I certainly was. It was an awful time in my life, and the harder I tried to fix everything, the worse it got. What I didn't realize at the time is that I had to fix myself before I could even begin to think about repairing relationships. I had to learn to love myself before I could truly love anyone else. I had to be willing to let go of the things I was so desperately trying to hold on to if I ever expected to have a chance at keeping them. I had to change myself before I could expect to change any of my relationships. I didn't do that. I didn't know how, and the reality was that I couldn't do it by myself anyway. I needed someone more powerful than me, someone capable of miracles, and that person was God. I just wasn't ready to call on Him yet, although He was waiting patiently for me. So I suffocated my family, desperately clung to them, tried to control and change them, and all I did was push them away. The further they fell away, the more distant our relationships had become, the more troubled and depressed I became, and the more I drank. It was a vicious cycle that required a personal implosion and a human crash-and-burn if the cycle was ever to be broken. That's exactly what happened, and after I'd blown up as a human being, which included another hospital stay, jail, and a couple of weeks bouncing from cheap hotel to cheap hotel, guess who showed up to help me? My wife.

Now that is what I call love. I didn't recognize it then, but the enormity of her actions at that time were a supreme example of unconditional love. Not romantic love, but what I suppose is the kind of love that God feels for each of us. Here I was, this disgusting, hideous, unlovable creature that had ruined her life, broken up our family, and pelted her with hurtful words and actions. I damaged her soul, her spirit, her mind and kept her in a constant state of fear and anxiety. If anyone had a right to walk away from me and hope I'd burn in hell, it was Lori. That's not what she did though. Somewhere deep inside her she felt compassion. She saw a very sick man, not the one she married and fell in love with, but simply a suffering child of God. The heart she has for God and all his children allowed her to turn the other cheek and love when I wasn't capable of loving back. I think a part of her knew the things I'd said and the things I'd done weren't intentional, that they weren't the Mike she knew, and somehow she was able to reach out and care for the person who had inflicted her life's greatest wounds. She doesn't know this, but she helped save my life. I was out of options, no one else was going to show, and that gesture opened my eyes to the kind of person she really is. In some small way, it made me feel loved by the person I most wanted to be loved by. It made me feel forgiven on some level, and it gave me the strength and the confidence to finally do what I had needed to do for years. Let go and live!

CHAPTER 8

COLLATERAL DAMAGE

One of the common statements made by alcoholics, drug addicts, those addicted to pornography, or folks with eating disorders and all the harmful behaviors that surround those addictions is "I'm not hurting anyone but myself." That is the biggest fallacy around any addiction. I've even said it a time or two myself—and believed it. That statement couldn't be further from the truth, and the reality is that our addictive behaviors, compulsions, and associated actions actually do hurt those around us, especially the ones who love us, more than we hurt ourselves. We're just not feeling that hurt because we are continually dulling our pain by medicating it away with tequila, meth, Internet porn, and with blooming onions (and a diet Coke, please)! If we weren't so stoned out of our minds, we might actually see it, but we don't. If you suffer from addiction, later in this book you'll have the painful opportunity to put yourself in the shoes of all those affected by your addiction, and for once in your life you'll stare down the barrel of pain you've reigned upon everyone you've loved and been loved by. It's not a pretty picture and is an eye-opening look at your selfishness, and a tortuous and very real and insightful look at how your life, your behaviors, and an unwillingness to take responsibility for an addiction truly damage those closest to you. Oftentimes, it's serious and permanent damage. My experience was no different.

Most of my addictive years were spent blaming my wife, my kids, my parents, coworkers, and even God. If you had my problems, you'd drink too. Just leave me alone, I'm not bothering you, I'm not hurting you, just go away and stop trying to correct me, nag me, or tell me what you think I need to do! But my irrational behavior was bothering people and hurting people, and my actions were affecting others. In fact, there was a long and littered trail of injured bodies scattered in my life's wake!

After going through the process of identifying the harm I had caused, explained in subsequent chapters, I began to have a real awareness of just how I'd shown up in life, and in relationships. It was like I had been transported into Charles Dickens' *A Christmas Carol,* and the ghost of Mike's past took me on a ride into the unfortunate lives of everyone I touched. I was able to see my mom's agonizing worry about what happened in high school just about every weekend night between my curfews and when I actually arrived at home. I was able to empathize with her tossing and turning, hundreds of nights, wondering if I was alive or dead. Saw her heart break for what I'd become, felt her tears for the wife and children I was neglecting. I watched her face age when I disappeared for days on end. I robbed her of sound and peaceful sleep and caused great fear and anxiety in her every time she heard the phone ring after 10 p.m. Was it a desperate call from me, the police, or the undertaker? I watched her fret over the helplessness she felt and the anger welling up inside of her at my unwillingness to help myself. Watching someone you love disintegrating and throwing their God-given life away takes a toll on a mother, and mine was no different. I never gave that one thought while in the middle of my selfish addiction. Not one. I told myself, she's 1,000 miles away; I'm not hurting her. That was a lie created to make me feel better.

I cried out for "the ghost" of Mike's past to "Take me away, because I couldn't bear to see anymore." He did, and I was then transported into the heart of my father. It was easy to see the frustration on his face from an inability to help his son, the helplessness that can drive a man crazy, and the guilt that surely surged inside of him over the questions I imagined he kept asking himself, over and over: "Is this my fault? Where did I go wrong? What could I have done to prevent this?" I felt the sadness in his heart and the mourning that must come from watching a child deteriorate and plunge into the abyss of alcoholism. I saw a father, who at one time expanded with pride over a successful high school athlete, a college graduate, a son who was successful in business and who had built a family and blessed him with grandchildren, but who now had a sickness in his stomach for what his boy had become. I felt the anger and confusion about why his oldest son couldn't "pull himself up by his bootstraps" and lick this thing, like he'd licked adversity so many times before. I felt his heart break for his grandchildren and was consumed by his overwhelming fear of what was to become. Could I feel all of that in the "thick of it"? No. I couldn't. My thoughts were, "It's not his problem, I can handle this, and he shouldn't be concerned, this doesn't affect him." But it did.

"No more spirit! Take me from my father; I don't want to see anymore."

As much as I wanted these visions to end, those hurt the most were still to be seen on this journey. It was far from over. As we descended upon my only son, I could hardly bear the thought of seeing the pain I'd delivered to him. One thing that came to mind was, "How must have God felt, watching the world reject, belittle, torture, beat, and crucify his only son?" God was the one who allowed it, and it was part of His plan to save the world. It wasn't part of my plan to save the world, it was just me unintentionally hurting the boy I loved more than life itself. The guilt and sadness were astounding. The inability and desire to change the past brought tears to my eyes as I watched a confused young man struggle with how to deal with a sick and unpredictable father, with a family that was coming apart at the seams, and with his distraught mother and frightened sister as they struggled as well. I felt his humiliation, his embarrassment, and his shame for having an alcoholic dad. I watched him retreat inside of himself, withdraw from life, struggle in school (only for a semester, the kid is smart as a whip!). I felt his confusion, his loss of security, his feelings of neglect, his fear, and his own guilt from not being able to do something to stop the hurt I was causing those he loved. But there was nothing that he could do; there was nothing that anyone could have done. I could see sadness in his heart from being essentially fatherless and the regret of not having a strong and guiding role model in his life. It was a missed opportunity during a formative period in a boy's life. It makes me sick to think about it. Oh, for another chance, the ability to turn back time so I could tell my son how much I loved him, how proud of him I was and am. "Please, give me another chance to be his role model, his strength, his refuge, his cheerleader, and his shoulder to cry on." I wasn't that dad back then and it hurt him. So don't think for a minute you're not hurting those around you. You are, and it was becoming painfully obvious to me that I was too.

"Let's get this over with Spirit, where to next?" I cried. "To see your daughter," he bellowed.

An unquestionable "daddy's girl," who completely and utterly stole my heart from the day she was born. I've spent the last sixteen years wrapped hopelessly around her little finger. But despite my unbreakable love for her, I still tore her apart as she battled to reconcile her unconditional love for me against the person I'd become, and against a mother she loved equally. I put her in a position of picking sides, defining loyalties, and covering for my indiscretions. A position no child should ever be put in. Her fear, her heartache, and her sadness were enormous. Her desire and need for a loving, providing, and protective father were taken from her and replaced with the instability, selfishness, and madness of a father who was incapable of fulfilling his role. Her longing for a man to have as a role model for future relationships was demolished, and her insatiable desire to unconditionally love me were at odds with the man and father I had become. I watched her sink into a quiet depression as I fell further and further away from the family. She missed the old me so much that it left a permanent ache in the pit of her stomach. She had to grow up too quickly because of what I had become. She assumed the role of encourager, provider of hope, and deliverer of love, when no love was deserved or due me. She had taken on the role that I should have been playing for her. I became the child and she the parent, a responsibility no child should ever have to endure. Of all the pain and hurt my addiction and I dealt my daughter, the biggest had to be the fear my condition instilled in her. As a daughter, she needed to know that her father was a rock, a shelter against the world's storms, a trusting lighthouse in a world of darkness, danger, and crashing human waves. She needed to know and feel that she had a protector and a provider of security, some kind of authoritative force to make a child, especially a daughter, feel safe. If asked how I've hurt my one and only daughter, it's in that way. I took that security away from her, and it's not something that can be easily re-instilled, if ever. "Enough, enough! My heart is heavy! I know I've hurt the next person on our journey; please don't make me see how much, Spirit."

I had to though, in order to see, to understand, to acknowledge, to learn and grow, and to not continue to hurt her anymore. My ex-wife, Lori, was the person I was closest to in this world, in part because of the life and experiences we shared, the vulnerabilities we've exposed to one another, and from the insights we have into one another's personalities. Our intimate emotions opened us up, especially her, to the most stinging hurts one human being can inflict upon another. As the Spirit and I peered into her soul, I could see so much sadness and reflection on the life that could have been, for the family that could have thrived, for the future that was cut short by my hideous existence. I sensed the overwhelming fear, the insecurity, both financially and emotionally. A security she needed so desperately. I saw the anxiety she lived with on a daily basis, the instability of wondering from day to day when the "other shoe would drop." I heard the frustration and weariness in her voice from having to raise two children by herself, from having to guide and nurture them through rough waters alone. I sensed her anger for having to go it alone without the help of a strong and supportive husband and father. I felt her disgust as she watched me become just another helpless child to take care of. Her longing for a husband that adored her, honored her, protected her, guided her, and was the spiritual leader of our family. Her disappointment in not having that man, the man I should have been, in her life. I felt her tiredness in trying to keep it all together, alone, and without the help of a man who long ago promised to be her equal, to be a self-sacrificing and giving partner. Her heart heavy and her soul needing to rest, but there was no time for rest. There was too much to do, too much to worry about, too much to prepare for, and no one to help. She must have felt betrayed, let down, dealt a bad hand in life, all because of me. She felt deceived because of all my lies and omissions, "less than" by my attempts to control, and invalidated psychologically and emotionally by my attempts to negate her thoughts, feelings, and emotions. I decimated her ability to trust, not just me, but others, most likely men, and I hardened a heart that had so much love to give. I badly hurt the one I loved most, the woman God gave to me as a partner.

So I can no longer tell myself that I'm not hurting anyone but me. I hurt everyone that crossed my miserable path, and they have been hurt WAY more than I've ever hurt myself. I have to live with that and do my best to repair those wounds by understanding and always remembering.

"Spirit, let me wake up and be different! I don't want to be that person from the past. I want to be who God says I am and the person He designed me to be. I want to be the opposite of who I've been!"

Those aren't the only people we hurt in our addictions; they are just reminders of the people often hurt the most. They're easy to identify. Just look around at the people you're closest to. Look for the people who love you the most and you'll see the wreckage and collateral damage your actions have caused.

The others? There are plenty of them as well. When you hurt someone's daughter you hurt them. When you default on a business dealing, you hurt the individual's reputation that you've been dealing with at that company. When you're hurting yourself, you're hurting your siblings. When you neglect your duties at work, you're hurting your coworkers. When you let down your church friends, you weaken their faith. When you drive around high or drunk, you are endangering perfect strangers. When you lie to and avoid your friends, you hurt their feelings and make them doubt the legitimacy of what they thought was friendship. The list goes on and on. It's like the movie, *The Butterfly Effect,* based on the premise that when a butterfly flaps its wings, somewhere down the line that flapping has a cascading and exponential effect on a series of something elses. Everything we do in life is a butterfly flap, and every move we make, every action we take, every word we say, every decision we make affects someone, somewhere down the line. The question one must ask oneself is, "Does it affect positively or negatively?"

I wish I could say only alcoholics, addicts, and generally misguided "bad people" cause collateral damage, but that's not the truth. Just because I got sober two years ago and became a better person didn't mean that my capacity to hurt others ended. It didn't. What I have figured out about actions that hurt other people is that they come from the same source that caused me to drink, or another person to use, or binge, or surf for porn. They came from a spiritual malady discussed in great detail in a later chapter.

Here's an example. Last year, I decided to get remarried. I found the most wonderful Godly woman who absolutely adored me. She understood my past, accepted me for who I am, was the most self-less, giving, self-sacrificing person I'd ever met. She was the calming agent I desperately needed in my overactive life and mind. She was perfect in every way and someone who made me a better man. As we charged ahead full steam toward matrimony, I convinced Angela to quit her job, sell her house, pull her daughter out of school, and move her life to Tulsa to be with me a few months before the wedding. She loved me and trusted me, so she made the move. Two days into living together and a month before the wedding, I was overcome with fear, with doubt, and with anxiety. I was consumed with guilt over separating from a family that I had known and loved for twenty-five years and starting a new one. I became selfish and panicked about all the personal sacrifices I was going to have to make. I had been living alone for several years, was used to having my own space, my own routine, my own way of doing things. I didn't have to share with anyone and had the flexibility to do whatever I wanted, whenever I wanted to. Now, all of a sudden it dawned on me that I was going to be inconvenienced by having to cohabitate with two other people and a house dog. (I'm not a big dog fan and certainly not a "dog in the house" proponent.) I was worried about how my kids were going to view the marriage, was convinced that it was going to damage the newly restored and delicate relationships I had with them, and I was greatly concerned about the responsibility of having to take care of a new wife and her child. My selfishness and fear overtook me, and I made a very bad decision. I told my fiancé I wasn't ready to get married, and I couldn't live with them. They had to move out. That was a wicked and devastating blow.

Why I didn't figure that out before asking Angie to marry me, I don't know. Why I didn't think it through before convincing them to pack up the only life they knew and move to a completely new city, I can't say. It was incredibly shortsighted of me. I may have even blocked it out, out of loneliness, or because I loved her and just figured it would all work itself out. Probably neither. It was most likely that I'd allowed my relationship with God to lapse and had stopped relying on His wisdom and direction months earlier. But the day they moved in, complete with slobbering and shedding dog, I came unglued and trashed the best thing I had going in my life—and I wasn't even drunk!

When friends, church friends, family, and coworkers heard the news that the wedding was off and the girls and dog were gone, I started getting calls and "drop-bys" from well-wishers offering condolences, lots of free advice, and their infinite wisdom. Some months later it all kind of "hit me" that we humans don't really give much thought to the far-reaching implications of our actions. Here is a summary of the feedback I received. It's not just me.

"Well Mike, sorry to hear it, but no damage done; better to realize it now, than later, when it's too late."

"Thank goodness you had the courage to call it off. That could have become a real mess."

"I hate to say it, but I really thought you were moving too fast; glad you recognized it and changed course before any damage was done."

"If you weren't sure, then you made the right decision, and everyone will be better off in the long run."

"I know it's hard, but really, you've just done everyone involved a huge favor."

Seriously? A huge favor? Why don't you ask Angela, her daughter, Elizabeth, and if you speak canine, their dog, Scarlet, if they felt like they'd been done a huge favor? Not one person said, "That poor woman, that frightened and innocent child, and that confused dog!" I know, I know, I'm getting mad at my "well-wishers" when I'm the one who caused all of this to happen. My point is that oftentimes we don't consider the magnitude of our decisions and how they negatively affect others.

My selfishness, my fears, my doubt, and my anxiety caused me to hurt, and hurt badly, two wonderful and innocent people. Two children of God (and one dog). Angela was crushed and confused. She was frightened and in shock. She had just quit a job she loved, sold a house that had become a home for her and her daughter, and blindly packed up her life to move to a new city to be with a man she loved and trusted. The guilt she must have felt over uprooting her daughter from a stable environment had to be crushing. The self-doubt and confusion she must have felt about "What went wrong? How did

I not see this? What have I done? How could one day we be so in love, see a future life together, and then the next day we're out on the street?" It was a serious and devastating setback in her life and with her emotional well-being. I hurt her self-esteem, trampled her self-worth, and demolished a trust that had been carefully constructed.

What about her innocent daughter? Yanked out of the only town she'd ever lived in. Taken away from her school and friends, moved to a big city to live with a man she hardly knew, who despised her beloved pet! She was let down by a father figure and felt to blame for the breakup. She had been promised a better life, then had it ripped away from her in two days' time. She had to be unbelievably frightened and hurt. She trusted that her mother would protect her and make decisions that were in her best interests, and Angela did, based on the trust she had in me. I broke that trust because of my own insecurities, and it had a chain reaction that affected all kinds of people down the line, including her daughter, her son, her parents, her friends, her coworkers, and even her dog.

Not one person on my side of the equation really stopped to consider that. I didn't either at the time, but my actions, my self-will, and my disconnection from God caused a "firestorm" of pain and resentment that is going to take time to clean up. Not just with the people I've hurt, but within my own soul. The experience filled me with such guilt, shame, and remorse that I'd even put my own self at risk for another relapse somewhere in the near future unless I was able to clean up this mess, do my best to right this wrong, ask my God for forgiveness, forgive myself, and repent from this type of thinking and action.

I'm getting ahead of myself (especially in this book), and all these answers would come later, much later. You have to be broken enough, utterly defeated, and completely surrendered before you're able to have any kind of spiritual awakening. Your life doesn't begin to change until you've reached that bottom and have come to a place of despair that gives you enough willingness to reach out for God's help. It is from this humble point that real changes can begin to happen in your life. I was almost there as we digress a few years earlier to my own personal bitter end.

CHAPTER 9

BACK TO THE BITTER END

It's always the darkest before the dawn, but holding on until that first ray of light appears feels like an impossible task. I was so lost and it was so dark, I never thought the morning would come. My life was over and I was literally asking God to end it for me so I wouldn't have to do it myself.

I had relapsed badly again, was holed up in my apartment fading in and out of drunken consciousness. I had disappeared from the face of the earth, and hadn't been to work in almost a week. My phone was blowing up with texts, e-mails, and phone calls, none of which I answered or responded to. I was living to drink and drinking to live, and it was incredibly difficult just to make it to the liquor or convenience store for more booze.

I can't tell you what day of the week it might have been, or even what time of day. I was in my easy chair in an alcohol-induced comatose state when an authoritative knock pounded on my front door, rattling my small apartment. I didn't move. The knock came again, this time louder. I struggled to my feet, walked toward the front door, and eyed the peephole with no intention of answering it. It was a Tulsa police officer. A man I knew from the kids' school. I stepped back and tried to think for a minute. Maybe he would go away. I stood motionless and waited as the silence began to give me relief. A few seconds later I leaned in to peek through the hole again and "Wham," the entire front door came crashing in and hit me in the face. He'd kicked the damn door in and behind him stood my wife, a business colleague, my entire staff, and a few friends. The lack of my responses over the last several days led them to believe that I may be dead, by bottle or by hand. My wife came in while the rest of the rescue party waited outside. I sat down on the couch with my face in my hands and just wept. I was so scared, so lost. I begged her not to divorce me, but she just hugged me and walked out. She couldn't take any more, and once she saw that I wasn't dead, she washed her hands of me and turned me over to the small crew who I hadn't hurt enough (yet) and who seemed still willing to help. The rest of the entourage threw me into the backseat of a car and drove me straight to Valley Hope's thirty-day treatment facility in Cushing, Oklahoma.

I was in a stupor, a coma, one of the walking dead, and I just went along because I no longer had any resolve of my own. They could have led me to a cliff and walked me off the edge for all I cared. I had assumed an emotional "fetal position" and was practically carried through the front doors at Valley Hope. Four days in detox and three days into treatment, however, I started feeling better and just wanted out. "I've been here before, done it! It's not going to work." I called a friend who picked me up two hours later, against the wishes of EVERYONE. I was drunk again that same night, and after two more weeks of hell, I drove myself back to Valley Hope and tried again. This time I meant business, and I wasn't ready to die, but seemed to know that I couldn't go on in my present state. This time I stayed the full thirty days and actually felt pretty good, but thirty-day treatment centers don't solve thirty years of problems, and I was poorly armed to handle what lay ahead of me—a failing business, a divorce, broken relationships with kids, and a sea full of untrusting people.

While away at Valley Hope, my coworkers and church friends moved me out of my apartment and took care of my business. They had devised a plan whereby, upon my return, I would live with a church friend and his wife until I summoned enough stability to get back out on my own. I was open to it only because there were no other options. My new house parents had two rules—no drinking and no lying, or you're out. The "not lying" lasted about three hours, the "not drinking" about three weeks. I knew before even leaving treatment that I'd be drinking before long. I hated myself, I hated my life. I'd been reduced to living with a church couple, answering to them like a thirteen-year-old. I didn't know how I was ever going to pull myself back together and regain some semblance of integrity. I hated the situation, but didn't have much choice. I had no money, no home, and no one who wanted to get within 100 yards of the unlovable creature I'd become. To say I was miserable would have been an understatement. After a week in my new digs, I stopped at a bar after work and had three or four beers, went back to my church friend's house, faked my way through a short conversation, and excused myself for the evening. The next day, I smuggled a bottle of vodka back to their house and hid it in my room. I was off to the races again.

Later that week, my daughter was having her fourteenth birthday party and I was in charge of planning it. The previous week I was forced to purchase a new Jeep with money I didn't have so I'd be able to get around. I bought it for a couple of reasons. First, because with alcohol in my system I wouldn't be able to start my old truck due to its interlock system, and second, because the entire front end of my truck had been smashed in. I have no recollection of the crash. I've had two visions, maybe memories about it, but only one of them could have happened. One very vague memory I have was being on a side street and smashing violently into a parked car. The other was rear-ending someone at a stoplight. Both would explain the damage, and I have a faint recollection of speeding away from both. It's uncertain if either one of them was true. The only evidence was a truck with a seriously crushed front end.

Anyway, my wife saw the Jeep and knew what I was up to. She told me I wasn't allowed to pick my daughter up and take her to the birthday party I had spent all week planning; rather I was to just meet them there. I drank because of that and showed up a little buzzed. The whole party was surreal, and I felt like I was watching it from a million miles away. As I watched my daughter interact with her friends, open her gifts, and do her best to enjoy her special day, my heart broke for the person I'd become, for the pain and fear I'd introduced into her sweet young life. As dinner arrived, I sat with Lori at a table off to the side and felt like I was talking to a complete stranger. She had constructed the highest, most solid emotional walls to protect herself against me. It cut me to the core. She was done.

The party ended, I hugged my daughter, and knew exactly where my next stop was going to be, and so do you. Straight to the liquor store. After a half a fifth of vodka, I called the church friend I was staying with and let him know I was drunk. He said, "You can't stay here any longer," but I already knew it and couldn't wait to get out before I pulled more of my friends into the quicksand that was beginning to engulf my life and everything close to me. I drove back downtown to my building with some leftover pizza from the party and drank myself into unconsciousness once again. There was no plan for tomorrow, the rest of the week, or my life. I was sleeping on an air mattress in a tent on the third floor of my building in the Urban Campout, a 10,000 square foot indoor campground I'd created and rented out for indoor overnight campout parties. What a sight that must have been.

As I lay there next to a half-eaten pizza and nearly finished vodka bottle, my mind began unearthing every negative thing I could think of. Then, out of nowhere, I became overwhelmed with anxiety, panic, and disgust over something I'd done in the Urban Campout. Several months earlier I'd gotten this brilliant idea that I needed to purchase a handgun for the store. The business was located in a questionable area, and oftentimes I was in the building after dark. I rationalized the purchase as protection, but in hindsight, I realized I bought it because I thought it would make me feel differently. Somehow safer, more in control, more respected. It was a Smith and Wesson 9mm automatic handgun. It was always loaded and didn't have a safety. It was big and powerful, and that's exactly how it made me feel! The first few weeks after buying the gun, I stuffed it in my jeans, behind my belt, and covered it with my shirt. Carrying that gun around made me feel like a real man. I rarely took it out, except to impress people (who were not impressed). Having it stuffed in my pants was more than a little uncomfortable, however. One afternoon I was up on the third floor in the Urban Campout, setting up for an eleven-year-old boy's birthday party and overnight campout. I had been drinking all day, and I pulled the gun out and set it on the window ledge so I could crawl around in the tents to make sure everything was set up and clean for that evening's party. I finished my work just before the entourage of twenty-three little boys charged the campground for a night of wild fun. I chatted with the parents, but quickly excused myself to prevent them from detecting my drunkenness. An hour later, I went back upstairs to check on the party and was filled with a horror that I can't describe. One of the boys had found my gun, and he was chasing after a herd of a dozen other boys pointing it at them and yelling "Bang Bang, you're dead." About the same time I noticed this, the father of the birthday boy noticed as well, and we both headed over to extract the weapon. I was mortified and told the father it must have been left by one of our maintenance workers. He was skeptical and angry, but somehow I was able to disarm him, shortly after disarming the boy. I went downstairs with the gun in hand and left for the night, absolutely sick to my stomach. To this day, I wake up in the middle of the night in cold sweats predicting how that could have easily turned out. I wasn't just hurting myself anymore. I was putting other drivers in danger, the people I was driving around (usually my daughter) in danger, and now random children in danger! Another gulp of vodka and those nightmares would temporarily disappear. Three or four more and I'd be out again.

The next morning I woke up, finished what was left of my bottle, and decided I needed to go hide out. A cheap motel in midtown would do. I would hole up with my whiskey and try to figure it out.

I was still in charge I thought. That was laughable, but I believed it. I'm not really sure what happened over those next several days. All I know is that a few days later, I woke up lying in the bed of a different hotel. How and why I'd moved from one to another I'll never know. My brother had been furiously calling me, and I finally picked up and tried to describe to him where I was. It was January and it was very cold and snowing outside. The next thing I remember was being down in front of the hotel talking to my brother and my friend, Steve. They were unsuccessfully trying to reason with me. About what, I can't recall. The hotel clerk was standing nearby, watching intently. All I remember was Steve asking, "Do you want to go to jail? Do you want to go to jail?" I responded, "I don't care," and in what seemed like sixty seconds, I was handcuffed and pushed into the back of a police car. I had on a pair of shorts, a T-shirt, and no socks or shoes. As the door shut, I remember looking at my brother and asking, "How could you do this to me?" The look on his face was excruciating.

I was booked and charged with public intoxication. While sitting in the holding room amid a black caucus of fellow violators, I recall going off on some diatribe about how unfair the penal system was to blacks. I pounded the armrests and preached words like discrimination, prejudice, profiling, and gross unfairness. I was a drunken Malcolm X right there in Tulsa, fighting for the rights of my brothers! If they weren't so amused by me, I probably would have gotten the crap kicked out of me. Before long, the cold hard bunk in my cell was finally made available to me, and I climbed up top and burrowed in for what would be a sleepless night.

Jail is a frightening place. Only someone who's been there can relate. The feeling of helplessness is overwhelming. Being locked in a small cell was suffocating, and I was climbing the walls. Every minute felt like an hour, and the orange jumper I was clothed in only added to my humiliation. I couldn't take one night and can't imagine what goes through the mind of someone who's been given six months or a year. I actually think getting a "life" sentence would be easier. Knowing life, you could at least wrap your mind around your fate, and your future would be somewhat known. Mine was still up in the air, and my mind was taking me to the worst case scenario of what might lie ahead. In any case, it wasn't much of a wakeup call for me. The grip of alcoholism was too great. The loss of everything of value in my life, including my freedom, ran a distant second to the desire to make my internal and emotional pain go away. I imagine it would be like getting waterboarded. You just want that hurt to stop, and you'll do whatever is necessary to make it go away. In my case, alcohol always made it go away, temporarily.

The next morning I awoke shaking violently and had to get out of there. Being booked out of jail is a tortuous process. Three hours later, about ready to crawl out of my skin, I walked out the front door the same way I walked in, shorts, T-shirt, and no shoes into 20-degree snowy weather. The power on my phone was at 10 percent as I made a quick call to a cab driver I'd befriended over the previous three weeks. He answered, and I asked him to come pick me up. Thirty minutes later, he was in the front drive of the county jail. I asked him to take me to the nearest liquor store. I walked in and headed straight for the vodka. I'm sure I reeked and had to have been quite a sight. I was dirty, my hair looked like I'd just stuck my finger in a light socket, and the checkout was more painful for the cashier than it was for me. I couldn't get the money out of my wallet. She had to help me. As I climbed back into the taxi, I unscrewed the cap and was shaking so badly I could barely get the bottle to my lips without fear of breaking my front teeth. I was spilling it all over myself but managing to get some of the cure down. After a few minutes, I was able to take in some longer shots and after ten minutes, I was fine. The taxi driver just kept saying, "Take it easy, man. Take it easy. It's going to be all right." I could feel his empathy and wished his advice would do the trick, but knew it wouldn't. I had him take me to another cheap motel. I checked in with a credit card and began the same old routine again, no plan, no thought, just drink.

What I hadn't figured out was that my sources of funds had all but disappeared. The front desk called and said my card had been canceled. I tried another. It didn't work either. I wrote a check (that no one could read) and he wouldn't accept it. He wanted me out by noon the next day. What to do???

I was out of booze again, so I walked down to a liquor store a few blocks away. I grabbed another bottle, but a third card had been declined. I begged the cashier to let me have this bottle and promised I'd be back to pay her in the morning. She refused. I considered running out the front door with it but couldn't see a feasible escape route. I left and went next door to the grocery store, grabbed a case of beer, and was ready to walk out with it, but first decided to try the self-checkout aisle. I scanned the case, and the little light went off alerting the staff to check my ID. They did, punched in the code that I was legal, and then she walked off. I pushed "pay with credit card," slid my card in, and it came back declined, but spit out a receipt. I grabbed my case and rejection receipt and walked out the front door.

The walls were closing in. I had a few bucks in my pocket and had one last financial option, an ATM card on my business account. After getting a dozen beers down, I called my taxi driver friend. He came and picked me up and drove me to my business bank. I slid the card in, punched in my pin, and the message came back that I was no longer an authorized user on this account. That was it! I had ZERO access to funds, the hotel had given me until the morning, and I had twelve beers left before I was out on the street again. No one would take me in; they were done with me.

As I sat in the hotel room finishing the last of the Natural Light (if I was going to steal beer, why didn't I steal a better brand?), reality began to set in and I realized I was out of options. What do I do? It was a long shot, but I decided to call my wife. She picked up and I explained my predicament to her. She listened and said she'd call me back. An hour later, I was out of booze, out of money, and in a panic. I walked down to the hotel bar and ordered a drink, then another, then another. I had no clue how I was going to pay for it, but the bartender didn't hesitate to open a tab for me. Before long my phone rang. It was my wife. She was at the hotel, waiting outside my room and wondering where the hell I was. I told the bartender I was staying in room 212 (not my room) and had left my wallet up there. "I'll be right back to settle up with you shortly." (I didn't go back.) When I arrived at my room, my wife was waiting there. She looked stressed, weary, disgusted, frightened, sad, and was likely vacillating between feeling responsible to help and putting a bullet in my head.

I followed her down to the parking lot and to her car. She drove me straight to a local detox and treatment facility, parked, and walked me inside. I had an open beer in my hand and was immediately warned by another patient who was outside smoking that I couldn't have a beer here, so I chugged it, threw the can in the bushes, and headed inside to wait for a hopeful admission. The wait was long, and Lori realized that she had to pick Caroline up at 3:00 p.m., so she left, praying I'd be admitted. I wasn't, and the facility called Lori's cell and told her she'd have to come pick me up and they'd try to get me in the following day. I walked outside and sat on a bench, looking like the bum I was. A few minutes later, Lori returned from school with my daughter, who was sitting in the front seat. I poured myself into the back, crying, and still drunk. Caroline wouldn't turn around. She couldn't bear to look at me. I can only imagine how frightened she was. I said, "Caroline, turn around and look at me." She did and I said, "I promise you that you will NEVER see me like this again." The horror in her eyes was unbearable. My wife screamed at me to stop, that I was scaring her. I sat in silence for the rest of the trip, and my daughter never looked back again. It would be the last time I would see her for a long time. I had no idea where we were going and didn't really care. It was the worst day of my life. I was killing myself and the people I loved most. I was unrecognizable to them or myself, and the terror in their eyes was enough to make my heart just want to stop.

A few miles later, we stopped at another hotel. Lori asked me to get out. We went to the front desk, where she checked me in and paid the clerk. She walked me up to my room and said, "I have to drop Caroline off; I'll be back in an hour." An hour later she showed up with a sack full of food and a twelve-pack of beer. She said, "Someone from the local detox and treatment center will pick you up in front of the hotel tomorrow morning at 9:00 a.m. Be down there." Then she looked at me and said, "This is it Mike. This is the last time I am going to help you. It's up to you from here. Either you make your ride tomorrow morning or you die. I've done all I can and all I'm willing to do." And she left. All I could think about was the twelve-pack. I didn't even eat the food.

I drank nine of the beers and purposely saved three for the next morning. I would need them to get through the admission process at the detox facility before they began giving me withdrawal medications like Ativan or Librium. My ride arrived promptly on schedule, and I was both showered and ready to go. I didn't have another option. As it turned out, the woman who graciously agreed to transport me from hotel to rehab just happened to be the wife of the man who started the particular detox and treatment facility I was minutes away from entering. He was also the same man who had been my AA sponsor a few years earlier. He was a guy with over thirty years of sobriety, was known for sponsoring dozens of drunks at a time, and managed to do it all while building a successful oil company in his spare time. A year earlier, however, he shot himself in the head. It seemed he had a bipolar condition he'd apparently been suffering from for quite some time. I was floored. This guy had been my rock and had done a pretty good job of keeping me sober for one year of my life. I went to his funeral and relapsed shortly after. I kept telling myself, "We are all doomed! This poor guy fought to stay sober thirty years and then one day pulls out a gun and kills himself." I reasoned that the impossible battle to fight off alcoholism finally caught up with him. I wondered to myself if he'd just relapsed a few times and relieved some of that built-up stress of trying to stay sober, maybe he would never have gotten to that point! Later, that kind of thinking would prove to me I was more delusional and insane than he ever was.

In any case, I was summarily checked in two hours later and finally escorted to my room. I attempted to lie down on the filthy bed that resembled more of a cot. Believe it or not, I still had so much pride, ego, and arrogance that I called my wife again and said, "You have to get me out of this homeless shelter that thinks it's a rehab; I want to go to a long-term treatment center that is plush and more for people like me!" She was not happy or cooperative. Imagine that? To be honest, all she could think about was how she was going to get me to sign the divorce papers. She desperately needed to divorce herself from me before I took her and the entire family down. Fortunately, I'd smuggled my cell phone into detox and it hadn't been cut off (yet). So I started surfing the Web, looking for long-term treatment centers. I found one in Austin, Texas. It was an eight-to-twelve month program. I called admissions and a process began. It took eight more days to get approval. I stayed at the detox facility and entered their thirty-day program while I waited. Over that time, and for the first time in my life, I actually surrendered. I gave up on everything, and I reconciled the fact that I wouldn't see my kids for another year. I was ready to stop fighting the divorce, ready to let my business file bankruptcy. I just wanted to go away and hide.

The day before I was set to leave for long-term treatment in Austin, I called my wife and said, "I'm done fighting. Have your attorney draft the divorce settlement any way you want it and I'll sign it before I leave." She came down with her attorney that day and with still trembling hands, I signed away the love of my life. I broke down and all I could manage to get out before she left was "I love you. You were a good wife, and I'm sorry." The next morning, my brother picked me up and we went straight to the airport where a small welcoming party from the Burning Tree Long Term Treatment Facility was there to greet me.

The dawn had broken, but I couldn't see it yet.

CHAPTER 10

SURRENDER

This book began with a terrifying quote from Lamentations where we hear the cry from the beaten man, broken down by God. "God has brought me into the deepest darkness, shutting off all light. I cannot escape; He has fastened me with heavy chains. He has left me bleeding and desolate." He was a man in a complete state of utter hopelessness and despair. It was a verse that certainly described my life to a "T." I've heard it said that brutal honesty and truth about oneself is painful to hear, but can be downright cruel if offered without a solution. The message that comes from the scriptures in Lamentations certainly was painful to hear as the reading reminded me "that all hope was gone for me." My strength had turned to water and rendered me powerless over the bitterness and suffering I had been dealt.

But brutal honesty and truth with a solution show love and compassion. As haunting as Lamentations can be, it is far from cruel, as God shows his love and compassion with a solution. He goes on to say that "Only in suffering will you meaningfully abandon yourself and surrender to God's hidden faithfulness." The solution is to abandon yourself to God. Surrender to Him and his faithfulness. So began my journey from the "pits of a living hell." God offered me a tiny ray of hope, a way out of the depths of despair. It was the only ray of hope.

Surrender . . . It is defined by Webster as "ceasing to resist to an enemy or an opponent and submitting to their authority." Who was I fighting? Who are you fighting? Who did I need to surrender to? My answer was God! I was fighting God and everyone else that stepped into the wake of my path. The humorous realization set in as I laughed at the insanity and arrogance of thinking I could win a battle with God! I realized that, not only am I completely powerless in a duel with God, but I'm powerless over pretty much everything else in my life as well, certainly over everyone else, and unquestionably over alcohol. Very few things were within my control.

It often takes a tremendous internal struggle to establish that comprehension. Was I really powerless? Hadn't I been in control of my life? Didn't I accomplish so much of my own volition? After all, I was a successful student and athlete. I'd made my way through college and secured prominent positions in corporate America with personal determination, self-will, and independence. Hadn't I successfully maneuvered my way into a coveted Wall Street appointment, found and married a beautiful woman, had two amazing children, and established myself as a respected and adored person in my community? Hadn't I done all that with my own power? I sure thought I had!

One of my favorite books was written by Dr. Larry Crab and titled *66 Love Letters*. In Dr. Crab's book he asks God to tell him exactly what God wants us to hear from each book of the Bible. He realizes that the sixty-six books of the Bible are individual "love letters" to each of us from God, and each book has an important underlying message. In the "love letter" titled "Job," God tells us that we are NOT in control of either getting or keeping blessings. That what comes into our lives always comes with God's knowledge and with His permission. They are gifts given through God's grace, and we did NOTHING to deserve them! That is to say, if God gave gifts based on merit, aligned with what we deserved, we'd all be in hell! So thank God we don't get what we really deserve! It's the Lord giveth and the Lord taketh kind of stuff and has almost nothing to do with our own efforts!

So maybe I wasn't in control of all the great accomplishments in my life. Maybe they were blessings given to me by God. If that's the truth, then God does have a lot of grace, because I sure wasn't living a godly life. I most certainly didn't deserve all the wonderful things I had been given in my life.

One of the underlying tenets throughout Dr. Crab's book is that God will do anything He has to do to draw us closer to Him. He will realign, readjust, and redirect our lives in such a way that serves the purpose He has outlined for each of us according to His plan for our time here on earth. When we stray from that path, when we fall away from Him, He will do whatever He has to do to return us. Those actions are not always pleasant; most of the time they are not. If given more money, more happiness, more position, more power, I don't love God more, I love myself more! Real change in any human being does not occur without brokenness. When we fall away from God and begin to rely on ourselves, God has to break us, like the man in Lamentations, and that's exactly what happened to me. Maybe it's happening to you right now?

Still wrestling with this notion that I had my own power, I had to begin to embark on some honest reflection. Making that leap to accepting things as godly gifts regarding family, my career, my position in life, and all the wonderful material things I had was tough for me to do. I was willing to "thank God for the blessing he gave me," but still felt like I'd earned them through hard work, intelligence, and masterful persuasion. God had to get me to a place where He could prove to me that I was completely unmerited and powerless. He did that for me through addiction to alcohol! He may be doing that for you through divorce, the loss of a family member, a job, an eating disorder, a strained relationship, a different addiction, depression, or a self-esteem problem. Whatever it is that is going on in your life that's causing you unhappiness and pain is more than likely God's tactic to turn you toward Him. I've heard it said that we should be grateful and joyful when disaster strikes, when troubles and adversity come our way, when "bad things happen to good people," because we know when those difficulties arrive that God hasn't given up on us. He is teaching us. He is shaping us and drawing us closer to Him. We should be joyful and open to those misperceived opportunities. I know I'm going to have a lot of people arguing with me on this point regarding God "making bad stuff" happen to us in an effort to correct our behaviors. I'm not saying God is creating these personal problems; WE created these problems. God is just "allowing" them to happen. Remember, nothing happens without God's permission, so if you're going through something painful, you might have caused it, but God has given His permission and allowed it to happen for a reason. So back off Bible scholars!

I was listening to my brother vent one day about a string of difficulties he was facing in his own life. He was complaining about a guy he knew who didn't believe in God, wasn't saved, and didn't want to be. The man partied hedonistically, cheated on his wife, was dishonest in business, didn't take care of himself, and was selfish, self-centered, and offered no assistance to other human beings. He was rude, meanspirited, and one of the least compassionate people my brother had ever known. But somehow this guy fell into one blessing after another. He had ridiculous amounts of money, expensive homes and cars, took exotic trips, ate at the finest restaurants, and basked in the glory of complete self-indulgence. As my brother contrasted this man's life with his own, he got more and more resentful. He said, "Mike, I do my best to live right. I have a heart for God, I love my family, I help others, and I'm honest, giving, and caring. I read my Bible every day. I go to church. I pray. I do my best to trust and to follow Christ. But yet my problems continue to pile up on me. I can't find a job, I'm burning through my savings, I've got issues with the kids, problems with neighbors, and the list goes on and on. It just doesn't seem fair."

And then he realized "our treasures are stored up in heaven," not here on earth. That at least right now, Satan is not worried about his friend. The devil has him in the bag already. Why would Satan want to put troubles in this guy's life? Those troubles might actually drive him back toward God. On the other hand, my brother is a member of God's army and Satan knows that. He also knows that, like our friend Job in the Bible, if he can make Mark's life miserable, my brother might just turn from God. But God knows that with His help, Mark can only be strengthened by the trials and tribulations he is experiencing. God is molding my brother into a stronger Christian, and he should be grateful for that and should pray that when God is ready, unbelievers will be convicted in God's time and in God's way.

I've gotten a little off track here. The point is that we are powerless over many things that happen to us in life. The real control we have is how we react and respond to the negative occurrences in our lives. When we realize that troubles are God's way of teaching, molding, and making us stronger, we accept them with the gratefulness that God hasn't forgotten us, that he is giving us an opportunity to grow. Most importantly, however, difficulties remind us that we are not in control, that we are essentially powerless over the things that happen in our lives, and the result and objective of these trials is to place our trust and our reliance upon Christ.

There is a point every man and every woman must reach before they can get better and begin to improve their lives. That point is complete surrender of everything in their lives. It is a point where you become "willing" to let everything go—your spouse, your kids, your job, your friends, your money. It's a place where you are prepared to admit complete and utter defeat. A place where you finally believe, in your heart, that you are absolutely powerless over everything. An admission that your life is out of control and YOU can't fix it. A belief that you are not in charge anymore, you are NOT in control anymore, and you really never were. You just fooled yourself into thinking that you had some power over the trajectory of your life.

I'll give you a few examples that, upon review, began to convince me that I was powerless over the things in my life, and especially alcohol. Upon these realizations I had to finally come to the conclusion that

God was trying to change me and that I had to put my faith and trust in Him. Once that determination was made and I had surrendered to His power, I was finally able to bridge that gap of powerlessness to all areas of my life.

These examples are related to my powerlessness over alcohol, but they illustrate, to an extreme, the proof of real powerlessness in my life. Your examples may be something different, but are probably similar to many other areas in my life where I found myself powerless, like stopping my wife from filing for divorce or making my children behave and love me like I wanted them to. Like keeping the banks or city departments from making decisions that negatively affected my business. I had no power over all the bad drivers in the world or what decisions my kids' teachers and coaches made. Controlling the actions of fellow coworkers and even close friends was a futile effort, and I realized it was pointless attempting to direct how other people treated me, viewed me, or considered me as they managed their own self-centered lives. You could be in a situation in which a boss might want to fire or demote you, or upset at how an "ex" is managing the kids when they aren't with you, or asking a loud cell phone talker to "zip it" while you're trying to enjoy a nice meal with your significant other. This list could go on ad infinitum!

For me, admitting I was powerless over alcohol was the first step. As I reviewed my history, I was able to recall three key times where, upon review, I had to honestly admit I didn't have a choice, and this area of my life was far beyond my control.

The first was a camping trip taken with my extended family to Arkansas. It was a boy's trip. My dad, brother, brother-in-laws, and all of our kids, seven in total. Our plan was to travel to a remote campsite, set up camp, go for a hike, start a little campfire, and have a "roughin' it" kind of dinner before retiring for the night. We had plans to pack up camp late that next morning and head back to Tulsa.

After arriving, I was kicking myself for not honoring the Boy Scout's creed of "always being prepared," because I forgot to bring booze. I had assumed that dad, or one of the other men, had packed away some beer for the evening. When camp was set up, I began foraging around for something to drink, but soon found that no liquor, whatsoever, had been brought. I tried to fight off the urge, but within the hour was obsessing over having a few drinks. I tried to rally some drinking support from the others, but no one else was on board, and they seemed fine depriving themselves of alcohol for twenty-four hours. At my breaking point, I notified the group that I was going to town to bring back a few beers for the team, with the parallel notion in mind that I'd also pick up a little bottle of whiskey to get me through the night and into the next morning.

I had a brief thought of, "This is crazy. You are out in the middle of nowhere, you have no idea where the closest 'package store' is, and you'll be back in Tulsa in less than eighteen hours. Just wait!" But I couldn't. I had to have a drink, and I had no power over that choice. So off I drove in a mad search for alcohol. Since we were practically in the middle of nowhere, it took me over an hour to find some kind of civilization. Finding nothing open, I began to get desperate as the time ticked away and my absence from the family outing was getting ridiculously noticeable. When I'd exhausted all potential stores, the insane thought hit me that I would just pull up to a random farmhouse, knock on the door, explain to them our situation, and offer to buy any booze they happened to have in their cupboards. That is INSANE! But to me, it was a reasonable and resourceful action! After frightening two or three unsuspecting households and coming up empty-handed, I returned to camp three hours later to some very perplexed family members. Really? Could I not control myself or my situation for one night? That was embarrassing and a real eye-opener for me. It was the first time I realized that maybe I didn't have any power over my drinking.

Another time, and most certainly the most telling example, happened shortly after my wife asked me to leave the house. I had continued to relapse, and this was the first time I'd suffered a real consequence of losing my wife and kids by having to move out. I'd been living away for about two months, still drinking, but had fooled her (or so I thought) into thinking I'd been sober since leaving the house. As opportunity would have it, she called me and asked how I was doing. I responded with a resounding "great, sober, and getting it together." She was glad to hear it and informed me that she was planning on being out of town for a four-day weekend and asked if I would like to come home and spend the weekend with the kids while she was away. I jumped at the chance, knowing full well that this was my opportunity to prove to her and to the kids that I could be a responsible and sober parent and husband. There was nothing more in life that I wanted than to be reunited with my family, and this was my chance to show them I deserved another chance. I was determined to stay sober until that weekend, show up sober, have a productive weekend, and greet my wife upon her return with tidings of a successful weekend.

On the morning of her departure, she called me at work and informed me that she was about to leave for the airport. She then asked if I was sober and thought I was capable of caring for the children over the weekend. I confirmed I was and I could, but in that moment, feelings of anger, rage, and resentment overcame me. "How dare she ask me those questions? Did she think so little of me, have such little confidence in my resolve, did she not trust my ability to care for my own children?" After all, she was probably going off on a party weekend with her girlfriends and they would surely be drinking. It wasn't fair that she could drink and party, but I was under scrutiny and had a "no tolerance" drinking policy placed upon me. I took a deep breath and quickly reminded myself of my goals, which were to stay sober, care for and have a great weekend with the kids, and to show my wife I deserved another chance to move back home and resume my place in the family.

But that lingering anger continued to gnaw at me until an insatiable urge to start drinking enveloped me. I told myself I'd just drink enough to make the anger go away. I won't get drunk, plus it would maybe ease the anxiety, the awkwardness, and the uncomfortableness I was feeling about seeing the kids after a month of separation. Without a discerning thought or hesitation, I made an excuse to leave work, went straight to the liquor store, and bought a bottle of vodka. By noon, I was three sheets to the wind, and by 2:00 p.m. was passed out in my apartment. Around 3:20 the ringing of my phone awoke me and I noticed several missed calls since 3:00. I answered, and it was my son asking if I had planned to pick Caroline up from school, or had I forgotten? Still very drunk, I apologized and explained to him that I was very sorry, but I had been drinking and was in no condition to drive. He hung up the phone, called his grandmother, who decided to drive 160 miles from Wichita, Kansas, to take care of the kids all weekend. My anger, bitterness, and that one drink spiraled into an event that had me blowing a grand opportunity to reunite with my family. I had completely failed. The damage was monumental, bordering on irreparable, and guaranteed me another several months in the apartment that was beginning to feel more like a prison.

After a few more months of isolation and uncontrollable drunkenness, my parents finally decided to insist that long-term help was necessary for me, and I was in full agreement. I was killing myself and needed help. I was actually looking forward to a long-term solution. In reality, it was the only option left for me. They located a facility that would accept me into their ten-month program. The only problem was that this facility did not have detox capabilities, and it was required that I be sober for five days before admission. So my parents, not having any confidence in me achieving that goal, flew to Tulsa to stay with me, under lock and key, for five days before escorting me to Florida for the long-term help I desperately needed. I could do it. I wanted to do it.

The first three days were rough. Self-detoxing is not fun. There are the uncontrollable shakes, the nausea, the sleeplessness, the sweating, and the unbelievable craving. But my parents did not let me out of their sights for four days, and after that time I began to feel much better. On the fifth and final day of sobriety, they were feeling a little bit of confidence in my progress, but more than likely a lot of cabin fever, and suggested they might run to the bookstore for an hour and be right back. They point blank asked me if I would be okay for an hour alone. I confidently reassured them, and satisfied, they left the apartment.

Before their car left the parking garage, my shoes were on, keys were in my hand, and I was hell-bent on making it to the liquor store before my parents returned. "NO! I told myself, just one more day. You need this help. Don't do it." But I had no control, no power over what was ruining my life, and off I went. Within fifteen minutes, I'd secured a large bottle of whiskey, had half of it gone by the time I returned home, and hid the other half in my closet. I shut the door to my bedroom and decided to pretend I was taking a nap when they returned. It would give me time to sober up a bit before I had to face them again.

I made a fatal mistake, however, and upon returning had parked my car in a different spot because someone had taken the spot I'd left while I was at the liquor store. The minute they walked in, they knew!

"Where is it?" they asked. "We know you went out. Where is the liquor?" I denied it, but they knew I was drunk. I ran to the closet with my dad following close behind me, pulled out the bottle, and took as big a gulp as I could. I was acting like a starved and desperate dog eating a piece of raw meat, growling at anyone I thought might take it away from me. Dad grabbed the bottle from me, and I wrestled with him to get it back, begging for just one more swallow. I was too strong and too desperate, and he succumbed. After calming down and then passing out, I awoke to two very disappointed and discouraged parents. They asked me what I wanted to do and I replied, "I don't want to go to treatment." They then asked, "What do you want us to do?" I said, "Go home. You can't help me." They packed their bags and left. Later they told me that they had given up like everyone else had. That they had resigned themselves to the fact that I was going to die, and that if that was God's will, they were ready to accept it.

Powerless! I couldn't make it one hour! The love of my parents wasn't even enough. The notion of considering their feelings and empathizing with their heartbreak wasn't enough. The treatment opportunity I desperately needed was not enough. My God, I'd never laid a hand on my father. I'd always given him ultimate respect, and here I was arguing with him, fighting him for a bottle of whiskey. The pain in their eyes, the hurt, the torture I was inflicting upon them wasn't enough. I was completely and utterly powerless over alcohol. They walked away with sadness and a great sorrow that lay heavily on their hearts.

It was here, finally, that I began to realize that no one person could help me. That I was powerless in being able to help myself, and the only person I could think of that could possibly help me was God, and I thought He wasn't listening.

So, how does one "get this power" they so desperately need in their lives? If we're powerless over everything, then are we just randomly floating through our time here on planet Earth? Are we subject to the whims of nature, of the universe, of God, of Satan, of others? Or is there some way to find this power, a power greater than ourselves, greater than our environment, greater than this spinning world and all the people and influences swirling around on it?

The answer is singular. "There is One, may you find Him now!" That's it, the only answer to the powerless question. God has the power, and our quest lies in figuring out how to harness this power that God wants to give each of us over our lives.

Unfortunately, we can't just ask Him and receive it. There are certain conditions that must be met before God becomes willing to transfer this power to you. In Galatians, the Bible tells us that "We are not free to change ourselves or things simply by exerting our own willpower." It won't work. We have to be willing to stay in step with God and allow ourselves to be changed by the power of God. We simply can't do this thing called life on our own! We need God's power, God's strength, God's wisdom, and God's direction. To get those things, we have to completely surrender to our own selfish natures, to our own egos. We must first "Die to ourselves and let Christ live within in us, so HE can manage our lives." In simple terms that means . . . we have to admit that we are not in control of our lives, that we are powerless over everything except our own thoughts, perceptions, and actions. We are going to forfeit those thoughts to God, so He can change them. When our thinking has been changed and directed by God, we see that actions always follow thoughts, and when it's God's logic and understanding that is leading your mind, the actions that follow have God's power! Once we make that decision to follow God's will instead of our own, we FIND THAT POWER!

With that power, we are able to see that God is bigger than any of our problems. That with His power we are overcomers and capable of effectuating miracles. We can find that by surrendering our own lives and giving up what false sense of power we think we have, we are actually gaining a power that is infinitely greater. The Big Book (AA's Bible) says that when we've reached a point where we have dismissed the idea of operating our lives under our own perceived power and have accepted the power of Christ, we are no longer totally powerless, that we can make certain things happen as long as certain criteria are met. If our motives are good, if we are not self-seeking in our thoughts and actions, and if we are helping others, we will have an unlimited supply of God's power to accomplish the most amazing things. Along these lines, we can assert our newfound power all we wish. When we are following God's will, we also have God's power, and that power can accomplish anything. It can heal any hopeless addiction, like mine. It can restore any relationship, it can allow us to become miracles in the lives of others, and it can give us the confidence and peace to know that all of our physical needs will always be met!

If you can identify with the foolish need to be in charge, then surrender to Him. Stop fighting and trying to control everything in and around your life. Die to yourself, destroy your pride and ego, submit yourself, and accept the power that God wants to give you. It's not a cochairman proposition, and as long as you think you have, or you can exert, a little power and control over your own life, God will step away and His power will no longer be available to you.

And THAT was my problem, and I was beginning to figure it out. But it's easier to conceptualize than to practice. I needed more convincing and a much broader understanding of where and why my life was so unmanageable and just "how" I could use this newfound power to better manage it. I would soon find out!

CHAPTER 11

THE UNMANAGEABILITY OF LIFE

Have you ever heard anyone say, "My life is so unmanageable right now," or "I just can't manage everything going on in my life," or maybe, "I've just done such a poor job of managing my life"? Of course you have; people say it all the time, and when you ask them to be more specific, they say things like, "My job is out of control and I can't keep up with all the work," or "I just can't be the wife or husband I'm supposed to be; it's too much work," or "I'm so bad with money, my finances are out of control," or they might say, "I just can't control my kids; they run me over and won't listen to anything I say," or possibly, "My house is always a wreck, and I just don't have the time to keep up with it," "I can never stay up on everything going on at school," and things like, "I've got to shed some of these responsibilities; I just can't focus on them all, and I'm doing a poor job at everything!" Sounds typical, sounds normal, but when I press it a little further and say, "That's all understandable, but what's REALLY unmanageable with your life?" most people just look at me like I wasn't paying attention (because I'm usually not), and they respond, "I just told you!" Then I reply with, "No, you just told me 'the results' of your unmanageability, not the root of what's so unmanageable in your life." Blank stares and crickets ...

My responses used to be exactly the same, and I was no stranger to returning that "blank stare" when someone tried to explain to me what the real unmanageability in my life was. When asked that question, I'd say things like, "My marriage is suffering, I have financial problems everywhere I look, I'm losing friends, my business is suffering, or I'm always sick and never feeling healthy." But what I found was that those things were only "the truths," and the results of a much deeper problem. The real unmanageability of my life resided at a deeper level and in a place I never thought to consider.

To explain it from an alcoholic point of view, it works like a cycle. It's a vicious cycle that revolves in the life of an alcoholic, drug addict, gambling addict, sex addict, or even with an eating disorder for that matter.

As an alcoholic, I have a threefold illness. It's a sickness of the mind, the body, and the spirit. Non-alcoholics and addicts have the same illness; it just manifests itself differently. Let's start with the "Spirit." Your spirit is just your emotions, your feelings, your psyche, if you will. When my spirit is off-kilter, I'm usually feeling one or any combination of distasteful emotions like jealousy, self-consciousness, fear, worry, insecurity, embarrassment, guilt, shame, anger, or nervousness. It could also be a combination of remorse, regret, or morbid reflection. Maybe even restlessness, irritability, or discontent. You can add more, but you get the idea; it's just the range of negative emotions or feelings one experiences from time to time.

When I'm feeling those negative emotions, they're uncomfortable, and I don't like them one bit. I want to make them go away, and as an alcoholic, the first thing that comes to my mind is, "A drink or two will make these painful feelings go away!" If you have an eating disorder, you might choose "a triple fudge sundae and a bag of Doritos to make you feel better and mask the feelings of say, depression or shame." Or you might think, "I'm so angry with my husband, some shopping will take care of this discontent." A few hours at the blackjack table used to take care of my restlessness and boredom. One might even decide that pulling up some pornography on the computer might make your irritability disappear. And it does. All those solutions actually work, temporarily. We use them because we need relief and we don't have a better solution.

So when the negative emotions overtake us, we look for relief, and quick relief, which comes from the behaviors illustrated above. But what happens after the spiritual or emotional component of our sickness appears is what we call the "mental obsession" or the second part or fold of our disease. A mental obsession is "a thought that outweighs all others."

The mental part of our problem seizes control of us once our spirit and our souls begin to exhibit these uncomfortable feelings we've just discussed. It is a powerful and persuasive overtaking! As the mind begins looking for solutions to treat our emotional malady, it begins to tell us things, and to rationalize. It commences to "lie" to us about how this problem should be handled. Our minds have a vague notion of the consequences, but not significant enough to stop us with sufficient force before we find our solution. For the alcoholic, the mind tells you things like, "I'm just going to have one or two. No one will know, I can control it this time, I deserve it, it'll be different this time," or defiant thoughts like "screw it!"

It works exactly the same way for the shopper, when she (or he) tells herself things like, "I'm just going to browse, or I'm only going to spend $50, or I deserve a new dress." For the person with an eating disorder it might be, "I'll just get a small burger, no fries, and I'll work out tomorrow." Or "What's the use anyway; I'll never be able to control my diet." Maybe he or she says, "No one will find out, so what's the big deal."

The mind is a very powerful thing! It's incredibly persuasive, a master of justification, and genius at self-manipulation. It controls our actions because actions follow thoughts, and if the mind creates a strong enough thought (and it will) because it has a very uncomfortable and urgent problem to solve, the body follows with an action. We have very little, if any, control over the power of our mind.

This brings us to the third part of our disease, the body. The body is simply the physical component of the threefold disease. This is the only part of the disease that may act differently between an addict and a non-addict, but I'm not so sure. As an alcoholic, as soon as my mind begins to tell me the "lies" and I begin to believe them, my thoughts become actions, and I take that first drink. Once this occurs, the physical body takes over, and for an alcoholic or a drug addict, a physical craving develops. It is much like an allergy of the body, and the body requires not just one drink, but one after another after another. An analogy that best describes it would be a man who has been starved for food for thirty days and comes upon a gourmet feast. He knows that gorging himself will make him sick, but after he eats that first chicken finger, his appetite takes over and he eats and eats until he gets sick. The same is true with an alcoholic or an addict. That first drink sets off a physical reaction, and he drinks until he passes out or something or somebody stops him.

It works much the same way for a person who buys things to relieve an emotional nagging, like anger. Their minds tell them, "you deserve it, you're only going to spend $50," and then you make that first purchase and it feels so good, you buy something else, then something else. They can't stop until their credit card gets declined or their spouse catches on and stops them with suspicious inquiries. The same result occurs with someone watching pornography. A quick look turns into a three-hour marathon. The gambler, looking to eliminate boredom, rationalizes by saying, "I'll just take $100," but he visits the ATM machine three times before finally exceeding his credit limit and trudges home unable to make his rent payment.

These physical reactions are called "sprees." An alcoholic goes on one just the same as someone who's shopped too long and spent too much, and the same as the overeater who intended to have a Happy Meal, but bankrupts the buffet instead.

Now we've come full circle and are back to the very thing we started this chapter with, unmanageability! We see what most people see as the unmanageability in their lives. What we're really seeing is the outcome, the consequence, the by-product of the unmanageability of their lives. We're seeing the results of our behaviors and NOT where the problem truly lies! We are seeing what the cycle calls the "truths," and the "truths" for an alcoholic are: "I can't keep up at work, my job is always in jeopardy, my marriage is a wreck, I'm losing friends, I'm making stupid financial decisions, I'm going to lose my kids if I don't get it together," and so on.

For the man who decides to gamble a little to relieve his discontentedness, he finds that his "truths" are: "I'm going broke, my wife is angry, my kids ignore me because I don't spend any time with them," or "I can't seem to save for my retirement."

The person who sought out pornography to relieve his irritability might think: "My wife is leaving me, my sex life with her just isn't what it should be, my son caught me on the computer and doesn't want to be around me," or "I'm in trouble at work and might lose my job because they found porn cookies on my desktop."

The shopper would say my "truths" are: "I have credit card debt that's out of control, I'm fighting with my husband about money all the time, I'm in trouble for lying about how much I spent, etc., etc."

Most people would say that yes, my drinking is unmanageable, my eating habits are unmanageable, my gambling is a little out of control, my finances are a wreck because of my shopping, but these are just the symptoms, the results of your behaviors. They are the "TRUTHS." When we see what we've done, whether it's getting drunk again, overspending, or gorging ourselves with food or pornography, we swear to ourselves we'll never do it again. We make firm resolutions to stop these behaviors, and we mean business! You could hook each of us up to a lie detector and ask us if we'll ever do those things again and we'll say, "NO WAY," and we'll pass. We're that convinced!

As we complete the circle, guess what happens? We exacerbate the cycle and stoke the flames of our illness. It's bad enough that we're already experiencing all the feelings we discussed inside the "spirit" part of this cycle, the negative emotions. But when we emerge from one of our sprees, things get worse. We feel more shame, more guilt, more worry. We get more insecure about our relationships and ourselves, we get fearful that others will discover our behaviors or will scold us or put consequences on us for committing them. We have great feelings of remorse and worthlessness. Things are worse, emotionally, than they were before we started trying to find our own solutions for relief.

And so the cycle begins again! What can I do to make these uncomfortable emotions go away? I'm feeling so bad, what will make me feel better and fast? Hmmmm . . . Maybe a drink, maybe a gallon of ice cream, maybe some blackjack, or a trip to the mall?

Queue the mental obsession and we're off to the races again! We get to a point and to that point very quickly where we can NO LONGER differentiate between the "LIES" and the "TRUTHS." Our minds are so complex and crafty that we can't put two and two together. We can't comprehend that taking one drink, looking at one naked photo, spending thirty minutes at the mall can and usually will result in wrecked families, broken relationships, health problems, and lost jobs and homes. We just want that emotional pain to go away, and everything else is but a faint concern.

I wrote earlier in the book that pointing out a problem to someone and offering a solution is a sign of caring, compassion, and love, but pointing out a problem and not offering a solution is just downright cruel. So here is the solution because I care about you.

The answer to the question asked in the first paragraph of this chapter, "Where is your life unmanageable?" is in the spirit or the emotional portion of the cycle! So if I ask you again, I don't want you to say, "I just can't get along with my spouse." I want you to say, "I have a lot of feelings of insecurity, resentment, shame, or fear that I can't seem to get a handle on and it's ruining my marriage." I will most likely do a handstand, because then I'll know you've "got it!"

That is EXACTLY the right answer! The unmanageability of our lives resides in our broken or damaged spirits! And if we can solve those spiritual problems, those feelings and negative emotions, the remainder of the cycle is moot. It is destroyed, and we can spot the differences between a lie and the truth about our lives without any effort or confusion at all. And guess what? We aren't having marital problems anymore, we aren't underperforming at work, our kids love and respect us and think we're cool, we get healthier, and our finances are under control!

"Okay, great Mike, now we know where the problem lies, but we're getting frustrated, angry, irritable, and worried because you won't give us the solution!" Before you begin thinking about chugging a twelve-pack, buying a lottery scratcher, and then going to the mall to buy a bunch of junk, only stopping for a few minutes in the food court to eat funnel cake and grande burritos while undressing all the pretty girls walking by with your eyes, I'll give it to you!

The solution is so unbelievable easy and effective that you'll be blown away by the process that will completely change your life! Here it is . . .

When you begin experiencing any spiritual malady, whatever it is—jealousy, anger, self-consciousness, irritability, insecurity, etc., etc., etc.—you do three things:

First—You recognize and acknowledge those negative feelings, take a quick moment, and toss up a quick prayer to God. You simply say something like, "God I'm feeling very fearful right now. Please remove this feeling from me."

Second—You immediately discuss those feelings with someone else. Hopefully you have a close friend, a spouse, a family member, but it could be a complete stranger if the circumstance warrants. You don't want to walk up to a complete stranger and say, "Excuse me sir, but I'm feeling very depressed, resentful, and angry right now," especially if you're in a post office or the security line at the airport. But if you've been waiting in line at the DMV for long time and are getting resentful, you might tactfully share that with someone behind you. After asking God to remove those feelings, you'll be amazed at some of the responses you'll get. I once did that and the person behind me said, "I know, but don't you feel sorry for the people that have to work here?" and I almost immediately felt gratitude that I didn't as I looked at the poor woman behind the counter. She looked exhausted at having to deal with the never-ending stream of angry and problem customers.

Third—You turn your thoughts to someone you can help. No matter where you are. Just stop for a minute and think to yourself,

"Who can I help today?" Or "God, please show me someone I can be of service to." Again, you will be surprised about what simply "pops" into your head. You might quickly realize that your wife has been swamped all week and you could pick up her dry cleaning, or go home early and make dinner. You might think, my friend, Joe, has been going through a tough time. I'm going to call him and see how he's doing. Or you might notice a woman at the back of the DMV line who looks like she's in a bigger hurry than you are, and you can offer her your spot in line.

That's it! And I am GUARANTEEING you it works, and works every time!

Here's why. First of all, you are putting God in charge right up front, and you are drawing on His power. Second, your motives and your requests are pure and good. You want to remove the bad, to remove evil from your spirit that, left unattended, will cause damage, hurt, and sin. God doesn't want that, neither do you, nor do the people you will be affecting. Third, you are vocalizing your feelings to an impartial and unemotional third party. You will find that once you've let those feelings go and dumped them on someone else, they cannot hurt you anymore, and they no longer have any power over you. More times than not, you'll realize immediately just how ridiculous you are being and how silly it was to feel that way. Even if you don't realize it, God will give that third party words and responses that they never might have shared otherwise. They may respond, like the person waiting in the DMV line, or maybe with a comment like, "I always feel bad when I know people are waiting on me, and they are all the time!" Finally, by turning your thoughts to someone else, you immediately "get out of" the place most of us like to reside—ourselves! You'll see again and again throughout this book that "most of our troubles are rooted in our own selfishness." Our spiritual maladies, like restlessness, anger, and worry, are a product of our selfishness. Our desires are not being met, and we're not getting what we want. Maybe we're being inconvenienced by others. By turning our thoughts to someone else we can help, we are instantaneously removed from our own selfish thoughts, from our self-centered thinking, and instead focusing on, and acting on, someone else and what we can do for them.

It's so simple! You don't have to send up big elaborate prayers. Just a quick "Hey God, can you remove this?" You don't have to schedule ninety minutes with your therapist, just text, or better yet, call your sister and say, "Hey girl, I'm feeling so much worry today and wanted to talk to you." She might text back Matthew, chapter 6: "Look at the birds in the air. They do not sow or reap or store away in barns, yet God feeds them. Are you not more valuable than they? Who can anyone of you, by worrying, add a single hour to your life?" You don't have to turn your thoughts to things like joining the Peace Corps or rescuing babies from orphanages. Instead, do something small and helpful, like helping an old lady put her suitcase in the overhead bin or letting someone cut in front of you in traffic.

Okay. One last quick personal example and then I'll stop beating this dead horse, but I shouldn't, because if there is one pearl of wisdom in this book, it's this solution, right here in these last few pages. There are many other important points to make as you'll realize, reading on, and it's all vital in opening up the clearest path to God possible, but this one, by itself, is enough to change your life!

When I left the treatment center in Texas (the last, by the grace of God), I decided to go out to Colorado to spend a few weeks with my parents. I wanted to decompress and ease back into the real world and hoped to make some much deserved amends to my folks. Not having had a car while in treatment and needing to go to Colorado with no money, my brother was kind enough to call the local Greyhound bus station and buy me a one-way ticket to Albuquerque, New Mexico, where my folks would pick me up and then take us up to their home in Pagosa Springs, Colorado. I'd never traveled on a bus and was accustomed to driving my own car or flying. However, the past several months had humbled me considerably, and I was grateful to have paid transportation and more thankful that my parents welcomed me for a visit.

That gratitude didn't last long as we transferred in Dallas and awaited our next connection. It was about 6 p.m. and a voice over the loud-speaker announced that all of us going on to Albuquerque were to report to line number four and stand with our luggage while we awaited a signal from the doorman, who would show us which bus to load. Six p.m. turned into 7:00 p.m., and 7:00 p.m. turned into 8:00 p.m., and we were still standing in that same line. We started hearing rumblings of delays, overbooking, and mechanical problems. I began to get frustrated and even started cussing the bus system under my breath. By 9:00 p.m. that frustration had turned into anger and severe irritability. The spiritual malady was upon me and upon me hard! I didn't like these feelings and wanted them to go away. I'd just left five months of rehab and you're not going to believe it, but my eyes turned immediately to the terminal bar and the gay crowd happily surrounding it, laughing, talking, and smiling. "A beer would make this frustration, anger, and irritability go away" I thought. And then it hit me! I closed my eyes and said, "God, I need you badly right now! I'm frustrated, angry, tired, irritated, and I'm uncomfortable. Please remove these feelings from me." Then I looked at the girl who had been standing patiently in line in front of me for three hours. We had been exchanging a little small talk throughout the evening, and I said to her, "I'm getting so frustrated and angry." She turned to me and said with a smile, "I know. My boyfriend is shipping off to Afghanistan early tomorrow morning from Seattle, and with this delay I won't make it in time to see him before he deploys for sixteen months."

Ouch! Here I was, going out to Colorado for a few weeks to sleep late, eat well, relax, hike, and enjoy the beautiful mountains with my parents and was complaining and upset over being twelve hours late. She was missing the opportunity to see someone she loved before he went away to defend our country and risk his life. Man, I felt like a schmuck! Thanks, God!

Since parts one and two of the solution worked so well, I decided to go for the trifecta and thought to myself, "Who can I help?" I didn't have a phone and couldn't call anyone, so I decided to focus my attention on the masses in the terminal and see who looked like they could use a hand. As my head swiveled around, my eyes stopped and fixed on a small group of people attempting to board a departing bus. I zeroed in on a Hispanic woman with four small children. She was crying, her baby was crying, and she was struggling to maneuver her large amount of uncooperative luggage. I quickly sacrificed my place in line and moved through the glass door and out on the bus tarmac (if that's what it's called) and asked her if she was all right. It seems she had left her husband and was taking her children to live with her mother, and the bus they were supposed to be on was oversold. She was overwhelmed, tired, scared, and didn't know what to do. So I grabbed as many of her bags as I could carry and said, "Come on, let's go inside to the ticket counter and see if we can get this figured out and get you and your family rescheduled on another bus." We did, and when she was all settled again, I wished her well. She thanked me, and I could see what appeared to be gratefulness in her eyes. It was probably the first nice thing someone had done for her in a long time. Who knows her story? Maybe her husband was abusive; maybe she was flat broke and holding on to the four most important things in her life. She was probably frightened, afraid of what the future held for her and her children, and on her way to a two-bedroom trailer they would call home for a while. I don't know, but I'm probably not far from the truth.

The amazing thing to me was that I wasn't patting myself on the back for being such a Good Samaritan! The surprise was that she was helping me and didn't even know it! That quick prayer to God, that thirty-second conversation with the girl in front of me in line, and that simple little ten-minute offer of help to the woman had completely removed my feelings of frustration, anger, and irritability. They were replaced with immense gratitude, immeasurable joy, and comforting peace.

With that spiritual malady being properly and effectively managed, I was no longer in danger of allowing the mental obsession to convince me that a beer would solve my problems (because I HAD NO PROBLEMS!), and without that beer, none of the painful "truths" would materialize. I thanked God for giving me His power and pouring His grace upon me.

I've had many experiences just like that one, and nearly every significant negative spiritual and emotional feeling I've had since that day has been miraculously solved by that simple formula. My reason for sharing that specific one with you is because that is the absolute first time I ever put that strategy into action, and I wanted to show you that it doesn't take practice, it doesn't take years of trial and error or hundreds of experiences to perfect the operation of this solution. It worked the first time I used it and every day since. It will work for you.

A word of advice, however, parts two and three of the solution can be difficult, especially for men. As men, we are conditioned NOT to share our feelings, NOT to show weakness, NOT to be vulnerable, and NOT to seek help. We're big, tough, and strong. We don't need anyone's help; we can manage on our own. We're not about to let another male competitor see us in a time of need or weakness. So we keep our spiritual maladies to ourselves, we tuck them away, and have the toughest time expressing our feelings. That's dangerous, because it's no more than pride and ego standing in the way of our emotional fitness. You know what they say pride cometh before! So how do we get around this resistance as men (and even women) to allow ourselves to be vulnerable? We find people we can trust, those who won't judge us, people with humility who understand that we're all flawed and we need to lean on them. But that's not usually enough for a man. For me, I like to beat around the bush, hoping that my confidant will pry, dig, and draw my troubles out. So my close friends and I have all agreed to use a "code word" to alert each other when we we're feeling low and need to get something off our chests. That word is "Iron," because the Bible says, "Iron sharpens Iron," and we all know that none of us is going to voluntarily puke up what's bugging us or where we're hurting. So we just text the word "Iron," and then it becomes the responsibility of the textee to contact me and start digging. "Hey Mike, what's going on?""Hey, nothing, it's all good, I'm fine, I got it figured out," I'll reply. Then he'll say, "Seriously dude? What's really going on? Just tell me?" "Okay, Okay I'm just really upset right now about this or that, or about him or her, or I'm just bored, lonely, or depressed and I don't know why." Boom! Conversation started!

Part three isn't actually as hard as part two, but it takes a little courage, requires some self-sacrifice, and oftentimes some personal inconvenience. When you ask God to show you someone you can help, or you turn your thoughts to someone you might assist, that person will appear, but you are still required to take some action by reaching out. Know that this effort is going to, mostly likely, cause you some mild inconvenience and a little bit of sacrifice on your part. But it's well worth the effort, and the good news is that the more you do it, the easier it becomes, and before long it simply becomes a part of how you live your life and manage your spirit!

Determining where the real "unmanageability" in your life originates, having God's power behind you, and knowing how to execute our simple solution will change your life beyond your expectations! Try it!

Chapter 12

God Could,
but Would He?

Having realized I was essentially powerless over everything in my life, and now beginning to have some understanding of where the real unmanageability of my life resided, I set upon a quest to find "this power" that could seemingly turn things around for me and restore me to a sanity I unknowingly lost along the way. Having made the humbling admission that I was not in charge, that no exertion of my best efforts had any profound effect on my environment and the people in it, I had to concede that I needed God's help, God's assistance, and His unlimited power.

Knowing and truly believing that God could restore me to sanity and supply me with this power was not a difficult gap to bridge. I certainly believed in a power greater than myself, believed in God, and absolutely accepted that He sent His son, Jesus, to Earth to die on the cross for our sins. In believing, I was saved, would have eternal life, and would not perish, at least in the next life, but I wasn't so sure I'd been promised any relief or grace in this one. I knew God "could" restore me. The big question that lingered in my mind was "Would He?" The other question I just couldn't come to terms with was along the lines of being "restored to sanity." If I needed to be restored to sanity, then that presupposes that I am currently insane! Really? God had already asked me to admit that I was powerless and couldn't manage my life, or my spiritual condition on my own, and NOW He wanted me to make a declaration of emotional instability?

I have seen insane people! They wander around aimlessly and carry on conversations with themselves. They have these maniacal laughs, they babble and mutter, they're mentally deranged, they're crazy, and they wear straitjackets, live in padded rooms, and drool a lot! That's not me, is it?

So I looked up the definition of the word "insane" and found it contained some descriptive words like immoderate, wild, absurd, irresponsible, foolish, and stupid. Then I remembered someone describing the definition of insanity to me as "continuing to do the same things over and over, and expecting to get a different result." That certainly described me; maybe I was insane?

There are dozens of ridiculous examples of this kind of "insanity." There's the guy who loses a wager when the opposing team hits a last-second shot to win the game, and then he bets the same way on the replay saying, "I don't think he can hit that shot two times in a row!" Or the person who places their hand on a hot stove and burns it, but does it again because they don't think it'll burn them a second time. A toddler only has to do that once to know he'll never touch a hot stove again, but as an alcoholic, I kept reaching out for that bottle, thinking to myself, "It can't burn me this time." Was a three-year-old smarter than me or more sane than me? I was beginning to wonder! Maybe I needed to do a little historical research of my life before dismissing the idea that I might actually be insane. I had to, because unless a person truly believes they need help, they won't be open to accepting what might be offered.

As I reviewed my life, thoughts of "insane" behavior began to flood my memory, and I realized this wasn't going to take long. I thought of all the times I'd withdrawn $500, gone to the casino, lost it all in thirty minutes, then returned to the ATM machine, done it again, then again, before leaving and telling myself, "That was stupid, foolish, and irresponsible. I'm never going back into that casino again." Casinos are designed to eventually put you on the losing end of the stick. But within weeks, days, and sometimes within hours, that mental obsession would take over and I'd start telling myself all the "lies" we talked about in the last chapter. "Last time was just some bad luck. I'm sure I'll win this time, it's just $500, I'm due, and besides, it's my money, I enjoy it, and after all, it's just another entertainment expense." Fifteen hundred dollars later, I was on my way back to the parking lot, swearing off gambling forever. Forever in comparison with the "life cycle of a fly," because I was back again, quickly subjecting myself to the same torture with the exact same result! Winning a hand or two, or a day or two, only exacerbated my insanity around gambling.

That insane obsession carried over into commodities trading as well. I'd put on a big position, lose, do it again, lose, and again, and lose. You'd think after a few times one would say to oneself, this isn't the job for me, or maybe I need to change my strategy around commodities trading; but no, my insanity around trading would eventually take me to the point of huge company losses, followed by termination. Sometimes voluntary, other times not.

What about relationships? I'd lie, deceive, manipulate, and use passive-aggressive behaviors to get what I wanted. Things would eventually blow up and cause some damaging resentment or trust or respect issue, and I would later say to myself, "That was stupid! I'm never lying again, I'm going to be up front, honest, caring, and unselfish," but again and again an uncomfortable issue would present itself and I'd find myself lying and manipulating people, especially my poor wife, over and over. My mind would tell me, "You'll get away with it this time, or she'll never find out, she'll never understand if I tell her the truth, anyway."

My insanity around alcohol goes without saying. I can't tell you how many times I've picked up a bottle and days, hours, or even minutes later have found myself on the wrong end of a DUI, lost money, a detox facility or a rehab, a further damaged relationship, and a soul filled with incomprehensible demoralization. But within days of sobering up, I would be convinced that the outcome from a few drinks would be different the next time around. It never was.

I recall one Halloween night when my wife and I had been invited to a party. There would be drinking at this party, and after being sober for a few months, I was miserably unhappy about situations like this. I'd been out of my second rehab for about a year and had experienced a string of mini relapses that all ended badly. I didn't want to go to the party. It just wasn't going to be fun for me without a couple of drinks. I explained my dilemma to Lori and then launched into a diatribe filled with manipulation and self-denial. I reasoned that I just wasn't fun anymore, that I was a better and more fun person after having a few drinks, and miraculously she seemed open to the idea that maybe I could try to "drink again," but keep it under control! I'm not sure why she concurred. Maybe she had just given up on me, or maybe my argument was partially accurate, that without alcohol, I was a miserable dry drunk, and if a few drinks made me more tolerable, well then, maybe it was worth the risk. Maybe at that time she didn't yet understand the disease as she does today and thought it was a matter of "willpower." Maybe she just thought that anything was better than I was at that time. I don't know. It's possible she hoped I could eventually learn to control it. Drinking at one time was a very fun part of our lives and was the social lubricant that kept our marriage idling with laughter, fun, comfort, and ease. Maybe she was longing for the "good old days" and the memories of less-complicated times.

In any case, we attended the party, and I jumped at the opportunity to have a few drinks with impunity. I had five or six beers that night, laughed the night away, was incredibly sociable, lighthearted, funny, and we rekindled a dying passion within our marriage. "I knew I could do it! Alcohol was not in control of me any longer!" The insane thought that this time around it was all going to be different wasn't just a theory. I had proven it.

The next morning, I was scheduled to drive five hours to Kansas City to meet my wife's father, brother, and my brother-in-law for a weekend hunting trip. Having had a successful and controlled night of drinking, the first thought that crossed my mind that morning before I left on the trip was, "I've got this, and I should buy a bottle of vodka to take along for the hunting trip." I did, and about thirty minutes into the drive, I began to get bored and was feeling slightly off from the night before and decided a few shots while driving seemed harmless. By the time I reached Kansas City, the bottle was nearly gone when blue and red lights began flashing in my rearview mirror. Not long after, I found myself in jail, had my car impounded after blowing a 2.2, and was arrested for DUI. Those were the best things that happened to me that afternoon. The disappointment of my wife and her family were more than I could bear. I spent that night in a cell, retrieved my car the next morning, spent $400 in impound fees, another $1,500 on an attorney, and paddled back to Tulsa in a sea of murky guilt, shame, and remorse. The legal, relational, and spiritual damage caused from that one incident would take months, even years, to resolve. One would think that experience would be enough to teach me that every time I drank, the result was disastrous, but it didn't, and within a short period of time, the insanity had returned and I once again could not recall with any sufficient force the memory of what happens to me every time I drink. "It would be different next time." No. It wouldn't. I was officially insane. Get the white jacket and reserve my padded room! In retrospect, that may have been the best place for me. An insane asylum would have been preferred to where my drinking would later lead me.

Having seen in black and white, in real-life experience after real-life experience that I was the living definition of insanity, I finally had to accept it. I was doing the same things over and over, expecting different results, but always getting the same painful outcome. I was being foolish, stupid, and irresponsible just as Mr. Webster described me in his definition. Do you find yourself doing the same kind of things? Making the same mistakes, but expecting a different result? Pick your poison. Mine was alcohol, gambling, and lying. Maybe yours is pornography, infidelity, overeating, overspending, or avoiding responsibility. Does it classify as insane behavior based on what I've told you?

Mine did. So okay! I'm insane. I get it! I agree! I had also convinced myself from earlier work that I am powerless in and of myself, that my life and my spirit are completely unmanageable by me, and the only person who could give me power, a power that could help me manage my emotions and restore me to sanity was God. That all brought me back to my first question. Would He?

I honestly didn't think He would. Why would He? This question took me on a deeper quest into understanding who God is, who my God is, and it took me on one of those "lay down on the sofa" kind of introspective psychology trips! So hang on, I'm going to get pretty "deep" here, but this little exercise may make you think about your relationship with God, where it originates, and hopefully you can break that "idea or notion" of God, such as the concept I needed to dispel. But it takes an open mind and an honest willingness to forget everything you ever learned about God; everything you ever thought about Him; all the preconceived notions you've held about who, exactly, He is, and about the prejudices you've held that have created the kind of God and the kind of relationship you "think" you have with Him.

Prejudices? About God? Who am I to judge God? Of course I don't have any; or did I? Do you? Back to the notebook for some more self-evaluation.

Someone asked me to write down what my prejudices were against God, against religion, against other so-called Christians, and the following is what I found out about myself. It's an exercise that I think is worth your time, because just like everything else you'll hear in this book, you can't change, you can't be different, until you know what you're changing from! You have to know who you are, what you believe, where you've been. You have to know the kind of person you no longer want to be. You must have a complete awareness of self before any real change can occur. I had to understand exactly the kind of person I was before I could see what needed to be adjusted in my life. We'll go over this in greater detail in the chapter on "personal inventory," but this is a start.

What were my current prejudices against God?

Well, He won't help me when I need it. He is constantly convicting me with troubles in my life in an attempt to teach me, to change me. He isn't "with me" or "on my side" because I'm not living or acting the way He thinks I should. He's ashamed of me. He doesn't love me because of the person I have been. He doesn't want to hear my prayers, let alone favorably answer them.

How does God feel about me?

He is sad and disappointed in the choices I've made. He is worried about how "lost" I've become. He is angry about me being a "lukewarm" Christian. He is hurt by all the pride, ego, and selfishness in my life.

Okay, so what are my prejudices against religious institutions?

Their doctrines and practices are monotonous, boring, and robotic. They have no real practical application to my life. They think they know everything and are quick to disregard other belief systems. They focus too much on collecting money. They spend too much effort on trying to make me feel guilty, rather than energizing me in a positive way to follow Christ. They are hypocritical and place unattainable standards on their members.

What about other so-called Christians?

They are hypocrites. They look down on others, especially non-churchgoers. They are inflexible and judgmental. They think they are better than me. They are really just weak people. They hide behind religion and God. They use religion and "God's will" as an excuse to not face difficulties in life. They are too accepting and tend to get "run over" all the time.

Wow! Where did these beliefs come from? Are they accurate? Are you ready for some free Freudian kind of psychoanalysis? Maybe they came from your own father. God is our heavenly Father, and it's just logical to consider that the only reference we have in how to view Him is in how we view our own fathers, and in how we characterize our relationship with our earthly and biological fathers.

Take, for instance, someone who has grown up without a father. That person probably has feelings of abandonment. So they think God will, or already has, abandoned them as well. A child who has been beaten and punished by an angry father may be of the opinion that God is violent, mean, angry, threatening, and frightening. Another person who has no intimate connection with their father may feel like intimate connections with God are not possible. Or take the child who learns that in order to make dad happy, you have to be good in school, in sports, around the house, and stay out of trouble. That kid spends all his time trying to please daddy and therefore feels like they should do things that please God in order to "win" His love and acceptance.

When considering my own relationship with my dad, I began to realize that my view of God was highly correlated to that relationship "I thought" I had with my own father. I knew my dad loved me, but he didn't say it much to me as a child, and he wasn't quick to comfort me when I was hurt or down. He was, however, always there for me and provided me with everything I needed. He was consistent, coming home every night at dinnertime, helping me with sports, doing everything a father is supposed to do around the house.

As long as my behavior was good, he allowed me to do pretty much anything I wanted. Even when my behavior was bad, he rarely, if ever, disciplined me. I respected him greatly and was very proud of him, but we did not have what you'd call an "open relationship." We never spoke of feelings, emotions, or life. Our conversations were of the educational variety and on the surface. My dad didn't like to see failure and could be mildly critical at times. He rarely affirmed positive results and had a life philosophy that one should always focus on the worst-case scenario, so that whatever happened, you'd would be pleasantly surprised!

He was a man who believed in God, but didn't show it and was uncomfortable opening up about his faith to the family. He was also someone who hid his emotions. I rarely saw him overly happy, sad, hurt, or excited.

He was a man who intimidated me to a certain extent. He always "took the lead" in projects and events, and subjected me to the role of "gopher" or "assistant." He had high, unspoken standards, and I felt that he was greatly disappointed when I did not meet them. I always felt like my father wanted to show more love, compassion, and openness to his family, but he didn't know how and just wasn't able to do it. I'm certain his inability to communicate on an emotional level was a direct result of the relationship he had with his own father.

When my dad reads this, he's going to be upset. "So before you revise your will Dad, let me tell you where I was not only wrong about you, but how it translates into how I have been wrong about God." First, let me connect the two, and then I want to talk about how, today, I am beginning to see how both of my fathers feel about me.

Let's make the connection. With my own father, I feel that when I don't do what is expected of me, my dad will be angry, critical, and confrontational. I believe that God will do the same. If I'm not being the best Christian I can be, God will be disappointed with me.

I always felt that if I wasn't meeting my father's expectations, he really didn't want to communicate with me in a positive way. He would point out my faults, be critical of my mistakes, and rarely affirm any successes. An example would be scoring twenty-five points in a basketball game, but the only thing I heard from my father was, "What happened when you threw that one pass away?" So God must not want to communicate with me unless I'm meeting His expectations. God is critical of my performance in the same way.

My father has always provided me with everything I've ever needed, and I feel exactly the same way about God. He will always provide me with what I need. But the requirement is that I must be pleasing him.

And because my relationship with my own father was not open and vulnerable, my relationship with God can't be either. Due to the choices I've made, my father is not happy with me, so it makes sense, God wouldn't be either.

So I avoided God. I agreed to attend the Catholic Church because I only had to show up for an hour a week. I could mindlessly recite the same creeds over and over, leave early, and feel like I'd fulfilled my religious commitment.

I avoided God because I believed my bad behaviors and lifestyle were not pleasing to Him. I believed that a "wedge" had been driven between us. Since I wasn't willing to give up those habits, it seemed to be a pointless exercise to call on a God who didn't want to have anything to do with me.

I have stereotyped most church people as hypocrites. Partying and cussing on Saturday nights, cheating on their spouses and their taxes, putting on the "halo" Sunday morning, and saying things like, "I'll pray for you. We feel so blessed. I wish someone would start a Bible study. I would so love that." All the while making sure everyone saw them drop that "big check" into the offering plate or flashing their "angel tree" underprivileged charity tag for all to see. So I avoided God for fear that others would see me, just like I saw them, as a hypocrite.

I have even gone so far as opening the debate of other religious cultures. Muslims, Buddhists, Scientologists, and even primitive people from the jungles of Africa who have never been exposed to our brand of Christianity! I'd say to myself, "Who knows who God is?" "Who am I to say?" After all, where you're born, the family you're born into, the schools you attend, and the people who surround your life teach you about God, and that becomes your conception! I just happened to be born in the United States, into a Christian family and around a Christian community. I was a Christian. But what if I had been born in Motuo, China, and been raised by Buddhists, wouldn't I believe in Karma, Nature, Enlightenment, and Reincarnation? Who's to say these people aren't right? So I avoided God, deciding to rely on the notion of "Who really knows?"

Many of my views of God come from the relationship with my own father, and those views couldn't be any more false regarding either father! Think about these parallels in your own life. Is your conception of God the same as the one you hold for your earthly father? You'd be surprised! But it's not, and the way your own father feels about you probably isn't remotely close to the truth either! We have this great advantage on Earth, where we have the opportunity to ask our own fathers, "how they really feel about us." I've never done it, but should! I imagine if we all had the courage to follow through with that assignment, we might just begin to see a different kind of God! The kind of God I now see!

Today, I see a God who loves me, despite my actions. He wants what's best for me. He has a plan and a purpose for my life. He loves me unconditionally. He forgives me of my sins and forgets them. He is constantly using my experiences to shape, mold, and teach me. He wants to have a close relationship with me and wants to comfort me when I'm down. I am His masterpiece. I am perfect in His eyes. He will never leave me. He will never forsake me. He wants me to prosper and has given me everything I need to succeed in life.

I've realized that I cannot love well enough, act good enough, pray hard enough to ever win God's approval. I cannot "out sin" God's forgiveness. His forgiveness and His grace are free, and all I have to do is surrender myself to Him, admit my weaknesses, and call on Him. He loves me unconditionally, wants the best for me, and is proud of me. I know now that when I call on God to intervene on my behalf, He not only can, but He will. God is my hope when the world around me sees none, when I see none.

That's not even close to how I saw God! And guess what? If you ever get the nerve to ask your own father how he feels about you, I'll bet a dollar for a dime your dad will say and feel the exact same way! All those prejudices we formed about not only our own fathers, but about God our Father, will melt away. They were fabrications of our own minds, grounded in assumptions and selfish self-pity. We don't know how they felt, because we never took the time to ask them! (Note to self: Confirm with your old man.)

So we know now that we are powerless over almost everything in our lives. We can't manage our spirits without help. We know God can, and after figuring out "just who God is, and how He feels about us," I think we should understand that He "will" help us if we'll let Him! What will it take for you to allow God to give you the power you so desperately need? What will it require for you to allow yourself to trust Him, to let Him heal you, to change your life, or to give you direction?

That answer ended up being pretty obvious to me. I had to relinquish control. Needing or wanting to be in control is the opposite and at odds with having faith. It's reasonable and human for us to want control in our lives, but when we're reasonable, we don't allow the power of God to come into our lives. Our own sense of reason, emanating from our desire for control, prevents us from having any power that can heal us, make us more effective servants of God, or allow us to accomplish miracles.

The Bible proves this time after time. Was it reasonable for the little shepherd boy, David, to offer to fight Goliath? No! I'd have bet against that victory every time. David knew he didn't have the power to win that battle. But He knew who his Father was, and he knew that if he was willing to trade reasonableness for faith, that God could and would give him the power for victory.

Was it reasonable for Gideon to cut his army down to 300 men, brandishing crude weapons and silly horns against an army of 10,000 well-equipped soldiers? No. If Gideon was reasonable, he never would have climbed out of his cave! But he, too, knew God could, and he knew God would. His faith gave him victory as well.

How about Moses, parting the sea, or tapping a rock for water? Reasonable? No, but Moses submitted to God, knowing he could accomplish neither, let alone lead his people out of the wilderness, but he knew, like all the others, that with God's power, God could and would if He were sought.

Reason is fine, but faith brings real power that yields miraculous results!

So what is it going to cost you to admit your powerlessness? Admit you don't have control over anything? Realize that you are not in control of your life? Most people would think a lot! For me, it cost me my pride, my ego, my arrogance, and the fantasy that I was in control. It cost me feelings of self-importance and a false sense of security. It also cost me a whole lot of worry and fear. Really? Why were those things so valuable to me? That's like wanting to hang on to a bad case of hemorrhoids or a high balance on a 28 percent interest credit card! I was hanging on to things that were keeping me sick, keeping me insane, and keeping me from having a relationship with God and the ability to tap into His power!

Admitting that I couldn't successfully navigate this life with my own power helped me extinguish my foolish pride, my off-putting ego, my arrogance, my worry, and my fears. Those were all things that were nice to get rid of. Relinquishing control also gave me less stress, more humility, peace, serenity, ease, comfort, and removed all my insecurities and fears. Doesn't sound like it cost much at all, does it?

Shame was a direct contributor to my distance from God. When we become consumed with remorse about our decisions, our actions, and our lives, a relationship with God can never develop. Over time we rack up such a long list of sins and become so damaged from our actions that we can't see how God could possibly forgive us. We become locked in a prison of shame, guilt, and remorse. We hate our pasts, we hate ourselves, and there seems no hope of escape. The irony is that we are the ones holding the key to our own prisons! Even the "Eagles" knew that when they sang, "So often times it happens, that we live our lives in chains, and we never even know we have the key."

We believe that if people were exposed to the "real us" they wouldn't like us at all, and I knew that God knew exactly who I was, and I was absolutely certain he didn't like me. I was dying in this secret cell of shame, plagued with guilt about irresponsible and sinful behaviors. I carried that "rock" around with me everywhere I went, and its weight destroyed everything and everyone I came into contact with. We get to a point where we just can't comprehend "Why He would love us." We hide from others so they can't see our true selves, and we hide from God. We're sure there is no way God could love someone as evil and undeserving as we are. But God does love us! He just hates our sin!

You see, shame follows a pattern. First we experience intense emotional pain, and then we begin to believe the lie that this pain and this failure is "who we are," not just something we've done. These feelings trapped me into believing I could never recover, that I didn't deserve to recover. So I tumbled through life trying to cover up, soothe, and relieve these wounds by drinking them away, which only made things worse. Are you drinking your shame away, eating it away, shopping it away, or hiding from it in a world of pornographic images?

I found that God uses this pain we experience from our own choices to draw us back to Him. That God will do WHATEVER it takes to restore you to sanity and to redirect you toward living the life He has designed for you. It's our sense of guilt and our sense of insignificance that prevent us from seeing just how much God loves us.

We must accept our unchangeable past and recognize that what we've done is NOT "who we are." Once we admit our powerlessness and decide to completely rely upon God for our strength, do we then begin to see that God can and will change our lives. We are not who others say we are, we are not even who we think we are, we are who

GOD says we are, and He says we are His masterpieces, and He has the power to make us His new creations—people who are no longer defined by their pasts.

In Isaiah, chapter 64, verse 8, the Bible says, "We are the clay and God is the potter. We are the work of His hand." No believer is so broken that God cannot put him back together again. Sometimes God has to break down the defective pottery we've made out of our own sinful wills (like the ashtray I made in second grade), and rebuild and rework us through our life experiences, mistakes, and pain to create something much more valuable (like a Ming Dynasty vase!).

All that is possible through surrender! Admit and believe that you are powerless on your own. See that you are not strong enough to manage your own life by your own human efforts. Believe that God can give you the power you are lacking, and know that He will when you're ready to rely on Him and are willing to turn your life and your will over to His care.

CHAPTER 13

TURNING IT OVER

I am powerless. God CAN provide me with the power necessary to manage my life. God WILL furnish me with that power "if" I'm willing to turn my will and my life over to Him. If I do, He will restore me to sanity (because we've already determined I'm insane!), and direct my life according to His purpose and plan for me. And that's a fact jack, as Uncle Si would say!

So what exactly does it mean to make the decision to turn your will and your life over to God?

The word "decision" means to "Take prompt and firm action; to abide; to commit with force and resolve; having no reservations." We are making a prompt and firm decision to turn our will and our lives over to God with NO reservations. It's a whole-hearted commitment, a "no turning back" kind of deal. A decision is NOT saying to God we will "sort of or temporarily" put Him in charge, but since we're not sure how it will work out, we're reserving the right to withdraw that action. I have owned several of my own businesses, and over the course of my career I've hired managers and made "decisions" to put them in charge of specific areas of those businesses. My intent was to allow them to run those parts of the business as they saw fit, to leave them alone, let them do their jobs, and to trust them as they directed and managed what I had given them. However, almost immediately, I questioned their actions, their decisions, and their plans, and was always worrying about what they were doing. I never fully trusted them and almost always overrode their decisions and undermined their authority by doing what I thought was best. Invariably, they all got frustrated, angry, stopped being autonomous, independent, and lost their confidence. If they didn't quit, they'd condition themselves to check with me on every decision, or on every action they took, completely mitigating the very reason I hired them in the first place. I would become frustrated and come down on them, only realizing later that I was the one who had created their inability to manage! They eventually stopped trying to manage the parts of my business I had allegedly entrusted to them, the responsibilities always fell back on me, and the business suffered as a result.

God feels the same way. When we make the decision to turn our will and our lives over to Him, then micromanage God, second-guess His decisions, and take back control when it suits us, or when we're not happy with His plan or direction and change it, God gets frustrated and probably feels like quitting (but He never does!). I imagine He says to Himself, just like my managers did, "Mike doesn't need me, he wants to do it on his own, his own way. I'll just let him."

That's not making a "decision." It's also not taking prompt and firm action, or committing with resolve, and certainly not "having no reservations." That's what the Bible calls being "lukewarm." And God hates that, almost as much as my managers did!

So if we want God's power and his direction, we have to make the decision to commit to Him with no reservation, with complete trust and confidence, and with a willingness to support and abide by the authority we have given Him over our wills and our lives.

Just what do we mean by our will and our lives? Our wills are our thoughts, and our lives are our actions. So when we make that decision, we are turning over ALL of our thinking to Christ. We are turning over every action we take to Him. Since thoughts precede words, and words precede actions, what we're really giving over to God are the notions that form in our minds. We are opening up our minds and allowing every crazy thought that pops into our heads to be directed by God.

Just as we've proven to ourselves that we are powerless over addictions, our lives, and over other people, we now have to prove to ourselves that "our will" and the running of our own lives have hardly been a success. Admitting and acknowledging that we've fallen short of God's glory is yet another step toward a humility that is required to reach the power of God.

This was a difficult admission for me, and I wasn't so sure. After all, had I not been a successful businessman? Had I not been married for more than twenty-four years? Did I not have two great kids, lots of friends, a house, cars, money in the bank, and a pretty good reputation? A quick glance at my life told me that, although I had some problems, I was a pretty darn good success! Wasn't I in control of all that? Didn't my own self-will get me all these things?

A look to any outsider would certainly say so. The reality, however, was that I was always in collision with somebody or something, even though my motives were generally good. The truth was, I was really a selfish self-seeker, trying to wrest happiness and satisfaction from this world by any means necessary. That self-willed drive caused me to step on the toes of family, friends, business counterparts, and even people I didn't know! And they retaliated. On further review, I realized that all the things I considered successes in my life were simply a fragile "house of cards" I was desperately trying to hold on to and manage. My marriage was a disaster. I didn't have any "real" relationship with my children, business success was achieved through lies and deceit, and all the material possessions I'd gained were at the expense of someone else. My life was really NOT a success when run on my own self-will, and it was time to quit playing God. The day had arrived for me to become less interested in myself, my own little plans and desires, and more interested in what I could contribute to life. I sucked at running my own life, and it had become obvious to me! An honest look had shown where it had really landed me. Divorced, separated from my kids, broke, despised by many, poor-spirited, and an alcoholic! I had to be convinced that "my way, my will" wasn't working, and when I did, I found the humility to "really" make that decision and turn it over to God. No more trying to run my own life. I was ready to accept whatever God had planned for my life, no questions asked. My will was getting in the way of my recovery and ruining my life! Is yours? Do you find yourself as mentally and physically exhausted as I was? Are you tired of trying to run the show, keep it all together, and manage everything and everyone so "your plan" will come off just right? Life shouldn't be that hard, and it's not, when you give God the power to run your life.

People have asked me, "When you made that decision to turn your will and your life over to God, how did you do it? How did you operate? How do you get direction from Him?" It's a good question. It's not like you wake up the next day after making this decision and sit on your butt waiting for a message or an instruction. An operations manual doesn't just fall out of the sky, and that funny little "8 ball" we all had in the '70s doesn't work either (even though I wanted it to)! You have to wonder, like I did, "just how does this process of allowing God to run my life work?" He doesn't e-mail you a manifesto or text you a "to-do" list. He doesn't leave you a voice mail about what your next steps are to be. So how do you hear God? How do you know what His will is for your life? All great questions. The simple answer is that it takes a very open mind, a trusting spirit, some intuition, and a lot of work! But there's a process I'm about to share with you, and when you're disciplined about following it, God's direction gets easier and easier to spot, comes more frequently, and gets more and more clear as you become proficient in listening!

I've found that God speaks to people in many different ways, five ways to be exact. First, He can speak to us audibly. That doesn't happen very often, or ever, for most. But it does happen. We see in the Bible that God spoke to Adam in the Garden of Eden. He spoke to Noah about building the ark. He spoke to Abraham, Moses, and even to Saul on the road to Damascus. So we know He can speak to us audibly. I've never actually heard his voice, but if that ever happens, I'm pretty sure I'd do exactly what He told me!

Second, God speaks to us through circumstance. Often Christians refer to this as "God opening and closing doors." For instance, you may be asking God or looking for direction in your marriage, with a job, a move, advice on a relationship, or in making some kind of commitment. God doesn't give you any verbal advice, but things (circumstances) begin to occur. Your spouse might file for divorce, or they might suggest you go to counseling. Your position might be eliminated, or someone might contact you out of the blue about a new work opportunity. A friend might reach out to you for help, or the commitment you were thinking you'd make suddenly comes into conflict with a more important matter with a child. The job you were praying for gets filled by someone else. The house you thought felt right gets bought out from under you, or that "perfect someone" you thought was your soul mate suddenly decides to move to Michigan (unless you live in Michigan, then they go to New Mexico). The circumstance closes a door. That is God saying, "No, this isn't what I want for you." Then, when you get discouraged, out of nowhere a better house comes available, you lock eyes with that little "hottie" after church on Sunday morning, or you meet a guy in line at the Arby's who just happens to be looking for someone to fill a job that you're perfectly qualified for. These are all circumstantial directions from God. Once you figure out how to recognize them, accept them, and keep your eyes open for ever-changing new circumstances, you'll begin to see how God communicates uniquely to you in these ways.

The third way we hear God speaking to us is probably the most common, but also the most difficult to detect. God speaks to us through our own thoughts. Most of the time the only other person in my head is me. My head gets filled with thoughts, ideas, desires, inspirations, and objectives. Where do they come from? Oftentimes they are nudges from God. They are His Holy Spirit feeding my mind with guidance from God. But not always! Occasionally Satan sneaks in there and fills my head with logical thinking that is designed to undermine God. So until you get proficient at recognizing these thoughts as God's, you have to put them through the litmus test.

When it feels like my thoughts and feelings are originating from a God directive and are strong enough to stay lodged in my brain for months, weeks, days or even hours, I begin to ask myself some questions. Does this thought make good sense? Is it reasonable? Is it a fundamentally sound, wise thing to do? Is it self-seeking in nature? Is it a selfish thought? Are my motives behind it good? How will it affect others? Is this thought grounded in the notion of helping others? How does my gut feel? Is my intuition feeling right about it? Does my heart like it, or does it leave me with a sick, uneasy feeling?

These are all questions you have to investigate before taking action on God's behalf. If any one of them fails, it's probably not God's will for you. God did give us brains to use, but he also gave us His Holy Spirit in the form of a conscience or intuition. If you've passed the first logical thinking test, checked your selfishness at the door on this one, if your motives are good and the thought benefits are all involved, you're halfway there. Most people stop after completing the "logical" portion of the test. But when your head (your logic) doesn't match your heart (your intuition, gut feeling), then you have a problem. I can't tell you how many "logical assumptions" I've made, then gotten that "something just doesn't feel right" about this decision and gone ahead and proceeded anyway. In nearly every case, the outcome did not turn out favorably! So make certain your "right brain" is supported by all four chambers of your heart!

The fourth way in which God speaks to us in an attempt to direct our lives comes through other people. God uses other people and our interactions with them to speak to us. When you open up your mind, fully engage your focus on what others are saying to you, what they're asking of you, and how they're living their own lives, you'll be amazed how much of God you can see in them. When you stop viewing people as just other human beings sharing and invading your space here on earth and start looking at them as "messengers of God," you'll be blown away by how God may be using them to speak to you.

I can name hundreds of examples, but the one that brought me to the point of complete submission to God's will and proved to me that God uses other people to speak to us came from my fifteen-year-old daughter. I was in yet another long-term treatment center for alcohol addiction and was recovering nicely. I was improving and getting stronger physically, emotionally, and mentally. I had accepted my powerlessness over alcohol, understood where the unmanageability of my life resided, knew that I needed something more powerful than myself to get better, and had rededicated my life to Christ. I was on fire and ready to turn my will and my life over to God. Some really miraculous things were happening to me, and I was having one spiritual experience after another. Feeling that God had finally intervened on my life, I was certain I had been healed and was ready to check out two months into an eight-month program. I was tired of bunking with three other guys, tired of being told what to do all the time, tired of feeling like I was trapped in a prison. I was ready to see my children; they needed me. My plan was to return as quickly as possible, to attempt to patch things up with my newly divorced ex-wife as well, and I was sure she was ready to talk reconciliation.

On the work side, I was chomping at the bit to retake the helm of my business because it couldn't survive without me, and I wanted to show everyone that I was strong enough to do this on my own. I was ready to return healthy, take back my responsibilities, and prove that I had "overcome." There are a lot of "I's" in those statements! Logic, self-confidence, and arrogance were prevailing, and I was crafting with the skill of a seasoned attorney my rationale for leaving early, even bending the word of God to suit my personal and selfish desires. I'll admit that although my logic was good for leaving, my heart, my gut, and my intuition were telling me a different story. Allowing my own selfishness to prevail, I penned an explanatory letter to my daughter, detailing my progress and informing her that I would be home within two weeks. Everyone at the treatment center was telling me this was a bad idea, from other clients, to staff, and even AA members I'd met at outside meetings who had no vested interest in keeping me in treatment. I ignored all the signs and all of God's messages to me. He spoke to me through my heart, and my instinct gave me this sick feeling about the decision I was about to make. My heart did not match my head. God was speaking through other people, many other people, telling me it was better to stay and finish the work. Over the course of the next week, I dug in my heels and my resolve to leave. I allowed my pride and my ego to make my decisions rather than seeing the messages plastered by God all over my forehead!

Several days later, I received a letter in the mail that immediately changed my life. It was from my daughter, Caroline. I opened the three-page letter, and this is what the first paragraph said: "Hi Dad! I'm so excited that you are coming home. I can't wait to see you, I miss you so much. It was so great to hear about all the cool things that have happened to you. I have a question, though? Is this time going to be different or is it just going to be like all the other times?"

That was a dagger through my heart. One sentence broke and melted my heart simultaneously. It broke my heart, because she didn't trust that I could be changed, could be better, could be different, or could be healed. It broke my heart, because her statement told me that she was doing fine without me, and that she didn't need me as much as I thought she did. She didn't want me back unless this time was going to be different. The letter crushed my ego, my pride, and my arrogance. It showed me that I was wrong and that I was not following God's will. I cried for an hour realizing that although I'd made some progress, I still had much work left to do. It was a major setback for me, but also a major turning point in my recovery and in my life. I was very disappointed with myself for ignoring God's messages, for ignoring God's will for me. I, who had solemnly made the oath "that I will from this day forward turn my will and my life over to God and let him direct my life" had failed, and failed miserably at my first real test. It was here that I realized my life and will hadn't truly been turned over to God. I had gone halfway, confirming the lukewarmness about me. "Yes! I was willing to turn my will and my life over to God, provided that God's will matched mine!" And when it didn't, as in this case, I was deferring to my own selfish will, and I was disgusted with myself.

After sulking for a few days, I realized some incredibly important things about myself and about how I was going to have to change my life if I ever hoped to get better. First off I had to be willing to accept God's will whether I liked it or not, even if it was inconvenient. I had to be willing to do things I didn't want to do, not get things I wanted to get, and lose things that I thought I already had. You see, our "wills" are driven by our own selfishness, and our selfishness is driven by fear. When you're trying to get to the root of the "self-will" problem and to a place where you are honestly ready to turn your will over to God, no matter how that looks, you have to fix the problem at the root. The problem is not the exertion of my own will. It's not my selfishness. It's my fear!

What am I afraid of? What is anyone afraid of? What are you afraid of? Think about it before you read on. What are your biggest fears? You need to recognize them, because they are causing you to be selfish, and that selfishness is causing you to exert your own will. When you're exerting your own will, you're not following God's will for you, and because of that you do not have access to God's power. Without God's power you stay sick, you stay addicted, you stay unhappy, and you stay restless, irritable, and discontented.

Fear comes from two things. #1) Fear comes from "not getting what you want," and #2) fear comes from the thought of "losing something you already have." When I'm afraid of not getting something I want I exert my will in any way possible to get that thing. I don't care who I hurt, who it affects, or what I have to do, right or wrong, legally or illegally, to get it. That causes problems! A lot of problems! When I'm in fear of losing something I already have, I do the exact same things. I exert my will and do whatever it takes to hang on to, to keep the things I have.

Here is the relevant example. I wanted to be with my children. I wanted to reconcile with my wife. I wanted to regain control of my business. I was inconvenienced and uncomfortable in the treatment center and I wanted to be free. I obsessed about sleeping in my own bed, being able to drive my own car, and the ability to come and go as I pleased. The list of "what Mike wanted" goes on and on. That was selfish behavior, and because of that selfishness I chose to ignore God's will for me, exert my own, and leave the treatment center.

Those original fears almost caused me to make a colossal mistake! If I would have left so quickly, I would have missed out on some of the best parts of the program. I had learned enough to know the equivalent of how to dismantle a car engine, but not enough to know how to put it back together again. I would have certainly been drunk within a few months had I left so soon. I also didn't consider the effect my will would have on others. My ex-wife and kids needed time away from me to heal themselves. Going back too soon would have just further damaged those relationships. My business was actually running better without me, and returning as a still "insane" man would have had me resuming my same mode of operation that was sinking it in the first place. Most of all, I would have disappointed God by not following His will, and I would never have received the power I so desperately needed to survive.

The other fear was that by being away, I might lose what I already thought I had—my relationships with my children and ex-wife. The reality is that my early return would have lacked having the power of God on my side, and I would have lost them anyway. I would have been exactly the same broken person I was before I left, and that person was already losing them, if he hadn't already.

So how do we solve the "root" or cause of this problem called fear? You got it! Another admission! This one should be easy for you, because if someone as arrogant as me can get it, then anyone can. Here is the question you must ask yourself: "Do you think God's will for your life is better than your own will for your life?" Duh! Show me someone who isn't willing to agree to that question and I'll show you someone who unequivocally does NOT believe in a God.

Once you make this admission, the most incredible thing happens! Fear disappears! Because when you believe that God's will and God's plan for your life is better than anything you can desire, you no longer have to care about the outcome of anything! And THAT'S HOW YOU KNOW YOU'RE FOLLOWING GOD'S WILL!

When you are completely open to the outcome of any situation, knowing that however it turns out, it's God's will, and His will is infinitely better than yours, how could you possibly be fearful of the outcome? It is only when we have a vested interest, when we are exerting our own will, driven by selfishness, that we fear an outcome (and probably should fear it)!

A perfect example is a football wager. Several years ago, Harvard was playing Navy. I have never been in the service and I could never get into Harvard, so frankly, I could not have cared less who won that game. God could allow either team to win, and I had no fear about the outcome of the game. But all of a sudden I thought to myself, "I'm bored and a little depressed (the spiritual malady!). I think I'll bet $500 on Navy because soldiers have to be tougher than Ivy Leaguers. It will relieve my boredom, give me a little excitement, and pull me out of this afternoon funk I'm in." So I placed my wager on Navy, and suddenly I had a vested interest and began to become filled with fear. I was afraid I was going to lose $500 I didn't have to gamble with. I became selfish, lusting after the $500 I could win if the boys in blue pulled it off, and I immediately started behaving selfishly. I was cheering on Navy, cussing Harvard, throwing things at the TV, screaming advice to the coaches and players. I was trying to exert my own self-will and control over something I had absolutely no control over! There is not one thing I could do or say to change the outcome of that game, and so instead of being bored and a little depressed, I temporarily exchanged those feelings for a giant dose of fear!

How often do we do the same thing with God? Only He knows the outcome, and whatever He decides the end result to be is what will be best for us. As it turns out, the outcome was exactly the right thing for me. Navy lost and I was out $500 I didn't have. God wanted to teach me about bringing the unmanageable things in my life to Him. He wanted me to pray to him, "God, I'm bored, I'm depressed. Please remove these feelings from me." He wanted me to call a friend and tell them how I was feeling; then He wanted me to ask Him to show me who I could help that afternoon. Had I done that, God would have removed my uncomfortable emotions. The person I called would have said, "Hey, me too, why don't you come over and let's watch that Harvard/Navy football game together, and while you're here, maybe you can help me put together this Ping-Pong table I just bought for my kids!"

Had I done that, I would have had NO FEAR about who would win the football game, my boredom and depression would have been taken away, I would have had the satisfaction of helping a friend, and I would have been $500 less broke! Whose plan was better? God's or mine?

Finally, the fifth way we can hear God speak to us and understand what His will for us is comes through the Bible. The Bible IS GOD'S WORD! It IS His instruction manual to us on how to live our lives, handle our problems, and make the best decisions. When we read the Bible, God is speaking to us, right there in black and white! Some avoid this method, like I did, by saying things like, "The Bible is confusing, hard to read and understand, and it's impossible to find anything in there that's pertinent to the situation at hand." Technology takes away those excuses! With apps like LifeChurch's "YouVersion," the word of God is instantly available on your computer, iPad, or iPhone. You can Google anything. You can search for information every which way from Sunday and get instantaneous answers. You might type in "My marriage is struggling and I don't know what to do." And up will pop a host of messages from God, like Proverbs 10:12, "Hatred stirs up strife, but love covers all offenses." Or 1 Peter 3:7, "Husbands live with your wives in an understanding way. Show them honor." Or Ephesians 5:33, "Husbands love your wives as you love yourself. Wives respect your husbands."

So let's review . . . We've admitted we are powerless and can't manage our own lives, and we now believe that GOD can and will give us that power if we call upon Him. We must, however, be ready and willing to turn our wills and our lives over to God completely and with no reservation. When we do, we begin to hear His voice, and we begin to see His direction in our lives. Those messages from God are: 1) conceived in our own thoughts; 2) come through intuition led by His Holy Spirit; 3) are found through careful observance of circumstance; 4) often come through interaction with other people; and 5) finally, heard through the Bible, God's own word.

Every day I take time to meditate and to listen to the thoughts in my head that guide my day. I check my heart to see if it matches and supports those thoughts, making sure they are in harmony. If so, I run my thoughts by a few close friends to allow God to speak through them. Then I keep a vigilant watch of the circumstances happening in my life, looking for opening and closing doors. Finally, I am asking God to give me answers and guidance through His word, with a little technological help from YouVersion and Google! When all the stars are aligned, I feel confident that I am doing God's will, and my day falls into place so easily and effortlessly. If it's not, and I'm fighting it, struggling, running into one roadblock after another trying to follow what I think is God's will, it's probably not. It should be easy! God does not make terms too hard for those who honestly seek him with a faithful and righteous heart!

We are now beginning to hear you God! But it's still not perfectly clear, and we sense that we have more work to do. And we do. There is more to know and understand about God's will, but we will find it.

CHAPTER 14

MORE ABOUT GOD'S WILL

I was afraid that one chapter on surrendering our lives and our wills over to God wasn't going to cut it, so I'm going to dedicate another chapter to exploring that notion a little further. The truth is that the "art of turning our lives over" is probably an entire book in itself, and if I ever get it completely figured out, maybe there's more to write, but for now, a second chapter will have to do!

The reason this subject deserves another chapter is that the unwillingness to surrender our wills and our lives to God is the single "biggest block" that keeps us from being able to communicate effectively with Him. Do you remember my analogy about static and interference on the telephone lines that were keeping me from clearly hearing God and from Him hearing me? Well, operating a life solely on self-will and resistance to accepting God's direction for your life is about 50 percent of that static problem. It's a permanent ice storm that "cakes" those transmission lines with a shell of hard-packed ice, making it virtually impossible to hear what God wants for us, and is a pointless attempt to get a message or a prayer transmitted to Him. Once we melt away that ice by giving up our own lives, clear communication begins almost immediately.

When we stop our self-seeking behaviors, when we stop trying to wrest happiness and satisfaction out of this world by trying to manage everything and everybody, do we finally stop producing confusion and begin to create harmony. It's a delusion to think that of our own power and self-will we can direct the world about us and get what we want! We can't. Once we stop trying to "play God," we will find that this personal surrender becomes the keystone that allows us to pass through the "arch of freedom." When we learn to stay close to God, listen and be aware of His direction, and take action based on that direction, do we then find ourselves on solid footing in this life. Once we learn to become less interested in ourselves, our plans, our little designs for life, and we become more interested in what we can contribute to life through hearing God's will for us, do we begin to feel this new power. It is here that we begin to face life successfully, feel a peace that we could never find on our own, and begin to lose our fears. It is here that we begin to exert a power that had evaded us for so long—God's power.

Let me give you a Biblical example. In the last chapter we talked about self-will originating in a fear that manifested itself into selfishness, which then caused us to exert our own wills. A great example from the Bible would have to be the classic story of Jonah and the whale. God was calling Jonah to go to Nineveh and rebuke the people for their sins and to demand that they repent of their evil ways, lest God destroy them. Jonah knew this was God's will for him, but he chose not to listen, despite not only hearing God's voice directly, but also by experiencing all kinds of circumstances that were redirecting him back toward what God wanted him to do. He became caught in a terrible storm, was thrown overboard, and was swallowed by a whale! Jonah was exerting his own will because he was in fear! He knew the people of Nineveh were wicked. He knew that if he followed God's will, he would most likely be mocked and treated as a fool. He also knew that he might be attacked or even killed. He was afraid, and that fear caused him to exert his own will rather than follow and trust God's. I don't blame Jonah; I'd have most likely done the same thing. The request God asked of him would be like asking a Jewish person from New York to go to Nazi Germany in 1943 and tell Hitler and the rest of the Third Reich they were making a mistake and to apologize to the world and stop their aggression against the Allies and the Jews.

In the end, however, Jonah conceded, trusted God (although he wasn't given much of a choice!), and proceeded to Nineveh to follow God's will. The interesting part of this story to me is that when he arrived, the people didn't mock him, they didn't attack him, and they certainly didn't kill him. One theory is that the acid in the whale's belly actually bleached his skin and hair, and the people of Nineveh were fascinated with his appearance. Then after hearing his story of rebellion and the trials that followed, they feared the Lord's wrath and repented. God actually used Jonah's resistance and resulting tribulations to help Jonah accomplish his mission! It makes me wonder if Jonah's refusal to obey God's will wasn't part of the overall plan. In any case, God is certainly mysterious, and Jonah was able to use his misery to become a ministry for God.

If you'll remember the example from my own story with the foolish expansion of the eBay business, you'll see similar parallels. God was telling me to close the business, cut my losses, and move on to something else. My gut was confirming the same. My smart friends were asking hard questions I couldn't answer favorably, and my wife was telling me it wasn't prudent to expand before the first store was profitable and the concept had been proven out. If I would have been reading the Bible in those days, I surely would have turned to Proverbs and found God saying, "A fool and his money will soon be parted!" But I wasn't listening to God back then; I was running my life on self-will, driven by fear, and just like Jonah, I was tossed overboard into a raging sea of alcohol and debt and was swallowed up before finally being spit out so I could surrender to the right actions. Why did I ignore God's will and all the signs He sent me around this business? Because I was scared!

I was mostly in fear that after being employed on Wall Street and in the high-flying commodities industry, people would consider me a failure, now operating some "hokie" eBay store, a high-tech pawn shop! I was fearful they'd think I was a "wash up" after coming back from rehab, and I was worried that other competitors would get bigger than I was and grab more market share. I was scared I'd let my wife down, worried I wouldn't make as much money as I used to, and afraid one little store would impress no one!

Those were all the "fears" that allowed me to ignore God's warnings. Those were the fears that kicked my self-will into overdrive, and they were all rooted in selfishness. I wanted to be respected and admired. I wanted to impress other people. I wanted to be considered the "eBay King" of Tulsa—more market share, more money, and more attention. So I forced the opening of a second store. It wasn't easy, there was much pushback from everyone, it was a struggle, and it did not go smoothly or cheaply. When it didn't perform, I pushed and forced the opening of a third one, getting stronger messages from God through my own thoughts, intuition, and others, but self-will was in charge. When it was all said and done, the business was a complete flop, I lost a ton of money and eventually phased it out.

In retrospect, had I any relationship with God, many of my self-inflicted struggles may have been prevented. Had I surrendered my will and my life over to His direction, I would have had no fear. Because if I had turned my will and my life over to God, I would have known that His plan will always be better than mine, and I would have never forced the direction of that business. I had a vested interest in the outcome, though. I needed it to be successful so I could impress others, so I could continue to make the kind of money I made in the energy business, and because of those fears, I trusted myself, not God.

Why wouldn't one trust God? There are lots of reasons I didn't. First of all, I was too ashamed of my past failures to see "why" God would be interested in helping me. Second, I wasn't willing to let go of my false sense of self-sufficiency. I wouldn't allow myself to trust Him, because I trusted myself more. And third, I felt like I needed to clean up my own life before I could approach God, develop a relationship with him, and work toward developing a trust in Him. The problem with all that logic is that we will NEVER be at a point where our lives are clean and our way of living is perfect. We are imperfect people and will always be mired in sin. That is not a requirement of God. God's grace allows us to come to him as we are! Imperfect, sinful, and broken.

Why should we be willing to trust God? The answers are simple and true. Because God can be trusted. He has never let anyone down who has truly sought after Him. Because God wants us to seek Him as a place of safety and refuge and he has ALWAYS provided that. We should trust God because He is "unconditional love." He loves us no matter what we've done or who we have become. We should trust God because He tells us that He wants the best for us. Finally, we must know that we can depend on God. He will never let us down.

If you had a friend who never let you down, EVER, who always provided you with a place of personal and emotional safety and refuge, a friend who loved you unconditionally, no matter what you'd done, and was someone you could always depend on, no matter the circumstance, would you trust that person? Of course you would. Is that person better than God? No! How is it we can trust another human being completely, yet fail to put our full trust in a perfect God?

Let's say that same situation presented itself today. I would immediately turn to God and pray, "God please show me your will for me as it relates to this business, and if opening another store is how I can best serve you, then please remove the obstacles in front of me so that I can better do your will." Then I would have immediately gone to the litmus test. I would have thought it through logically, and through that process I would have recognized some of the flaws, but more importantly, I would have recognized what was driving me—arrogance, desire for self-importance, and money. My motives were not good! Red flag number one! Second, my intuition (God's Holy Spirit) was not only nudging me away from expansion, it was literally punching me in the face. I ignored my gut feeling about expansion. Third, if I would have just listened to one of the dozen or so people who told me expansion was a bad idea, I would have pulled in the reins. But I didn't do any of that. I wasn't listening to God. I was running my life on my own self-will, driven by selfishness and fear. And as it does every time, it ended badly for me.

It's not always easy though. When you are truly following God's will, things can become difficult for you, and you will face obstacles. That is just Satan trying to tempt or discourage you away from God's plan. Be strong, check your signals, continue to ask God for His strength and guidance, and "stay the course!" If it's really God's will, nothing can stop you. God is more powerful than any of Satan's efforts. It's been said before—God does not make terms too hard for those who seek Him and His will. God will never give you more than you can handle (I just found out that God never said that!). If it really is His plan and His will for you, it's not going to be that hard to follow. If, however, you find yourself fighting and struggling to follow what you think is God's will to make things happen, and you just keep running into one roadblock after another, then it's probably NOT God's will for you. When we're relaxing, taking it easy, trusting God, and things are beginning to happen, then we know we're on the track of God's will for us. When we're fighting it, it's probably time to "scrap" our plans and reconnect with God for clarification!

Let's look at some of what God tells us about relying on our own self-will and following His will for us, then we'll wrap up this chapter with a daily prayer we can petition God with each day to help us focus on His will, on taking us "out of ourselves" and allowing us to better see the direction God wants to give each of us every day.

When searching through the Bible, you'll see that self-will reared its ugly head from the "get go." Our friends Adam and Eve kicked it all off by foolishly deciding there was more happiness to be found on their own and without God. The decision they made to eat the forbidden fruit made a mess out of their lives, just like the decisions we make based on our own wills make a mess out of our lives. Genesis reminds us that every time we try to live on self-will, striving for our own happiness without relying on God, disaster strikes! When we believe that happiness is rooted in something other than doing God's will and serving His purpose, we find that the happiness we think we feel is just an anesthetic that tries to numb the pain lodged deep inside of us that we can neither bear nor eliminate on our own.

In Proverbs we are told to seek the wisdom God provides and that we are not smart enough to chart our own courses in life. In Judges we see how we, as human beings, fiercely resist God's will and are shown just how stupid and evil it is to live for ourselves.

In Isaiah we see how God rewards our foolishness, our insanity with pain, but that pain is redemptive and intended to drive us back toward God and His will for our lives.

In Pastor Craig Groeschel's book, *Altar Ego,* we are encouraged to pursue and seek God until His desires become our desires. We should commit to make every part of our lives available to God. God wants us to be BOLD, to take risks in His name. He is calling us, empowering us, and leading us to follow His plan. We are reminded that God has given us everything we need to fulfill His purpose for our lives, and when we obey God's will, God will surprise us with solutions, answers, and provisions that once seemed impossible. We know when we seek God's will, miracles happen. In his book, Craig points out that ultimately when we bring ourselves to a point where we are fully obeying and following Christ, we are no longer who others say we are, we are no longer even who we think we are. We have instead become who God says we are!

In another of Craig's books, *The Christian Atheist,* he explains to us that personal surrender boils down to trusting that God knows better than us. We are reminded that God's ultimate plan for us is not always our personal happiness. Our desire for happiness is a dangerous path to trek because it lights the fuse of self-will. Many of us pursue what we believe will satisfy us, but it never does. Sometimes what we think will make us happy is just the opposite of what God's will for us is! Although it can be hard to see at times, God wants and has something infinitely better for our lives, and we have to step aside and allow Him to show us. The Bible says that no one can serve two masters. He will hate one and love the other, or he will be devoted to one and despise the other. You cannot serve God and yourself. To find true happiness you need to choose one master. Do you believe more in yourself or God? Which master will you choose, or would you rather vacillate between hating God and loving yourself or being devoted to God and despising yourself? The conflict never ends well!

To summarize the last two chapters, I illustrated the often insane behaviors of a man (me) who desperately needed to be restored to sanity in order to stop being irresponsible, foolish, and delusional. I expressed how God could restore anyone, and that He would restore those who would earnestly seek Him. The meaning behind "turning our wills and our lives" over to God was also discussed—our wills representing our thoughts and our lives symbolized through our actions.

Additionally, it was discussed that to be true followers of Christ we have to be "all in" and make a prompt, firm, and complete surrender to Him. Living half-in and half-out is considered lukewarm to God, and He is intolerable of such behavior. A life led by self-will results only in pain, frustration, and disaster, and God's plan is always better than ours. It was comforting for even me to reiterate all the reasons why God can and should be trusted. My sincere hope, over these past two chapters, is that I've effectively demonstrated that holding on to self-will and a distrust of God are the largest obstacles keeping anyone from communicating successfully with God.

So, let's make that "decision!" Let's open our eyes, raise our awareness, listen intently, check our signals, and begin to watch the miracles happen in our lives. It takes practice, and no one but God will ever be perfect, but as our faithfulness and diligence grow, God's voice and instruction will become clearer to us and we will begin to know what to do when a situation arises. It all starts with a simple prayer. Say it each morning and repeat it throughout the day when you become unsure of yourself. It goes like this:

God, I offer myself to you. Build with me and do with me as you will. Relieve me of the bondage of self so I may better do your will. Take away my difficulties so that the victory over them will be a witness to those I can help with your power, your love, and the way of life you have designed for me. God, please reveal your will to me and give me the strength and courage to follow it.

Let's break that prayer down to better understand just what we're praying for. When we say "God, we offer ourselves to you," we are saying that we are giving "ALL" of ourselves to God: all of our thoughts, all of our actions, holding nothing back. We are not turning over ourselves just when it suits us. We are ready and willing to accept anything God wants of us no matter how wrong, painful, or inconvenient it might sound.

"To build with me and do with me as You will." Here we are giving God permission to do with our lives what He thinks is best. We are willing to accept WHATEVER that is, no matter what we think about it.

"Relieve me of the bondage of self" means we're asking God to remove all of our selfishness, all of our self-seeking motives, and we're asking Him to redirect our thoughts and our actions away from ourselves and toward others.

"So that I may better do your will." Referring back to the previous line, if we are being selfish or self-seeking, if our motives are for our own personal benefit, then we are NOT in a position to do God's will. We are in conflict when these characteristics are present, and in this line we are acknowledging that we cannot do a good job of following God's will if they exist.

"Take away my difficulties." Here we are asking God to remove the difficulties that exist in our lives, the problems we are having, and the obstacles that are blocking our paths and bogging us down. It could be problems at work, with finances, with relationships. It could be with addictions, children, parents, the law, or any difficulty we're facing. We are resolutely asking God to use His power to remove them from us.

"That victory over them will be witness to those I can help with your power, your love, and the way of life you have designed for me." This is the most powerful line in the prayer. Here is where we ask God to use us. By removing our difficulties, He is making us an example of victory to others. He is allowing others to see how we've "overcome" our troubles, and is allowing us to witness from our experiences in order to help others overcome their troubles through finding and relying on Christ. This line is "our calling," it's "our purpose," and it's how God shaped our lives in an effort to help others. This is one of the most powerful tools God has given us, and it cannot be wasted or hidden. Others must know how we've "overcome" struggles in life. This is our greatest responsibility!

Lastly, "God, please reveal your will to me and give me the strength and courage to follow it." This final line is just a reminder to ourselves and an ongoing request to keep ourselves focused on God's will and away from the dangers of drifting back into self-will. It is also a reminder that we cannot be effective if we are bouncing between God's will and our own. We can't afford to be "lukewarm"; we have to be all in. All the time and all the way!

Say this prayer every morning and throughout the day when life becomes uncertain, and I promise it will change your life and open up a line of communication with God that you never dreamed could exist. When we do these things, here is what we are promised.

When we sincerely take such a position in life, all sorts of remarkable things follow. We have a new employer; being all powerful, He provides us with what we need if we keep close to Him and perform His work well. Once established on God's solid footing, we become less and less interested in ourselves, our little plans and designs. We become more and more interested in seeing what we can contribute to life. As we feel this new power flow into us, we begin to enjoy peace of mind as we discover we can face life successfully. As we become conscious of God's presence in our lives, we begin to lose the fears of today, tomorrow, and the hereafter. We are reborn!

Now comes the real work! It's one thing to be reborn, to be a new person, and to set out on a new course, but to know where you're going, you have to know where you've been. That foreshadows the painful process we begin in the next chapter! It is the most difficult part of our personal journeys, but the most rewarding. Being able to see the "truth" about yourself, being able to see exactly how you've shown up in life, in relationships, at work, and in your community is not always a pleasant thing to uncover. It wasn't for me, but once I "bit the bullet" and took a pride-swallowing, ego-destroying look at myself, it showed me exactly the person I NO LONGER wanted to be, and just as mirrors reflect their opposites, it gave me the first glimpses of the person I DID want to become. It was a crystal clear vision of someone so very different than I used to be, and once I had completed my personal and introspective inventory, I almost had a crystal ball in my hand that showed me exactly how to best navigate my life as I walked hand in hand with God. So buckle up and get ready for a hard look in the mirror!

CHAPTER 15

DO I DARE
LOOK AT MYSELF?

B efore we begin, let me tell you that if you choose to embark on this journey, you'll need a workbook to help take you through this process. You can find it at KillingMrHyde.com. If you would rather just read on, this chapter will show you my own personal journey and the surprising findings that followed. An entire book could be written on the subtleties of this exercise. What I hope you'll glean from this chapter is more of an overview of how the process works and an understanding of how important and life-changing making this commitment can be for you. It was for me. Had you asked me to describe myself before taking this introspective journey, I would have painted you a very different picture of who I really was, but of someone I truly believed was real. In fact, that delusional self-portrait was not accurate at all, nor even close to what I found out about the kind of person I had become.

Once completed, you'll have a comprehensive list of personal character defects, a basketful of eye-opening realizations about yourself, and the first clear picture of just how you've "shown up" in life. You'll clearly see the person you no longer want to be, and you'll have a crystal clear vision of exactly the person you do want to be, the person God intended for you to be.

Here is the interesting thing. Every defect of character you have originates from a resentment you've been holding on to! Who we're angry with shows us more about ourselves than anything we've ever been taught, have experienced, or any predispositions handed down to us environmentally or genetically.

Since I love analogies so much, let me give you a real-life example. I once had an overstock business that dealt primarily in outdoor gear—hunting, camping, fishing, and backpacking goods. We bought semi-truck loads of overstock goods, discontinued items, scratch-and-dent items, and store returns. When we first started this business we were very selective about what we purchased; they were small hand-picked loads at good prices. As our business grew, we saw price opportunities in buying full semi loads of equipment. We could buy the inventory very cheaply, but each truckload required a considerable amount of sorting, repair, and organization. In our zest for profits, we found that we could buy one of these overstock loads, scrape off 75 percent of the good stuff, sell it for a profit, and push the remaining 25 percent of the "crap" into a corner of our warehouse, then go out and buy another truck and do the same thing. It worked great at first, but eventually that 25 percent of "crap" started piling up. It was disorganized, and it began to take up more space and more of our time managing it. We had to rent more warehouse space, then more, and eventually it reached a point where we had more "crap" than good saleable merchandise. Good items were getting co-mingled with bad items, and the "junk" was always in our way, preventing us from operating very efficiently. The mess began to eat up our once tidy profits.

I just couldn't bear to throw any of it away though, or to fire sale it, because it all had some kind of value to me. I might need a part on something broken to make something else new. Someone would always pay a little something for damaged items, and at worst, it had scrap metal value. I was always telling myself, I'd address it, sort it, organize it, and get it ready for sale, but every new load we received took up all our energies, and the problem continued to compound itself. Eventually, we had two large warehouses full of junk. We were running out of room for new items, and the cost associated with liquidating it became too great. Before long, we were overwhelmed, and eventually we went out of business.

Personal inventories, inventories of our own "crap," work exactly the same way. We start out with so much good, but little by little the crap begins to infiltrate our lives. We want to get rid of it, but we hold on to it because it has some value to us. It serves some purpose for us. Eventually the character defects in our lives commence to overtake the good, and we are no longer personally profitable or productive. Then we, too, go spiritually bankrupt. Letting go of these things is something we must do to survive, just like my overstock business. I needed to let go of the items that were killing my company. I needed to bite the bullet and sell them at a loss, give them away, or simply trash them. That was hard to do, because just like some of our character defects, the items in my warehouses had some value to me. Had I made the tough decisions and let go of the things that were weighing me down, I would have saved a lot of money on warehouse rent, labor, and general maintenance. I would have been more focused on the valuable parts of my business, been more efficient and effective, and certainly more profitable.

Our personal lives are no different. We can hang on to so much crap that the not "letting go" can kill us. The clinging to that baggage can render us useless, and its spiritual and emotional costs are bankrupting our lives. It overshadows the good in all of us, making our valuable qualities secondary as we begin to be quickly defined by our crap. That's what my business looked like at the end. What started out as a fresh outdoor gear business ended up looking more like a giant garage sale. When you're peddling good merchandise, you have happy customers who keep coming back; when you're peddling junk, you have one problem after another. Your customers get upset, you have to deal with returns, you eventually begin to develop a bad business reputation, and in the end you go bankrupt. It works exactly the same way in our personal lives; we start out with good intentions, with good personal qualities, and then little by little we start accumulating negative traits, behaviors, and character defects. People like us at first, and then they begin to become disillusioned. We begin stepping on their toes, taking advantage of them, dumping all our "crap" on them, exuding negativity, and before long, we've not only lost the trust, respect, admiration, and love of our friends and family, but we also render ourselves completely useless to them and we lose them, much like I eventually lost all of my customers. To survive, we have to rid ourselves of this unnecessary and damaging inventory from our pasts, but as in my business, there is a lot of work that needs to be done in order to see exactly what the inventory is and where all the baggage exists. Once you've identified it, then you can develop a plan, with God's help, to systematically remove it so you can begin to live a more profitable life.

So let me begin with the end result. When I finished the process, and I will explain this to you later in this chapter, I found the following personal inventory items I desperately needed to dispose of in order to continue to be a human-going concern:

- I place dependence on others, rather than on God.
- I am dishonest; I'm a liar.
- I put blame on others for my problems or failures.
- I am selfish and self-centered.
- I care too much about what others think of me; I place higher expectations on others than I do on myself.
- I manipulate people to get what I want.
- I lie to myself; I can't see the truth about myself.
- I don't follow or listen to my intuition or God's Holy Spirit.
- I don't trust that God knows what's best for me.
- I am entitled.
- I lead a double life; I have two sides, two faces.
- I think I need material things to make me happy, to feel accomplished, for self-esteem.
- I don't trust other people.
- I portray a false image to others.
- I don't know what it means to be a good father.
- I think I know what's best for myself and for others.
- I condemn others.
- I am self-seeking in every situation and relationship.
- I put undue/unrealistic expectations on others.
- I am lazy and don't want to work hard.

- I always look for the easy way out. I cut corners in life, at work, and in relationships.
- I have a lot of self-pity. I am always feeling sorry for myself.
- I don't like to be held accountable for my actions.
- I go to great lengths to cover up my wrongful actions.
- I mislead others into wrongdoing so I can feel better about myself.
- I don't know how to be a partner in any kind of relationship.
- I want praise for work I did not do, or did not do well.
- I am a controlling person.
- I think I'm superior to others.
- I need others to rely on me to feel valuable.
- I avoid others because I'm afraid they'll hurt me.
- I don't know how to be intimate.
- I don't stand up for what I believe in. I have no integrity.
- I am arrogant.
- I don't like to take responsibility for myself and my actions.
- I demand a reputation I do not deserve.
- I divert/deflect attention away from my own shortcomings.
- I am afraid of communicating what I want or need.
- I am unwilling to ask for help and take on things I'm not equipped to manage.
- I seek out people who will cosign my B.S.!
- I like to "play the victim."
- I am ungrateful.
- I rigorously justify my own wrong actions.
- I take advantage of others.
- I compromise my faith out of personal selfishness.
- I am not open to compromise.
- I get my own happiness at the expense of others.

- I don't consider the impact or the feelings of others in my actions.
- I lack transparency and I am not genuine.

Would you like to be my friend? My spouse? My kid? My employer? My coworker? My neighbor? My customer? I hope not! After I realized all these things about myself, I didn't care much for me either!

But the crazy thing about it was that I had NO IDEA this was the kind of person I was! I had no idea all these traits existed and how badly they were affecting my life and keeping me from having a relationship with God. These were the individual things blocking me from being able to communicate with God and preventing me from serving the purpose He had outlined for my life. This was the "static" on my telephone line.

So just how did I figure it out? It wasn't easy and it wasn't pleasant. I had to dig through the inventory of my life, pull out each item, examine it, then choose to keep it, repair it, or discard it. I needed God to help me with all of that. The important part was just knowing, because if you don't know who you are, then you won't know how to change, or who you want to be. Through this exercise, you learn who God intended for you to be!

As mentioned earlier, this entire exercise begins with resentments, and here's how it works and exactly how God helped me figure it all out.

Step One begins with a quiet place, a pen, a notebook, and a prayer. "God, please show me the people I have resentments against that You would have me look at." Then sit quietly, and as the names pop into your head, write them down. Just the name only, not why, not anything else, just the name. The first time you say this prayer, there may be ten or fifteen names that pop into your head. Write them down. "God, who am I angry with, who am I holding a grudge against, who am I not forgiving, who has hurt me, who would I like to get revenge against, who do I hope 'gets theirs'?" More will pop into your mind. Write them down. Your mind may go blank after a while. If so, get up and walk away for ten minutes, an hour, or maybe a day. Then go back, sit down, and do the exact same thing. "God, please show me the people I have resentments against that you would have me look at. God, who am I angry with, who am I holding a grudge against, who am I not forgiving, who has hurt me, who would I like to get revenge against, who do I hope falls down the stairs, loses his job, or gets left by his wife?" More names will pop into your consciousness. Write them down. Walk away. Come back. Do it again, then again, and again.

The amount of names that fill your notebook will grow as the number of names that enter your mind decreases. When no new names come to mind, walk away one final time. This time wait a day or two, then just to make sure you've listed them all, we'll add one more twist to this part of the exercise. The next time you go back, say the same prayer, but in the middle of your prayer, add a specific period in your life. For example, "God, please show me all the people I have resentments against from grade school that you would have me look at." Write em' down. Walk away, pray it, and do it again. Then, "God, please show me all the people I have resentments against from high school that you would have me look at." Then college, a particular company, a love relationship, a friend, a business associate, a child, a teacher, a coach, an institution, or even a principle. I think you get the idea. Just take a chronological journey through your life with your resentment glasses on and see who pops up! The goal is to come up with a comprehensive list of all the people, institutions, and principles that you have some kind of resentment against. The more thorough you are, the more information you are going to get about yourself.

That's the first step in identifying and evaluating your personal inventory. It really only takes a few days, and if you think of a few others as you work through the rest of the process, write them down and add them to your list. The number of people on your list will vary based on your age and your life experiences. I've seen as few as thirty people on a list and as many as 250! When I finished, I had about 120 names written down. My list really made me laugh! When I first entered long-term treatment, one of the counselors said to me, "I think you're a very angry man, a very resentful person." I was offended and responded, "No way! I'm not angry at anyone! I never get mad, I'm not holding on to any resentments." Boy was I wrong!

Step Two: After completing Step One, take a break and let your list marinate for a few days. Once you have an hour or two of free time, go back to it. Start with the first name on your list, and next to the name write, "Why am I angry at this person?" Then write down your answer. More than likely you will have multiple resentments against the same person, especially someone you've been close to. As you go through the next part of this process, you'll need to treat each resentment separately. When you're finished, you may have started with 100 names, but could have 150 or more resentments from having been angry with the same person for several different reasons.

I'll give you one of mine. This is the example I'll use throughout this chapter and for the duration of the inventory process. I'll use it to explain exactly how this process works and precisely how to extract the information needed in order to identify the character defects you need to rid yourself of. The workbook, if you choose to order it, has much more detail.

One of the names on my list was my ex-wife. Next to her name I wrote why I was angry or resentful toward her. I was angry because she complained about the way I built and managed my business. She didn't like the way I ran it, she second-guessed my decisions, criticized them, and was pessimistic about my chances for success. She had no confidence in my abilities. She was skeptical the business would succeed and complained that it was not making money. She was always nagging that the business was more important to me than her or the kids. That's it for Step Two of this process. Don't write down or think about anything else on that resentment. Then go to the next person on the list or continue on with the same person if you have more resentments against them. If there are multiple resentments against one person, you will have to spend a little bit of time thinking about your relationship and experiences with that person. Here again, you can ask God to show you what specific resentments you have against this particular person. Pray and listen, write down "why you're angry." Do it again, then again, until you can think of no more resentments against this person.

Once you have completed the "why I'm angry at this person" reasons for each name, you're done with Step Two. Depending on the number of names on your list and the number of multiple resentments you have for a single person, this process could take a few days, maybe a week. When it's done, you're ready to move on to the third of four steps. If you happen to think of a new name along the way, or an additional resentment for an existing name, write it down. Then let it rest and "sit with it" for several days. Now you're ready to move into the third part of the process. It's what I like to call the "self-righteous column," and it's really an ego and pride booster!

Step Three: In the third part of this analysis, or the third column as it's called, you are going to ask yourself seven questions related to this resentment. Each question is related to how this resentment affects certain parts of your personality. Each question is then followed with a Part B question, "What is my fear around this situation?"

The first question is related to your "SELF ESTEEM." "How do I see myself in this resentment?" Then you follow up that question with, "What is my fear surrounding this resentment?" In my example, I was resentful toward my ex-wife because she essentially didn't think I knew how to run my business.

So for "self-esteem," here's how I saw myself in this resentment. "I am a hard worker, a risk taker, a creative entrepreneur. I know how to manage a career and build and grow a business. My track record has shown that I have been and can be successful. I'm darn good at what I do!"

Now, what is my fear around this same notion? "My fear is that I will fail in business and I will disappoint my ex-wife."

The second question revolves around how this resentment affects my "PRIDE." The question is, "How do I think others should 'see' or 'view' me in this situation?" Then, "What is my 'fear' around that?"

In this particular resentment, I answered, "My ex-wife should see me as someone who is very hard working and successful at creating, building, and managing businesses. She should have confidence in my abilities and trust that I can make it a success."

My fear "Is that my ex-wife thinks I don't know what I'm doing. That she doesn't trust me or have any confidence in my abilities."

The third question asked relates to how this resentment affects my "AMBITION." The question is, "What did I want to happen in this situation?" Then again, "What is my fear around that?"

I wanted my ex-wife to be proud of me for my past accomplishments. I wanted her to have full confidence in my abilities. I wanted her to wholeheartedly support me. I wanted her to encourage me and to be proud of me.

My fear? I was afraid she had no confidence in me. I was afraid she didn't respect me or my abilities. I was afraid she wasn't proud of me or any of my past accomplishments.

Question four has to do with my emotional "SECURITY." "What did I need to have happen here so that I could be okay emotionally?" Then, "What is my fear?"

To be "okay" emotionally I needed my ex-wife to tell me that she was proud of my past accomplishments. I needed her to verbalize her confidence in me and my abilities. I needed her to acknowledge and understand how difficult it is to build a business. I needed her to encourage me and support me with her words and her actions.

My fear? My ex-wife doesn't trust or respect me or my abilities. She's not proud of me. She's not grateful for anything I've done in the past. She doesn't want me to succeed. Maybe I am a failure?

The fifth question addresses what we call "PERSONAL RELA-TIONS." The question you ask yourself is, "What are my deep-seated beliefs on 'how' this relationship is supposed to work?" Then once again, "What are my fears around this?"

Since this relationship is spousal (depending on your person, it could be your views on how parental relationships work, or children, employers, friends, etc.), this is how I believe a wife is supposed to be in this particular situation. Wives should wholeheartedly support their husband's efforts to provide for the family. They should respect, honor, encourage, and be grateful for their husband's abilities to provide and lead a family.

What is my fear around this? I'm afraid my ex-wife is not grateful for me or what I've done to provide for my family. I'm afraid she doesn't respect me as a person, a provider, or a husband. I'm afraid she is disappointed and annoyed with me.

Question six is about "SEX RELATIONS." No! It doesn't have anything to do with hanky-panky! But it would be easier to analyze if it did! It's similar to the last question. It's "What are my deep-seated beliefs on how this 'gender' is supposed to be in this situation?" So in my case and example, "How is a woman supposed to behave in this situation?" Again, "What is my fear?"

In my view, women should rely on and have a certain dependence on their men. They should honor their men, respect their men, and do whatever they can to support their men, admiring and being grateful for them as a provider and leader of the family.

My fear was that my ex-wife couldn't rely on me, that she wasn't grateful for my efforts, she didn't respect me, and didn't want to honor me. She didn't want to be dependent on me.

Finally, question seven has to do with your "POCKETBOOK." "How did the situation around this resentment affect my pocketbook or my finances?" "What is my fear?"

I borrowed and spent a lot of money to prove to my ex-wife that my business could be successful. I took a lot of financial risks to make that happen. I sacrificed a lot, financially, to make it all work.

My final fear was that my financial stress and burden didn't register with her at all. She would have no empathy for the financial suffering I was under to make a business fly. She would be angry with me for not being more financially productive and prudent.

That's the third step or third column, however you want to look at it. When I finished I was pretty pumped up. I was feeling incredibly self-righteous and ten times more resentful than before I began! How dare she? I AM a hard worker. I DO know how to run a business. I AM successful. She should be proud of me. She wasn't supportive, encouraging, confident, and understanding. She wasn't acting like a good wife or a good woman for that matter. I took a lot of risks and I suffered for her sake and all I got from her were disdain, complaints, and resistance. The woman had some nerve! I was really mad! I was really feeling put down, mistreated, unappreciated, hurt, and unloved. You're darn right I've got a resentment. It was well-founded, I thought. I really liked this part of the exercise!

Step Four: Now we're ready for the "sucker punch!" This is the drink from the fire hose of humility—the fourth step or column. Rather than going back to the next name on your list, we'll finish up this resentment with the final eye-opening work. Once we complete this one, we'll go back to the next name or resentment on your list and do Steps Three and Four for each one of those as well.

In the fourth column of this resentment, we ask ourselves just five more questions regarding this resentment. After we're done, we're going to get the first glimpse into "who we really are" and "what character defects we find in ourselves." After finishing this work on your resentment, you will have a crystal clear picture of not only who you are, but also of how you've shown up in life. You'll be able to create a list similar to the one I shared with you about myself earlier in this chapter, and a vision of who the new you could be will begin to unfold!

Question one is what we call the "REALIZATION." You ask yourself, "How have I done the same things I wrote down in column two or Step Two to this particular person (or to someone else)? How have I acted in the same way?" Be hard on yourself here, and be thorough in your thinking. Really think about your actions. It is not important if you acted like the person did in your column two to that same person. In many cases you didn't, but you may have acted like that toward someone else.

To summarize the example with my ex-wife, I was angry because (I thought) she didn't like the way I ran my business, she second-guessed my decisions, criticized them, and was always pessimistic about my chances for success. She had very little confidence in my abilities. She was skeptical the business would succeed and complained that it was not making money. She was always nagging that the business was more important to me than she and the kids.

Okay! So let me think . . . How have I acted in a similar fashion? Got it! I complained about the way she managed her real estate career. I told her she was on the phone, on the computer, and talking with other realtors too much. Her calls were not necessary or effective. I criticized her for giving away too much of her commissions to make a deal happen. I told her she was not a good negotiator, not a good numbers person, not organized or thorough. I constantly tried to tell her how she could do things better. How to negotiate her deals, how to manage her clients, how to improve her sales and marketing. I complained about her spending too much time in the evenings and on weekends focusing on real estate and that she was being neglectful of both me and the kids because of it. Hmmmm . . .

The second question asks how we were "SELF-SEEKING." "What were my self-seeking actions around the behavior I just mentioned in the paragraph above?"

I wanted my ex-wife to see that "it's not easy out there." It's not easy to provide for a family. I wanted to prove to her that I was capable and that she did need me, that she couldn't do it on her own. I built her websites without asking if that's what she wanted, created spreadsheets, and offered unsolicited advice on her real estate deals. I was an "I told you so" guy when things went badly in her business.

Third, we ask ourselves where we were "SELFISH." "What was my selfish thinking while I was taking the actions mentioned above?" I was seeking my own personal validation. I had a desire to feel needed and loved, a desire to feel important. I wanted her to fail so my efforts in business would look better and be appreciated. I wanted some respect, affirmation, and praise. All of my actions around her real estate business were designed to make me feel better. They were incredibly selfish and self-seeking.

Question four asks where I was "DISHONEST" in this dealing, or what lies was I telling myself that resulted in the above thinking?

I told myself that if she succeeded, she wouldn't need me anymore. I told myself that if I allowed her to think she was good at running a real estate business, she would see herself as a better business person than me, and a better provider for our family. I told myself that women or wives shouldn't be better at supporting their families than their husbands. I told myself that if I could keep her down, I'd look better relative to her efforts and she would respect, affirm, praise, and honor me more.

And finally, the fifth question deals with my real fear. "What am I really afraid of?"

I was afraid that my ex-wife would be more successful than I was in the business world and that she would no longer need me. That she would become financially independent and leave me. I was afraid that if she got stronger and more independent she wouldn't rely on me anymore and would wonder what value I really brought to the marriage. I was afraid that the kids would respect her more. I was afraid that the balance of power in the relationship would shift toward her, and because of all those fears I did my best to keep her down, to undermine her efforts, and to poison her mind by trying to discount her abilities against mine.

Well . . . she did do better than I did out there in the real world financially. She did get more independent, she really did bring more to the marriage than I did, she really did capture the balance of power in the marriage, and she really did put herself in a position where she didn't need to rely on me. And finally, she really did leave me! But it wasn't because of all of those things; it was because of all my selfish and self-seeking actions. It was because of my lack of support, encouragement, appreciation, praise, and respect for her. I allowed my greatest fears in this resentment to destroy the very thing I was afraid of losing!

That all came from one resentment! I couldn't believe how much the exercise taught me about myself and about the things I had NO IDEA I was doing. Now let's pull the meat off this bone! What we're really trying to find here are the ugly character defects about ourselves that surfaced with this one resentment. We are trying to identify that rotten inventory that exists in the warehouses of our character. Once we define it, we become aware of it, and then we begin to eliminate it, or at a minimum, tone it down.

In this specific resentment against my ex-wife, I realized several things about myself . . .

- I am selfish and self-centered.
- I think I know what's best for others.
- I want praise for work I don't do or don't do well.
- I am a controlling person.

- I need others to rely on me to feel valuable.
- I don't want others to hold me accountable.
- I am selfish at the expense of other people's happiness.
- I put down others so I can feel better about myself.

The above examples are what you call "character defects." They represent the "truths" about us that God doesn't like. They are undesirable traits and they are sinful. They keep us from God, and they prevent us from having a relationship with Him. They keep us sick with feelings of guilt, shame, fear, unworthiness, and depression. They create that spiritual malady we want to go away, feelings I tried to make disappear with booze! Maybe you do it with food, sex, gambling, or shopping? These were the items that were killing me, not the whiskey!

This is simply one resentment and one set of corresponding character defects, however. You have to finish them all to begin to see patterns forming, to begin to see a consistency in your shortcomings. Someone once said, "If one person tells you that you have a tail, you can probably discard it. If two people say it to you, that you have a tail, you might want to think about it. If three people announce that you have a tail, you better turn around and look!" The character defects and the things blocking us from God emerge from the processing of all our resentments. Patterns show up, I promise you, but looking at only one name on the list isn't enough to have any statistical accuracy. The "tail" is there; you just have to hear it enough!

After finishing my first resentment, several things crossed my mind. The first was, "How could I be angry and resentful at my ex-wife based on 'my perception' that she was criticizing my business efforts and questioning my actions around running it?" I did EXACTLY the same thing to her! What a hypocrite! Then I realized that my resentment was unfounded, that my anger was driven by my own fear, my own selfishness, my own pride and ego. Finally I was sickened by the way I saw I had treated her. Not only was I wrong to be resentful toward her, but I actually owed her an apology for my unfair and retaliatory behaviors!

Working this process allows us to see a little of our true selves, and I can tell you, I didn't like it one bit! From that ugly vision, however, a ray of hope, a glimpse of positive change was beginning to shine through. "I could see who I was! From that, it was possible to see who I no longer want to be, what I no longer want to act like!" I can apologize to my ex-wife and make amends to her for my wrongdoings. I can ask God for forgiveness, I can forgive my ex-wife, forgive myself, and know that I no longer have to be that way. I can flip those findings around and be just the opposite! The first clear-cut signs of my new life road map. I ask for forgiveness, forgive others, forgive myself, make my amends, and then begin to operate exactly the opposite way. (George Costanza may have been on to something!) Instead of being selfish and self-centered, I am giving and self-sacrificing. I am thinking of the needs of others. I can admit that I don't know what's best for others and allow them to tell me. I don't seek praise for anything I do; especially work I don't do well. I can stop trying to control others. I can allow others to grow and be independent. I can rely on God instead of needing other's approval and love. I can lift up others and be willing to sacrifice my own happiness for theirs. I can be loving, supportive, encouraging, helpful, respectful, and praise others for their accomplishments.

Now what about that guy? Is that someone you'd want as a spouse, a friend, an employee, a coworker, a partner, a neighbor? I hope so! It sure is better than the first guy I described to you!

Before we move on to the next chapters, which involve "fear" and "sex inventory," I want to share with you a few things God says about our defects or character, about the mistakes of our past, and about who He says we are and who He says we can be.

In the book of Ruth, we are told that God has the power to work through everything difficult in our lives to plant our feet on the road to joy. God can use the shortcomings of our lives to refocus us on the life that He has designed for us. In II Kings, God reminds us that every failure in life presents us with an opportunity to humble ourselves before Him and to stand tall in His grace. God gives up on NO ONE, no matter who they've been or what they've done! In 1st Chronicles, God uses life's difficult experiences to detach us from depending on happiness we think we can find through other people and material things. He uses them to bring us to a realization that only true happiness can be found by relying on Christ. That true happiness comes from doing His will, being of maximum service to the rest of His children, and by serving the purpose He has outlined for our lives.

God says that real searching, honest, fearless searching for the truth about ourselves generates lasting change in us. In Habakkuk, God tells us not to ignore the struggles and confusion that fill our lives, but to embrace them and make them our strengths as we overcome them with God's grace and God's power. Finally, in Philippians, God tells us to "hold nothing back, to give God everything we have, and that through the Holy Spirit, we will find a new power and a new way to live."

Pastor Craig Groeschel of LifeChurch sums it up so well in his book, *Altar Ego,* when he tells us that "We are each God's masterpiece and He continues to mold and shape us through our life experiences and challenges." Craig reminds us that "we are NOT what others think of us, we are not our pasts, we are not what we've done, how we've acted, or even how we've shown up in life. We are not even who WE think we are. We are who GOD says we are, and God says we are OVERCOMERS!"

So let's finish up our self-examination with a quick fear and sex inventory!

CHAPTER 16

FEAR

Fear is the number one driver of action for most people. Entire lives, thoughts, words, and actions are all usually motivated and driven by fears. That's really crazy if you think about it. We operate, position ourselves, and are reactive and proactive to the avoidance of fears that may or may not even happen! In most cases, they don't! Remember all the madness that occurred before Y2K? That fear consumed the entire world and created all kinds of crazy behaviors. How about the nuclear war fears from the late '60s and early '70s? I still remember the drills at school where we'd all be rushed to the basement, stuffed under a table, and told to cover our heads, like that was going to do anything if a nuclear bomb exploded near Lakeside Elementary! Fear causes us to behave in unhealthy, unstable, and negative ways!

Fears paralyze us. They keep us from being effective and from making positive progress. They block us from logic and they inflame irrational thinking. They generally propagate behaviors that actually help those fears become realities. Fears waste time and cloud our minds with negative thoughts. Negative thoughts lead to negative words, and negative words lead to negative actions. It's true, we do become what we think about the most. What usually happens to us is directly related to what we're thinking about the most! Something LifeChurch pastor Craig Groeschel once said really stuck with me. He said that if you follow up every thought, every negative or fearful notion with the words, "Because that's what I want," you'll begin to feel really silly about your fearful thinking. For example, one of my fears was that my newly licensed daughter would get into a car accident. When I used Craig's logic, I followed that fear statement up with, "because that's what I really want." What? Did I really want my daughter to get into a car wreck? Of course not. Then why did I think it, why did I obsess over it, why was it always in my thoughts? Well it was, and since it was in my thoughts, it was also in my words. I would tell my daughter, "Be careful, don't drive too fast, don't use your phone, don't get on the highway, don't drive at night, don't pass anyone, watch out in parking lots, be on the lookout for drunk drivers, and watch out for falling space rocks!" The poor girl was overwhelmed with negative information, was on edge, panicked, nervous, and paranoid every time she got behind the wheel. All good qualities of a good driver, right? My fears were actually making things worse for her; they were actually creating a lack of confidence in her driving abilities, and she was less likely to have an accident before I obsessively puked my fears upon her!

I also had a friend who once gave me the "so what" test when I expressed my fears. He made me boil down every fear to its "worst case" and then follow each iteration up with "so what then?" I would say, "I'm really afraid the bank is going to foreclose on me." He would reply with, "So what if they did?" Well, then I'd have to close my business. So what if you had to close your business? Well, then I'd have to find a new job. So what if you had to find a new job? Well, I don't know, I guess nothing. I'd just find a new job. "What else you got?" he'd ask. I'd think and reply, "Well people will think I'm a failure." He'd say, "So what if people think you're a failure?" "Well, then people won't like or respect me." "So what if people don't like or respect you?" I guess nothing.

So what are your fears? I'm reminded of my son, Steven. When he was about four years old, we'd give him his bath, put on his pjs, tuck him into bed, read him a few stories, tell him goodnight, and then jump into bed ourselves. Within a few a minutes, he'd come doddling into our bedroom with his "dog blankie" and say, "I'm afwaid of funder." We'd say, "Thunder can't hurt you, it's just angels bowling," and we'd send him back into his room. Five minutes later, he'd be back in again. "I'm afwaid of wightening." We'd say, "Lightening can't hurt you; it's just God's fireworks show," and send him on his way again. A couple of minutes later, he'd be back, "I'm afwaid of da dark." Getting frustrated, we'd tell him, "There's nothing to be afraid of; now go back to bed and stay there!" About 20 minutes would pass and we were relatively sure that he'd finally fallen asleep, but inevitably we'd hear the baby elephant quickly thudding across the hardwood, and there he was again. This time, he said, "I'm afwaid of evwefing," and we had to laugh and let him jump in the middle! You got us there, kid!

Looking back, I realized I was no different than my four year old. I was afraid of everything. Afraid of losing my job, my wife, my kids, my money. I was in fear of not getting that promotion, that bonus, that new house. Other people scared me, and I was afraid of what they might do to me. I was afraid of upsetting someone, of people not liking me, what might happen to my son in school or on the playground. I was afraid of not being able to maintain a reputation I thought I already had, about the future, of death, and of not making it to heaven. I was afraid of everything.

My adult fears were no different than my four-year-old son's childhood fears! They were irrational, unfounded, and illogical. There is no reason to fear thunder, lightning, or the dark. My fears were also irrational and illogical, and I began to wonder, "Why am I afraid of everything?" What causes fear?

It's really very simple to understand, but very difficult to practice. Fear comes from two things: First, fear comes from the notion of losing something you already possess, like a job, a spouse, a promotion, a house, a car, a child, a reputation, or so on. Second, fear comes from the thought that "you're not going to get something you want," like a vacation to the Caribbean, an award at the annual company meeting, or love from your spouse.

Doing a "fear inventory" isn't nearly as difficult as doing the resentment inventory we worked on in the last chapter. It does require a little bit of thought, and is just as important an exercise. As we learned through our resentment inventories, we need to understand, be aware of, and identify our fears before we can find the courage to walk through them. Knowing "what" we're afraid of helps us clearly see those fears, what is driving them, and provides a clear vision of how we can be different regarding fears. It's very simple and shouldn't take more than a few hours. All you do is grab a notebook again, sit down somewhere quiet, and ask God to reveal to you all of your fears. Then behind each fear, in parentheses, write down how it affects one of these categories and what's your character defect in that. The categories are Self Esteem, Security, Pride/Ego, Personal Relationships, Sex Relations, Emotional Security, and My Pocketbook. Here is the list I came up with for myself.

- I'm afraid of not getting what I want (Security—I'm being selfish).
- I'm afraid of personal rejection (Self Esteem—I care more about what others think of me than what God thinks of me).
- I'm afraid of losing what I have—my wife, kids, money, possessions, reputation (Security—I'm being selfish).
- I'm afraid of not being needed (Pride/Ego—I want to feel important).
- I'm in fear of the "real me" being discovered (Personal Relationships—telling God I don't like what He made).
- I have the fear of being held responsible (Personal Relationships—I'm trying to do it on my own and not relying on God).
- Fear of failure.
- Fear of being alone.
- Fear of being publicly embarrassed or humiliated.
- Fear of facing consequences.
- Fear of not being in control.
- Fear of change.
- Fear of the unknown.
- Fear of being broke.
- I'm afraid of what other people might say or do to me.
- I'm afraid of losing respect of others.
- I'm afraid of not being self-sufficient.
- I'm afraid of confrontation.
- I'm afraid of expressing my opinion.

- I'm afraid of being successful.
- I'm afraid to set boundaries with others.
- I'm afraid of disappointing others.

The list goes on. I had about forty individual fears. Many of them were derivatives of what I've listed above, but all were very real to me. When I looked across the list, I realized that "I was afraid of everything!" It ran the gambit from being afraid of losing a child to fears that damaged my emotional state, and I was even afraid of being happy and successful! I absolutely had to rid myself of these fears, because they were killing me. They were running my life, driving my thoughts, my words, and my actions. Fear-driven actions are never effective. My fears were paralyzing me. I was allowing them to dominate me, and as a result I was hurting everyone around me with behaviors that stemmed from my fears. I was actually aiding, encouraging, and promoting the realization of my own fears. The other thing I began to recognize was that because fear dominated me, I allowed others to dominate me. My fears rendered me useless, ineffective, unable to make a decision, and because of that other people could easily dictate to me "how things were going to be." I became very dependent on others—a textbook co-dependent. I relied on my wife to tell me when to get up, what to wear, where to go, what to say, how to act, how to deal with the children, and so on. At work, my fears made me a terrible leader; opinions and directions from everyone paralyzed my thinking, and I couldn't make sound or definitive decisions.

The real issue is that I wasn't relying on God! My life was driven by the power of my fears. Courage, by definition, is "walking through your fears." I had no courage on my own, but it was soon realized that with God's power, God's strength, and His direction, together we could find the courage to walk right through each one of my irrational fears.

Fear is based in selfishness. I wanted to keep all the good things I'd accumulated in my life, and I wanted to hold on to the gifts God had given me. I wanted to protect all my good fortune and hoard and guard "my stuff," and I became terrified of losing those things. Here's how that thinking was selfish. My wife did not belong to me, nor did my children; my job wasn't a given, and even the house I lived in did not belong to me. God provided all those things to me as gifts. When I treat them as gifts, when I am grateful for them, when I honor them, when I protect them, when I nourish them, God allows me to keep them. The other side of the selfish coin are my personal "wants." I want a promotion, a bigger house, more money, a big vacation, gifted children, a beautiful wife, a new girlfriend (not at the same time!), and accolades from friends and business colleagues. I want, I want, I want. SELFISH!

The real driver behind fear and its selfish motives is TRUST. What we're really saying when we have fears is that we don't trust God. What my son was really saying was that he didn't trust our assurances that thunder, lightning, and darkness couldn't hurt him. He didn't trust that we would take care of him, that everything would be all right, and that we would never let anything bad happen to him. I was no different. I didn't trust God to take care of me financially, socially, or relationally. What I was really saying was, "I don't think you know best God. You don't have my best interests at heart. I know what is necessary to be happy, secure, and peaceful." That thinking is pretty arrogant and stupid. Can you imagine sitting down with God and questioning His plans, offering what you think are better solutions, ideas, and directions?

Think about it. What if my son completely trusted me as a father? He would have slept pretty soundly at night knowing that I would never forsake him, never let him down, never lead him astray, always protect him, and do what's best for his little life. What if I had that same confidence in God? What if I trusted that whatever happened, it was for my good, for my benefit, even though it didn't seem that way on the surface? We've already proven to ourselves in an earlier chapter that we don't know how to manage our own lives, and we don't know what's best for us. We decided we wanted to turn our wills and our lives over to God. Then why don't we? Because we're afraid we might lose something we already possess that is valuable to us in some way and because we are afraid we won't get something we want!

Let me give you an example. I was terrified of losing my business. I had my whole life tied up in it. My money, my reputation, my identity were all contingent upon my ability to keep that business alive. I didn't trust that God knew what was best for me. I was driven by my selfishness. Selfishness for money, power, prestige, and reputation. My fears over losing it caused me to make all kinds of crazy, stupid, and sinful decisions, like lying, cheating, stealing, manipulating, and micromanaging. I was stressed, had anxiety, was on edge, nervous, and uptight all the time. I was afraid of losing it, because that's what I really wanted! (Thanks, Craig.) Well, I did lose the business, and guess what? The world didn't end. My worst nightmares didn't occur. In fact, I had an overwhelming sense of freedom, peace, and relief. The stress disappeared, the anxiety was gone, and I wasn't nervous, uptight, and edgy. All of those fears spawned feelings and emotions that led me to seek relief in the whiskey bottle. God knew that business wasn't the best thing for me. It wasn't part of His plan and was keeping me from being an effective servant of God. The business kept me buried in that spiritual malady that caused me to drink. It was keeping me in constant fear, filled with anxiety and stress. I was restless, irritable, and continually discontent with it. Those negative emotions kept me drunk and rendered me completely useless to anyone, especially to God and His plan for my life. My biggest fear occurred, and it turned out to be the biggest blessing I ever received. What was I so afraid of?

God gave me a new job, a better job, a more rewarding job. He gave me employment that allowed me to serve others and a platform to use my work as a way to serve Him. I made more money, met new friends, and I became a better employee and coworker. Had I known all this was available to me, I would have shut that albatross of a business down years before. My fear, selfishness, and my inability to trust that God knew better than I, and that He had a better plan for me, kept me in an embattled situation.

What if you had no fears? What if you completely trusted God with your life? How would that look? I remember reading a management book some years ago, and in it there was a business executive that no matter what news he received, he always responded with, "That's great news." His subordinates would come in and report that the assembly line equipment just went down and its bad, our best salesman just quit, our fiercest competitor just came out with a new product that's going to sink us. The CEO would always answer, "That's great news." After some time, one of his staff asked, "How can you always be so positive? How could any of this be positive news?" The CEO answered, "Because now we have the opportunity to upgrade our assembly line technology that will allow us to produce widgets more efficiently, more effectively, and at a long-term lower cost. Because, although our best salesman was good, he was disruptive to the rest of our sales force and was teaching them all bad habits. With him gone, we can retrain our existing sales force to sell our widgets the way we want them to be sold. We were compromising our sales integrity because this guy was so profitable for us. As for our competitor's new technology, this gives us an opportunity to revamp our R&D departments, to refocus our strategies, to sharpen our business models and stay competitive!" This guy was scared of nothing. He trusted that whatever happened, happened for his company's good. He didn't have selfishness or fear over short-term financial setbacks that would come from the expenses of new assembly line improvement, over lost sales from losing a best salesman, or over competition taking a bite out of his earnings for a short time. He knew that long term, these were all things that were good for his company.

Why can't we be like that with our own lives? I trust that whatever happens in my life is part of God's plan for me, and I'm willing to admit that God knows better than I do. That doesn't mean when bad things happen, there's not going to be some pain and some inconvenience. There usually is. It just means that if you trust God, open your eyes to His plan, and continue to be obedient, the changes will all be for your benefit.

So next time fear creeps into your life, think about a few things. The first is, "How am I being selfish in this fear?" because every fear is driven by some kind of selfishness. When you find it, ask God to remove that specific selfishness from your thoughts. Next, when that fear crops up, say to yourself, "Because that's what I really want to happen!" You'll laugh at yourself, and then ask God to redirect your thinking toward good, because God is goodness. Remember that what dominates your thoughts becomes your reality. So stop thinking negative and fearful things or they'll continue to happen to you. Ask yourself the opposite. "What do I really want to happen here?" Then replace those fears with thoughts of what you truly want to take place. When fears rear their ugly head, know that you are NOT trusting your Father, and remind yourself that God knows what's best for you. Humble yourself, forfeit your own selfish will, open your eyes, and open your mind to the "so whats?" So what if my boyfriend breaks up with me? I'll have free time to work on this project or that dream, I'll get to spend more time with my friends, and I'll have time to serve at the church, spend more time at the gym, or can read more. Maybe God has someone much better for me!

Don't let fear drive your life. Let God drive your life with positive thinking, affirming words, and healthy actions! Because that's what we really want!

CHAPTER 17

SEX!

Sex inventory! Always the attention grabber, but this kind of sex inventory isn't quite what you're probably thinking. It is, however, one the most important exercises you can embark on if you ever plan to be in or stay in a healthy relationship with the opposite sex. This inventory is a vital discipline that generates an awareness about yourself and how you are showing up in a current marriage or relationship. Just like the resentment inventory, until we know and can see exactly "who we are" in our intimate relationships, we won't know how we want to be in those love relationships. Working through this process is going to give you some incredible insight into the "kind of partner" you have been and by the end, a very clear directive of the kind of partner you want to be, and with God's help, the kind of partner you can be.

It works much the same way as the resentment inventory process, but takes much less time, unless you're Wilt Chamberlain or Gene Simmons and have been in thousands of love relationships! For those of you who purchased the "inventory workbook," a working section on the sex (as well as fear) inventory is included. We start again by finding a quiet place, asking God to reveal to us the intimate or romantic relationships from our pasts that He would have us look at. We ask Him to show us those we've hurt in our relationships and those who have hurt us. "God, show me who You would have me look at in all my love relationships." As the names begin popping into your mind, as you review your life and the people you've dated, gone steady with, been engaged or promised to, married to, divorced from, and maybe even had a little "fling" with, write them down. Just the names for now.

Once the list is complete, we go back to the first name and ask ourselves three questions about this relationship. "Where was I selfish in this relationship? Where was I dishonest? Where and how was I inconsiderate?" Write down your answers.

Just as I did in the "resentment inventory" chapter of this book, I'll reference one of my examples. Allow me to provide some background information. Her name was Annie, and she was one of my high school girlfriends. Annie and I dated for many months, and my motives and intentions were generally good. I was truly interested in her, I respected her, we shared many of the same interests, communicated very well, and cared a great deal for each other, at least as much as high school kids could. I was polite, romantic, not possessive or jealous, and was a very attentive boyfriend—for a while. It was really the first fairly mature relationship I'd ever been in. Before long, however, some of the other popular girls at school told me I could do better, and that they were surprised I was dating someone of her caliber, a second-tier player. I then overheard a former boyfriend of hers bragging (most likely lying) about his sexual escapades with her. I was jealous and immediately became disillusioned, feeling like I wasn't about to play second fiddle to anyone. I eventually began to withdraw from her emotionally, then began to "play her down" to my friends and the popular girls at school, and eventually cheated on her (not in a sexual way), before dragging out a break up because I was too weak to be honest with her about my feelings.

So to answer the first question, "Where was I selfish?" was found in the fact that I cared more about what other people thought of me than about this sweet girl. I was selfish because I wanted what others thought was better for me. I wanted a girl who fed my ego and made me look good in front of my friends.

Where was I dishonest? I told Annie how much I cared about her and I made her believe that we had something "really serious." I assured her of my love for her, that I would be faithful to her, and that our relationship was good and strong. I wasn't, I didn't, and I had no intentions of allowing this relationship to turn into anything serious. I didn't want to make any commitment and wasn't going to, but she believed I would, based on the lies I told her and the ways in which I led her on.

Where was I inconsiderate? I didn't consider that Annie might actually think this relationship was going somewhere. I didn't contemplate that she would get hurt by my actions. I wasn't chivalrous enough to stand up for my feelings for her in the face of others' opinions. I didn't bother asking Annie what she wanted out of this relationship, about her hopes and dreams, or her opinions about us. I was only considering myself.

The next round of questions we ask ourselves about this relationship are, "Did I unjustifiably arouse Jealousy, Suspicion, Anger, or Bitterness?"

In this case, the answer was yes. After Annie went away to college, I allowed our communication to lapse, continued to get distant and awkward when "feelings talk" surfaced. I stammered and stuttered when questioned about why I didn't call her back the night before and what I was doing. I knew she sensed something was up. She was definitely suspicious and probably jealous, even though she didn't show it. (Probably because she trusted me.) In the end, some bitterness was created in the break up because I wasn't "man enough" to be honest with her. She walked away confused, disappointed, and more than likely wondering what she did wrong, or worse yet, what was wrong with her?

Two more questions. The first one to ask yourself is, "Where was I at fault in this relationship?" The answer is that I was dishonest. I was so insecure and self-conscious about myself, I let others allow me to destroy what could have been a really great partnership. I was not open with my feelings. I was also at fault, because I never considered asking Annie about what she wanted in this relationship, or in life. I honestly couldn't tell you what her interests were, what her plans for the future were, how many kids she did or didn't want, what I could do to contribute to this relationship. Nothing. All I cared about was myself. I didn't want to be "girlfriendless," but also didn't want people thinking less of me for who I was going out with. I was thinking about the green grass on the other side of that electric barbed wire fence, and thinking about my own goals and dreams with absolutely no regard for Annie's. I was at fault for being completely self-centered and absorbed, and I'd made this a one-way relationship. Everything had to go my way for it to be right.

Finally, as we look at this relationship, we ask ourselves "What should I have done instead?" Looking back, the answers are pretty obvious. I should have been honest with Annie in all areas of my life, including the fact that I was only interested in having a casual boyfriend/girlfriend relationship and that I wasn't in it for the long haul. I should have examined my own feelings for this girl based on what I thought, not what others thought of her, and acted with integrity. I should have spent more time discovering her wants and needs, and considered her desires. I should have invested in this partnership and not made it "all about me and my selfish wants." I should have honored and respected Annie as a person and not treated her like a prize that I eventually became disillusioned with and tossed aside.

In the end, one could write that relationship off as "puppy love," and our break up probably didn't ruin Annie's life. In fact, she may feel very fortunate that it didn't work out! But my behaviors did cause some amount of hurt, disappointment, and bitterness. More importantly, I began developing habits and character defects that would hinder my relationships for years to come. And as the stakes got higher, women did get hurt, and hurt badly.

What did I find out about myself, about "who I am" in this one resentment? Let's see. I am dishonest, I am self-absorbed and self-centered, I have no integrity, because I allow what others think to override my own feelings, I don't share my feelings, I don't care about others' goals and dreams, I am unfaithful, I am jealous, I lead women on, I put down others to feel better about myself, I need someone in my life to be secure, and I don't consider the feelings of a partner.

That's just one piece of the sex inventory. When I finished my work on all the others, here is the list of relationship character defects that continued to show up for me on a regular basis. If I found one defect, in one relationship, that never surfaced again during this exercise, I omitted it. It wasn't a "tail." So here's how Mike used to show up in romantic relationships.

- I am dishonest with my partner.
- I only care about myself and my needs in a relationship.
- I have no integrity and won't stand up for myself, let alone my woman.
- I allow others to influence my feelings for a partner.
- I am jealous.
- I don't know how or am afraid to communicate.
- I lead women on.
- I don't consider the feelings of a partner.
- I use passive-aggressive behaviors with women to get what I want.
- I am controlling and manipulative.
- I don't accept others (my partner) for who they are.
- I am incredibly selfish.
- I don't like to take responsibility in a relationship.
- I'm insecure with myself.
- I'm not transparent or genuine with my partner.
- I put unrealistic expectations on my partner.
- I am needy and require an unhealthy amount of attention and affirmation.
- I don't bring God into a relationship.

How many of you are thinking right now, "I'd really like to go out with that guy!" If so, call me at 918-555-5555! Just kidding. I know the answer. There is no way any woman in her right mind would want to go out with the "jerk" I just described, but that was the truth about me. Can you imagine joining eHarmony and listing all those things to describe one's self? The reality is that any woman who would date or be attracted to a man with those qualities and attributes was certainly not anyone you would want to take home to mom! Sick people date sick people, and if you actually would want to go out with a guy like this, you had better get some counseling! (Which is what most women needed after dating me!)

The frightening thing was that I had NO IDEA this was the kind of guy I was! Had you asked me to fill out an eHarmony profile, it wouldn't have looked anything like that. I truly believed I was a "catch" and had everything a woman could ever want in a partner. I was completely delusional about myself and ignorant about what it took to create a healthy, loving, and solid relationship or marriage.

How could I, how could anyone expect to build a healthy loving relationship having this set of character defects? It wasn't possible, at least not for any period of time. When I finished my sex inventory, I felt horrible about how I'd shown up in all my relationships, especially my marriage. I was sick about the women I'd hurt and beside myself about what a horrible husband I had been. I owed so many apologies, and the amends I needed to make could only come in the form of changing myself. That all came through creating this "awareness" of who I was in a relationship, identifying my defects as they relate to intimate relationships, asking God to remove them, and creating what is called a "Sane and Sound Sex Ideal."

Before we make out our sane and sound sex ideal, let's do the obvious and flip our character defects and state their opposites. In my case, these traits would be the opposite of my relational character defects and the opposite of the guy I just described to you. Here are my inverses:

- I am always 100 percent open and honest, without omission.
- I care more about the other person in my relationship than I do about myself.
- I have great integrity, stand up for myself, and defend my woman at all times.
- I am committed to my partner and do not allow others to influence my feelings.
- I am faithful and dedicated to my partner.
- I am trusting of my partner and feel secure in our relationship.
- I respectfully and openly communicate my wants and needs to my partner.
- I do not lead women on.
- I consider the feelings of my partner first and always.
- I am direct, open, and loving with my communication.
- I am accepting, understanding, giving, and selfless.
- I allow my partner freedom and latitude to pursue her desires.
- I accept and appreciate my partner for who she is; I honor and respect her uniqueness.
- I am giving, selfless, and empathetic.
- I listen more than I talk.
- I take responsibility for all my actions and for the good of the relationship.
- I am secure with myself. I have self-confidence. I love myself.

- I'm open, genuine, and real in all my dealings and communications.
- I accept others for who they are, their abilities, and I'm proud of who they are.
- I am self-sufficient and independent. I give attention and affirmation and don't expect it in return.
- God is at the center of my marriage or partnership.

What about this guy? How about a date with him? I have a feeling that the eHarmony servers would go down if this kind of guy was posted! How great would it be if I could be this kind of a guy? How much joy could I bring to my partner? How much healthier, stronger, and exciting would my relationships be? It's pretty awesome to think about.

These are the ideals borne from looking at the opposite of our relational character defects. It's an inverted road map of how to be a good "dater," a good partner, a good lover, and a good spouse!

The Sane and Sound Sex Ideal is just a slight modification of this mirrored image of the perfect partner. In the Sane and Sound Sex Ideal, we ask ourselves two questions. The first is, "What am I going to bring to this relationship?" And the second is, "What should she or he bring to this relationship?"

Building off the "opposites" of my sex inventory findings, I mapped out my sane and sound relationship ideals. What I'm going to bring to the relationship is as follows: First and foremost I will put God at the center of any relationship I choose to enter into. I will make certain and be up front that my partner also has a strong belief in God and is a follower of Christ. I will make sure that my partner knows God is number one and she is number two. Kids should always be number three, because your strength and commitment to each other establishes the platform for effective caring, nurturing, and guiding of your children. Mom and dad, even mixed-family marriages, require the couple's dedication to each other over making their individual kids a priority. I will seek God's guidance on who I should date, become engaged to, and marry. I will bring God into our relationship, and we are going to pray together and for each other.

Remember the triangle diagram I talked about earlier in this book? At the bottom left was the husband, the bottom right was the wife, and at the top was God. The speaker measured the distance between the man and woman, then the distance between the man and God, then the woman and God. They were all the same distance apart. He then began to move the man halfway up the line and closer to God, but kept the woman in the bottom right hand corner. The man was growing closer to God, which was great. He measured the distance from man to God, and it certainly had improved. Then he measured the distance from the man, who was now 50 percent closer to God, and the woman, who was still in the bottom right hand corner, and they were at the same distance as when they started. They were no closer to each other, although the man had grown closer to God. But as the speaker began to move the woman closer to God, he pointed out that the distance between the man and woman grew closer. As each partner grows in relation to God, so they grow closer to each other. That diagram really spoke to me, and it proved to me that I not only needed to continue to grow closer to God, but I also needed to find a partner who was willing to do the same. If I could, I was assured that we would continue to grow closer together and our relationship would continue to strengthen. On the flip side, however, and even though the man and woman can grow closer together by seeking God, if one or both of them begins to fall away from God, so does their closeness.

The other ideals that mapped out what I was going to bring to the table were more along the lines of positive character traits, actions, and behaviors. I was going to be the kind of partner who:

- Verbalized my needs.
- Was secure with myself and had independence.
- Could be trusted. My actions matched my words.
- Was completely honest and offered full disclosure.
- Respected my partner's feelings; found out her desires, goals, and dreams.
- Would try to create an equal partnership.
- Focused on helping his spouse achieve her goals.
- Was unselfish and giving at all times.
- Was authentic, real, and transparent.
- Was focused on meeting my spouse's emotional and physical needs.
- Tried to be her best friend.
- Had genuine concern for her well-being.
- Had realistic expectations.
- Would honor, love, and respect.
- Was polite, considerate, and helpful at all times.
- Showed empathy and was always there to provide emotional support.
- Spent quality time with his spouse.
- Adored his wife.

- Built up his wife, made her feel special, important, beautiful, and wanted.
- Finally, was wholeheartedly committed before introducing sex into the relationship.

A rare find these days, right? Wouldn't you be the luckiest person in the world to have a partner like this? Of course you would. The irony of it all is that being this kind of person actually rewards you! Can you imagine how you would be treated in return if you brought these attributes to a relationship? They may be tired old clichés, but they're true: Do unto others as you would have done unto you. The love you give is equal to the love you receive. You get out of relationship what you put into it! It's all so elementary, but so hard to do. It's impossible to do by yourself; you need God's help, and to get God's help, you have to clear away the things in your life that are blocking you from God. Your self-will, your own sense of personal power, and your character defects are all blocking you from being the person God intended for you to be! God wants to help you, but you have to pick up a shovel and get to work.

Now you know how you used to show up in relationships or in your marriage. You know the kind of mate you used to be. Having seen the partner you no longer wish to be, you have looked at the inverse of your behaviors and are beginning to see a picture of the kind of spouse or dating partner God intended you to be. From that you can create a personality profile of just what you're going to bring to or back to the table in a relationship. The final question you have to ask yourself is, "What does my potential partner or spouse need to bring to the table?" How do you want her or him to "show up" in this relationship? It's important! It takes two to tango, and if you're the only one in the relationship being the partner God intended you to be, but your spouse or significant other is not, you still have a problem. So choose wisely if you're single, but more importantly, know what you're looking for! You don't go to a car lot and say, "Oh, that one's pretty, I'll take it." You don't, unless you're wildly impulsive. You see it, it catches your eye, you're infatuated with it, but you need to find out what it can offer you. How many miles to the gallon does it get? Is it reliable, comfortable, and dependable? Is it hard to start? Is it going to cause you a lot of problems? Are the repairs and maintenance going to be expensive? How does it respond when the weather gets rough? Can it hold a big family or is it a two-seater? Is it practical or is it just for show? Great exterior, but what's really under the hood?

Are you getting all my metaphors? It's silly, but how often do we see that shiny, attractive, sexy man or woman and fall madly in love and are ready to make a commitment before we know exactly if this model has the things we need in a relationship? If you don't know what you're looking for in a mate, you're going to end up getting something you weren't looking for! You know what you bring to the table, know what you want him or her to bring to the table. To do that, you have to define it by writing the same kind of "sane and sound sex ideal." Draw out your woman or man based on how that person fits you. Mine would look something like this:

- Must put God first in her life and me second.
- Must completely accept me for who I am, the good and the bad.
- Must be willing to make a complete commitment to our relationship.
- Must always be "building me up, supporting me, affirming

me."

- Must have a sense of self and be independent.
- Must be unselfish, kind, considerate, generous.
- Must be completely open and honest.
- Must be proud of me, defend me, and fight for me.
- Must want to honor and respect me.

You get the idea. Draw it out, know what you want and go get it! How can you know if someone is right for you if you don't qualify that person? The shine eventually fades, the excitement of the new model wanes, and when the newness of it all disappears, does your partner have everything you wanted to make your life richer?

If you're already married, don't go out car shopping, but put yourself and your spouse through the same tests. Challenge each other to look in the mirror and become the best partners you can be, moving yourselves up that triangle and closer to each other. "Pimp your own ride," and watch your spouse fall in love with you all over again!

CHAPTER 18

I CONFESS!

Confession? Maybe the Catholics are on to something here! I wasn't a Catholic, but my ex-wife was, and I attended the Catholic church for many years. One of their many obligations that I just couldn't understand was confession. I thought it was the most ridiculous and even sacrilegious practice I'd ever seen. Once a year, like clockwork, parishioners would trudge into the fancy oak "photo booth of the soul" and whisper their sins to a man sitting adjacent to them in a similar booth. Through a lightly veiled screen they'd come clean, or partially come clean, of their wrongdoings that year. The man on the other side would quietly listen and then assign them some menial penance, like saying thirteen "Hail Marys" or seven "Our Fathers." They'd walk out of the booth lighter than air, cleansed, and absolved of their sins. The relief they seemed to experience was always laughable to me. I felt like they were just relieved that it was over and they didn't have to come back for another year. That may have been correct in some cases.

The thing that bothered me the most was the power the people seemed to be advocating to the priest. He's not God. He doesn't have the power to forgive sins. How can you feel unburdened by a simple man you don't even really know? Seriously? If that's the case, then I'm going to knock off a liquor store, cheat on my wife and taxes, ignore people in need, and then walk into one of these miracle booths and have it all washed away! I just didn't see how confession to a priest was really helping anyone. Was it really clearing anyone's spirit? Did they really feel forgiven by God? It didn't make any sense to me.

One of my favorite movies is *Gran Torino* with Clint Eastwood. If you haven't seen the movie, it's a great flick! Clint Eastwood (Walt) is a rough Korean War veteran who has a very poor opinion of the church (and of everyone else for that matter). One of his deceased wife's wishes before she died was that he make a confession to a local priest. Knowing that he, too, had a terminal disease and his death was imminent, he finally makes the decision to enter the confessional and confess his shortcomings just prior to embarking on a neighborhood mission that he knows will end his life. From conversations with this priest earlier in the movie, you can absolutely tell he doesn't believe this young priest can absolve him of his sins and actually makes a mockery out of the whole confessional process. What he realizes near the end of his life is that his past has been weighing him down, and the only freedom he will ever find from that weight is by sharing those burdens with another person. It might as well be Father Janovich! As he enters the confessional this is the exchange we hear:

Father Janovich: "How long has it been since your last confession?"

Walt: "Forever. Bless me Father, for I have sinned."

Father Janovich: "What are your sins my son?"

Walt: "In 1968, I kissed Betty Jablonski at the work Christmas party. Dorothy, my wife, was in the next room talking with the other wives, and it just happened."

Father Janovich: "Yes, go on."

Walt: "I made a $900 profit selling a boat and motor and never reported the taxes, which is the same as stealing."

Father Janovich: "Yes, fine."

Walt: "And lastly, I was never close to my two sons. I don't know them. I didn't know how."

Father Janovich: "That's it?"

Walt: "Whatta you mean, that's it? It's bothered me for years!"

The priest was taken aback. Walt had killed many men in Korea, he despised the church and churchgoers, he was a racist, incredibly prejudiced, and had a ridiculously filthy mouth.

All those things didn't weigh on his conscious at all, but he was a prisoner inside himself by holding on to cheating on his taxes by about $105, cheating on his wife by kissing another woman, and by not knowing how to be close to his boys. Releasing those spiritually damaging secrets allowed him to find peace before doing what he was about to do. (I won't tell you, since you may not have seen the movie!) He couldn't find the relief in admitting those things to himself, or even to God for that matter. He could only find the release and freedom by discussing them with another human being.

I later realized that the Catholics were actually on to something with this confession business. It's not about giving a human man in a robe power to forgive sins; it's about the power of verbalizing your mistakes. It's a process that takes our largely theoretical sense of self and makes it real. The transformation to reality occurs when we share our shortcomings and sins with another. It's not about the priest; the recipient of our confessions can be any human being. It's about what that act does to us. It is the confession that gives us absolution, not the priest!

As we consider everything we discovered about ourselves in the resentment, fear, and sex inventories of the last chapters, we might be apt to go a little "easy" on ourselves for the faults, wrongdoings, and defects of character we've identified in ourselves. After all, what we've uncovered has been simply "self" discovery and hasn't been human tested thus far. Our findings are still greatly conceptual and only reside in our own minds up until this point. Verbalizing and sharing them with another may just be the way to gain some perspective on them. Getting someone else's opinion and even hearing ourselves verbally acknowledge them tends to make them more real. By confiding in another, we gain some perspective, and our defects gain some weight and depth. The purpose behind all the work we did with our personal inventories is to conquer the tendency we all have to deny the realities about ourselves. As I've said before, we are only as sick as our secrets. Confessing all these things to another, in the presence of God, breaks this pattern of self-deception. Sharing them with another does not give us the luxury of trivializing or downplaying our behaviors.

Sharing sins, wrongdoings, and character defects is important, because acknowledging them through verbalization is where the real power resides. Admitting them to another human being, priest or otherwise, makes them real and offers confirmation, through another, of how we view ourselves. It's difficult to have an honest perspective of yourself when the only point of reference you have is you. Openly admitting is the key to cementing self-awareness and the transfer of your burdens on to an emotionally unattached third party.

The Bible says that "Whenever two or more of you are gathered in My name, I will be there." So when you gather with a priest or another of God's children in His name, He will be there. As you share your shortcomings and wrongdoings, God will also be there listening, forgiving, and encouraging you to repent and choose a different path.

As we look to the Bible, we see in Psalms 51 that David brings his past out into the open in hopes of finding a way forward with God. He knew that he could not change the past, but found that with God's forgiveness, guidance, and power he could change himself, and the future. In 2nd Corinthians, Paul says, "I will boast all the more gladly about my weaknesses, so that Christ's power may rest upon me. For when I am weak, then He can make me strong." Confession brings us to a place of humility and a new reliance upon God. In 1st John, chapter 1, the Bible says, "We can confess to God for forgiveness," but that is only half the equation. We also need to confess to other Christians to ultimately help us overcome our sins." God tells us to confess to one another and pray for one another so that we may be healed. If a sick man goes to the doctor and refuses to confess his symptoms and his pains to the doctor, the doctor has no idea what medications to prescribe or how to recommend a cure. The same holds true for our spiritual sicknesses. If we aren't honest and forthcoming with our troubles, no healing can occur.

Okay! Okay! I'm sorry Monsignor Dorney! Confession does work and it is important!

Finishing the work on my resentment, fear, and sex inventory gave me a very general sense of where I was wrong, but it wasn't well defined. I was disgusted with my actions, my behaviors, my attitudes, my words, and could see that I'd really wronged a lot of people. I knew I was wrong, but I was having some trouble defining exactly what my flaws were, and it didn't become clear to me until I had the opportunity to share my findings, my troubles, my past actions, and my sins with a close friend. It wasn't just any friend, and the person you share yourself with shouldn't just be "any" friend either. It is imperative that you find someone who meets certain criteria. You need to find an impartial third party (that's why priests work so well!). You need another Christian—one who is non-judgmental and who understands exactly what it is you're trying to do; one who is willing to listen more than talk and question more than answer; someone who will be completely unaffected by what you share and will keep a confidence, hold you accountable, be direct, but loving; someone who is patient, empathetic, sympathetic, and supportive. If you're in AA, that person is called a sponsor. If you're a Catholic, that person is called a priest. If you're in a non-denominational church, that person might be called a mentor. If you're not a churchgoer, that person had better be a solid, understanding, and accepting best friend. In any case, choose the person or persons you share your defects with carefully. Once you find that person and begin to share your failures, the most miraculous things will begin to happen to you.

The first is what I like to call "the transfer of burden." Your secrets, your sins, your personal failures, your guilt, your shame, and all of your defects are a heavy, heavy load for you to carry. They weigh you down, they make you miserable, sad, lonely, unhappy, and make you feel unworthy. They drive you to seek relief in unhealthy ways. My relief valve was drinking. For others it may be food, sex, gambling, shopping, pornography, or the putting down of others to make ourselves feel better. That load will eventually kill you, either physically or spiritually, if you don't resolve it. These burdens keep you from having a relationship with God, and they prohibit you from being able to communicate with Him. These burdens have to be shed, but to transfer these burdens upon someone else seems cruel! It's not though! The weight of your sins, the heaviness of your guilt and shame, weigh very little at all to an impartial third party, and they weigh nothing to God! There is something so magical, something so healing, which comes from transferring your troubles on to another. The relief I felt in sharing my "ugliness" with another brought tears to my eyes and dropped heavy burdens from my shoulders immediately after those transgressions left my lips. I felt clean, free, renewed, and refreshed. I felt the spirit of God cover me as the stream of my tears poured on to the ground before me. My friend felt no pain at all. His heart was not a pound heavier, in fact it was lighter as he felt the joyfulness that came out of my newly freed spirit. We laughed, we cried, we hugged, and he even shared some of his own shortcomings that helped me feel not so alone. We left that rocky bluff over Lake Austin two cleansed men with a newfound freedom that wasn't possible to achieve on my own. I needed someone else, and because we were gathered on that bluff in God's name, God was also there taking on my burdens as His son did over 2,000 years ago. I had been washed clean, and it was as simple as sharing it all with another!

But it was more than that. My friend helped me define precisely how and where I was wrong. As he listened to each piece of my resentment, fear, and sex inventories, he would ask, "What is your defect there?" I responded a bunch of "I don't knows" at the beginning, and he would say, "Maybe you are the kind of person who wants credit for work you don't do. Or, maybe you compromise your integrity to get what you want, or to keep from losing what you've got." He might suggest, "Maybe you like to play the victim so you don't have to take responsibility?" Or, "Sounds selfish to me. What do you think?" Eventually I began to "get it," and as I read each piece of inventory, the defects of character I'd been exhibiting became clear to me. I'd say, "Oh, I manipulate others to get what I want. I portray a false image of who I am. I care more about what others think of me than what God thinks of me. I put unrealistic expectations on others. I act entitled and am always looking for the easy way out. I have too much self-pity. I don't like to be held accountable." The defects began to just pour out. The very things that were blocking me from God began to wash away on that rocky bluff in Austin. I felt closer and closer to God as each defect defined itself and fell from my heart. "Write it down," he'd say. "Write it down." What resulted after five long hours of sharing was the list of defects previously shared in the preceding three chapters. I could see the real me, right there in black and white, and it was painful. As the scales fell from my eyes and a crystal clear picture of my true self emerged, I could finally see the man I had been, the kind of husband and father, the kind of coworker, boss, and friend I had shown up as. I didn't like much of what I saw and was awash with an overwhelming sense of humility. I knew without a shadow of a doubt who I no longer wanted to be, and by simply reversing those defects could see exactly the type of man I intended to be. I knew, with God's help, it was going to be possible.

The dammed up emotions of years broke free from their confinement and vanished as quickly as they were exposed to my friend. As the pain inside of me began to subside, the tranquility of healing took its place, forever changing me. The presence of God was upon me, and I could see Him, hear Him, and could feel Him. I was the problem. I was the one responsible for the communication block that existed between God and me, but with His help that connection was about to become very clear.

This revelation and complete and utter paradigm shift occurred almost instantaneously. Pouring through my lists of resentments, I found myself in a position of granting forgiveness to everyone I thought had wronged me. My anger and frustration with all those people disappeared as I began to see exactly what my part was in all these resentments. As the humility settled in, I began to feel empowered by my past and found the ability to forgive myself for all the damage done. For the first time in my life I understood what Emmet Fox was talking about in his book, *Sermon on the Mount,* when he broke down the Lord's Prayer and specifically the line, "Forgive us our trespasses as we forgive those who trespass against us."

Fox calls this the turning point of the prayer. In it, he says that sin causes us to separate from God. I certainly had what I like to call "tier one" sins like lying, cheating, stealing, coveting my neighbor's wife and property, taking the Lord's name in vain, having the God of myself and the God of money before Him, disobeying my parents, and on and on, but the other sins that were separating me from God resided in all the character defects shared with my friend. I relied on myself and others, rather than on God, I manipulated others to get what I wanted and exhibited inordinate amounts of arrogance, pride, and ego. I put others down to make myself look and feel better. I felt entitled, cared more for myself than for others, was incredibly selfish, and that list continues . . . Fox explains that we need to "cut out" all these things in order to be one with God and to restore that lost connection.

He also goes so far as to say that we are obligated to forgive those we feel have wronged us and that forgiveness is contingent upon us being forgiven ourselves. We can never be forgiven by God until we have forgiven every last person on earth we hold anger toward. That includes ourselves. Don't even bother asking! I wasn't ready to forgive anyone UNTIL I took the time to work through my resentment, fear, and sex inventories. That exercise opened my eyes, allowed me to see "my part" in all those relationships, and finally gave me the willingness and the desire to forgive everyone I was holding something against. After forgiving them, I could then forgive myself, endeavoring not to repeat my past behaviors and actions. Then and only then was God able to forgive me, cleanse me, and make me a new person. Emmet Fox suggests that if your prayers aren't being answered, you should first check your consciousness to see if there is someone whom you have yet to forgive. Once you have identified that person and offered forgiveness, your demonstrations to God will open again.

Setting others free means setting yourself free, because resentment is simply a form of attachment, and it takes two to make a prisoner. Prisoner and jailer. The act of confession or sharing your sins with another gives you the insight and the courage to forgive others, yourself, and then to receive the ultimate forgiveness from our Heavenly Father. The goal of sharing our shortcomings with another human being is for our own personal healing and freedom from emotional bondage. It brings us to the point of extending forgiveness to others and to ourselves, and ultimately receiving true forgiveness from God. By opening up ourselves to another we no longer feel isolated, but rather experience a sense of being centered within ourselves. This practice relieves us from the heavy burdens we tend to carry, and in the process we begin to create a new self-awareness that becomes the critical component of our personal growth. Above all, however, is this new closeness and alignment with God that opens up a great and wonderful line of communication to Him.

There is more work to do, however, and becoming willing to lose your defects of character, your shortcomings, and your learned behaviors isn't as easy as it sounds as we find in the next chapter.

CHAPTER 19

INTRODUCING
MR. HYDE

I decided to title this book *Killing Mr. Hyde* because my ex-wife used to always say, "You're like Dr. Jekyll and Mr. Hyde," referring to how I was a completely different person when I was drinking or even living sober, but still in the emotional or mental manifestations of my disease. She was living in constant fear of just who was going to show up from one day to the next; even long periods of sobriety gave her little comfort.

Before we go any further, let me explain the difference between the two personalities to help you distinguish which guy was which! I have been familiar with the classic novel by Robert Louis Stevenson for as long as I can remember and have always thought that Dr. Jekyll was the bad guy and Mr. Hyde was the good guy. It just made sense. Dr. Jekyll sounds evil and sinister (cue the maniacal laugh), and Mr. Hyde sounds refined and respected, but it's exactly the opposite. Mr. Hyde is the evil one, and Dr. Jekyll is the good and honorable doctor. The reason I'm pointing this distinction out is because every time I want to say something bad or evil, I want to blame it on Dr. Jekyll, and every time I want to say something good, it must be Mr. Hyde. Not the case. Mr. Hyde, BAD! Dr. Jekyll, GOOD!

Anyway, my ex-wife would say she fell in love with Dr. Jekyll. "He is the guy I married. When he disappears and becomes Mr. Hyde, I long for his return." Early on in our marriage, Dr. Jekyll was mostly present, and Hyde would show up occasionally. But as I continued to drink more and more of "the potion," she saw less and less of Dr. Jekyll and more and more of Mr. Hyde. Her help and her hope diminished over time until she finally reached the point where she had to be honest with herself and admit that she didn't know who I was any longer. She was unable to recognize me as the man she married, the man she loved. She was living with Mr. Hyde, and it had become obvious that Dr. Jekyll would not be returning any time soon, if at all. She eventually left me, and in hindsight stayed much longer than she should have because I had turned into a dangerous, unpredictable man, like Mr. Hyde, and was putting her and our children at risk. I respect the length of her commitment and am often amazed that she hung on as long as she did. She must have really loved me.

In Stevenson's book, one can find many parallels to alcoholism, and an entire analogous comparison could be written, but I'll save that for a different day. For now, I'll share with you the part of the story that struck me the deepest. The following is an excerpt from a summary analysis of the story, then rewritten to describe how it paralleled my own life. I didn't have to change much.

Excerpt from Wikipedia: "At some point, Jekyll resolved to cease becoming Hyde. One night, however, the urge gripped him too strongly and after the transformation he immediately rushed out and violently killed Sir Danvers Carew. Horrified, Jekyll tried more adamantly to stop the transformations and for a time he proved successful by engaging in philanthropic work. One day, at a park, he considered how good a person that he had become as a result of his deeds (in comparison to others), believing himself redeemed. However, before he completed his line of thought, he looked down at his hands and realized that he had suddenly transformed once again into Hyde. This was the first time that an involuntary metamorphosis had happened in waking hours. Far from his laboratory and hunted by the police as a murderer, Hyde needed help to avoid being caught. He wrote to Lanyon (in Jekyll's hand), asking his friend to retrieve the contents of a cabinet in his laboratory and to meet him at midnight at Lanyon's home in Cavendish Square. In Lanyon's presence, Hyde mixed the potion and transformed back to Jekyll in Lanyon's presence. The shock of the sight instigated Lanyon's deterioration and death. Meanwhile, Jekyll returned to his home, only to find himself ever more helpless and trapped as the transformations increased in frequency.

Eventually, the stock of ingredients from which Jekyll had been preparing the potion ran low, and subsequent batches prepared by Jekyll from renewed stocks failed to produce the transformation. Jekyll speculated that the one essential ingredient that made the original potion work (a salt) must have itself been contaminated. After sending his butler, Mr. Poole, to one chemist after another, to purchase the salt that was running low, only to find it wouldn't work, he assumed that subsequent supplies all lacked the essential ingredient that made the potion successful for his experiments. His ability to change back from Hyde into Jekyll had slowly vanished in consequence. Jekyll wrote, that even as he composed his letter, he knew that he would soon become Hyde permanently, having used the last of this salt and he wondered if Hyde would face execution for his crimes or choose to kill himself. Jekyll noted that, in either case, the end of his letter marked the end of the life of Dr. Jekyll. He ended the letter saying 'I bring the life of that unhappy Henry Jekyll to an end.'" With those words, both the document and the novella come to a close.

My version . . . At some point, I resolved to quit becoming Mr. Hyde. As much as I no longer wanted to be him, the urge always gripped me too strongly and I drank. Once the transformation occurred, I would immediately run out and violently try to kill everything that I loved, including myself. Horrified after a spree, I tried even harder, with more resolve to adamantly stop these awful transformations that resulted from drinking. For periods of time I thought I had proven myself successful by throwing myself into philanthropic work, among other positive behaviors. I went to AA meetings, got a sponsor, showed up at church, joined small religious groups, read self-help books and the Bible, started working out, eating better, and refocused my attentions on family. After a while, I would reflect on what a good person I had become as a result of these human efforts and truly believed that I had been redeemed, somehow healed from my best efforts. But the ominous days would arrive, without warning, and I would realize that I had suddenly been transformed into Mr. Hyde yet again. These transformations were involuntary, and I could never explain their reoccurrences or see them coming. I had no control over them. All the human power I had thrown at the problem was utterly insufficient to stop them. Far from God and in trouble with everyone, I reached out to friends and family for help, hoping they could provide me with a solution to my problem. As hard as they tried and with exceptional effort, they could not. I returned to my hopeless existence to find myself ever more helpless and trapped as these terrible transformations increased in frequency and nothing seemed able to reverse them.

Eventually I ran out of the ingredients I thought I needed to maintain Dr. Jekyll. Good deeds, willpower, and a great desire to change didn't work any longer. They failed to produce any kind of lasting return of the good Dr. Jekyll (Mike). Those things just weren't successful in helping me return to the person I wanted to be. My ability to change back to Dr. Jekyll (Mike) from the awful alcoholic, Mr. Hyde, had slowly vanished. Realizing that I would soon become Mr. Hyde permanently, I wondered whether I would end up in prison or choose to kill myself. I noted, as did Dr. Jekyll, that in any case, this marked the end of the life, the end of the person my family and friends used to know and love. I was ready to bring the unhappy life of Mike to an end. With these words, my story would come to a close.

Frightening comparison!

I'm not going to spend a lot of time on this good vs. evil stuff, this internal battle that all humans have—that little devil on one shoulder, angel on the other analogy—but I do believe everyone has a good or God side and an evil or Satan side. It's all about the battle for your soul. God is obviously the more powerful influence, and Satan is no match for Him alone, but when we, as humans, "team up with" or facilitate Satan's workings inside of us, it makes the battle ever greater.

However, when we choose to join the battle with God, victory over evil, over our problems, and over our souls makes for an easy win against the hurtful ways in which Satan attempts to infiltrate our lives. We have the choice to tip the balance in how that battle plays out. The key is figuring out what you're fighting and where your weaknesses lie. What are your Achilles heels? What part of the battle is yours to fight, and what part of the battle do you need to call on the reinforcements of God? Going through the process of taking your personal inventory, identifying your defects of character, and understanding how to draw on God's power when human efforts are not enough to yield victory is an exercise that you must undertake to realize lasting success.

Once you find out who your "Mr. Hyde" is, then you know who and what you're fighting against. That's the person Satan wants to build up and grow, the soldier he wants to draw into battle with him. Satan wants to take your defects and use them against you and against God. The opposite of your Mr. Hyde is who God "says you are" and who God wants you to be. That is the person, your Dr. Jekyll, who you need to nourish, feed, focus on, and strengthen.

Satan knows your Mr. Hyde, and he knows exactly what to do to ignite it. Satan knows that if he can incite Mr. Hyde to come out and stay out, that you will fall further and further away from God. Satan's goal is to kill Dr. Jekyll! Yours is to kill Mr. Hyde.

When you've figured out who Mr. Hyde is (your defects of character), what his tactics are, when and how he rears his ugly head, with God's help you can immediately exterminate parts of him by calling on God for help. Other characteristics of him can be weakened, and many facets of him you may have to do battle with for a long time. But by continually engaging Mr. Hyde in the fight with God as your commander, you will weaken his stronghold and minimize his threat, as your Dr. Jekyll becomes stronger and more prevalent in your life. Through this combat mission, you will find yourself growing closer and closer to God and will begin to transform into the person that God intended you to be, the amazing Dr. Jekyll!

So who was my Mr. Hyde? Who is yours? If you will remember (of course you won't, so I'll reprint a few of them below; to see them all, return to Chapter Fifteen) all my defects of character from the inventory done a few chapters back, you'll get a very clear picture of who my Mr. Hyde was. My Mr. Hyde is partially described as follows:

- He puts blame on others for his problems or failures.
- He is selfish and self-centered.
- He cares too much about what others think of him.
- He manipulates people to get what he wants.
- He doesn't trust that God knows what's best for him.
- He portrays a false image to others.
- He is self-seeking in every situation and relationship.
- He has a lot of self-pity. He is always feeling sorry for himself.
- He doesn't like to be held accountable for his actions.
- He is a controlling person.
- He thinks he is superior to others.
- He needs others to rely on him to feel valuable.
- He avoids others because he's afraid they'll hurt him.
- He doesn't stand up for what he believes in. He has no integrity.
- He is arrogant.
- He doesn't like to take responsibility for himself or his actions.

- He demands a reputation he does not deserve.
- He diverts/deflects attention away from his own shortcomings.
- He likes to "play the victim."
- He gets his own happiness at the expense of others.
- He lacks transparency, and he is not genuine.

That's my Mr. Hyde. More importantly, who is your Mr. Hyde? What are all your defects of character? What kind of person do you turn into when your character defects are running your life? What tools are you making available for Satan's use? What defects are blocking you from having communication and a relationship with God? We all have them! We just have to identify and recognize them for what they are. Think about some of your most despised defects and let me ask you this:

"Do you want to get rid of them?" Did I want to get rid of all my defects? Of course I did; that's an easy question. But was it? After I took some time to consider that question, I realized that in most cases I really didn't want to eliminate my flaws. That sounds crazy, doesn't it? Who wouldn't want to exterminate the parts of their personality that had been deemed negative, unflattering, or damaging? After honest thought, I recognized that I really wanted to hang on to them! The reason? They served some purpose! Otherwise, why would we exhibit them? So it is important to comprehend that you can't just want to get rid of them. You have to be willing to sacrifice what they do for you! For example, I liked to play the victim, but what purpose did that serve? For me, it meant as long as I played the victim, I didn't have to take responsibility for myself. I could always blame someone else for my problems or get people to feel sorry for me or take care of me. Playing the victim served a huge purpose for me, and getting rid of that defect meant I'd have to start taking responsibility for my actions with my family, my job, and for my life. I didn't want to do that. It was too much work.

What about my defect of "portraying a false image?" Who wants to be a fraud, a fake, a dishonest or disingenuous person? I did, because by portraying a false image, I was feeding my ego and my desire to have other people like and respect me. By portraying a false image, I was able to avoid the humility that came with being a real and flawed human being. I didn't want people to see the real me.

Another defect I have is that "I often don't stand up for what I believe in," and "I lack integrity." That makes me spineless, weak, and someone who gets taken advantage of frequently. Do you think I want to keep those descriptions about myself? NO. BUT . . . not standing up for what I believe in and showing a lack of integrity allows me to avoid my greatest fear in life, CONFRONTATION! My distaste for it supersedes the alternative of being considered spineless and weak. I'd rather get taken advantage of than have to enter into a confrontation with someone. That's why I hang on to that defect!

Character defects are sinful, but sin can be fun and self-serving (for a while). Who doesn't like to feel superior to his fellows? Greed is good, according to Mr. Gecko. So we hang on to it and hide it behind the auspices of "ambition." What about lust? It's exciting, and we rationalize it by calling it romance. I love to gossip, even though I know it's wrong and sinful, but it serves the greater purpose of making me feel better about myself, or allows me to divert attention away from my own flaws. Every defect I have has some value to me, and oftentimes the notion of losing that value outweighs keeping the defect.

But here's the thing. All those defects make me sick. They incite and damage my spiritual condition. When I don't stand up or have integrity, I feel bad about myself, and I begin to form resentments against people I should have confronted. When I portray a false image, I feel guilt about being dishonest with who I really am. I insult God by not being proud of what He created. When I play the victim, which allows me to shirk responsibility, I feel unworthy, worthless, and my sense of self is diminished. Those feelings create an internal or emotional discomfort for me, I seek relief from those feelings in the bottle. Other people might find the solution with food, sex, shopping, or any number of unhealthy behaviors. Those personal deficiencies keep me from having a true relationship with God. They block my communication from Him because it's impossible to be in sync with God when you're doing things He does not want from you.

I wish it was as easy as recognizing these defects and "making a decision" to stop exhibiting them. I tried, and like everything else in my life, I realized I couldn't do it on my own. I couldn't stop drinking on my own, I couldn't fix my marriage on my own, and I couldn't be a good father on my own. I needed God's help, but first I had to make sure that I was "willing" to give up these flaws that had served me so well (or I thought had served me well) over the years.

The word "willingness" is defined as "to become ready, to consent, to desire, to wish for." That's the best we can do on our own, but it takes getting there before God will step in and help. The only decision I have the power to make is a decision to become "willing." It's important to recognize that although our character defects serve some purpose and offer some benefit, they are still traits we have to be willing to give up, even though they may represent some loss of personal value. We have to be willing to sacrifice something, to receive something better. Once we've reached that place of willingness, it is then possible to begin calling on the Power of God.

Being willing to give up these defects is a process. It's a grieving and mourning process, just like in any other death. As we ask God to help us destroy these parts of our personalities and lives, we need to take some time, stop, and mourn them. We need to recognize them for how "they served us," understand that they were just branches that needed to be pruned from our lives so that we could grow stronger in faith, in God, and to make room in our lives for more of the good, healthy branches that make us stronger.

Like everything else in life, willingness rarely comes without pain. As we talked about in earlier chapters, "Pain motivates change." That's why God invented it! I wish we were all smart enough, insightful enough, intuitive enough to become willing without having to experience the pain that accompanies change, but we're just not. Taking yourself through a thorough personal inventory, as we did in Chapter Fifteen, should have painted a clear enough picture of the person you used to be to break your heart. Facing that reality, that brutal truth about yourself, can be crushing, but it brought me and hopefully will bring you to a point where you are ready for God to change you. If not, well, I'm afraid you're not hurt enough. God will get you to the point of change in His time; everyone is different, and it takes what it takes. It took me a dozen years before I reached that point, but as painful as it was, every hurt I felt, every blow I doled out or that was dealt to me was another lesson that needed to be learned.

If you'll remember King David from the Bible, he had the same problem. He was quick to point out others' defects, but couldn't recognize his own and certainly wasn't willing to give them up and change. In Psalm 26:9, he prayed, "Lord, I am not like them, I live with integrity, so redeem me and show me mercy." He approached God on his own merit. I did the same thing. I'd say, "God, I'm a good man, a good person, why are you allowing these bad things to happen to me? Show me some mercy!" I wasn't willing to see my own faults and certainly wasn't willing to change. It wasn't until much later in King David's life when he was finally confronted with his own sins of adultery and murder that he was able to say in Psalm 51:5, "I was born a sinner and I realize that the sacrifice you desire God is my broken spirit." David finally reached a place of humility that only came from recognizing his own defects. He then found "the willingness" to allow God to change him. When we do, God does not judge us, he does not punish us, he does not ignore us. He forgives us, comforts us, cleanses us, and makes us a new person!

Another great example is in John, chapter 5, verses 5-9. We hear about the sick man who needs to get to the healing pool. Jesus asks him, "Do you want to get well?" His answer, of course, is, "Yes, but I can't get to the pool, someone always gets there ahead of me. No one will help me." His character defects of blaming others and playing the poor victim were the defects blocking the way to his healing! His own efforts weren't enough to get him into the pool; he needed Jesus's help! Jesus responded by saying, "Stand up, pick up your mat and walk." Instantly, the man was healed. Thirty-eight years of his own efforts did nothing for him but keep him sick. A willingness to recognize he couldn't do it on his own, a personal decision that he was "sick and tired of being sick and tired," and one request of Jesus healed the man. The point is that this invalid could only get himself so far because for so long he wasn't willing to own his defects and become ready to have them removed. His story is no different from yours or mine regarding our defects. He hung on to his, because they served his purpose. The Bible doesn't tell us, but I suspect there was a part of that sick man that didn't want to get well. Not getting well allowed him to not have to take responsibility for his life, to rely on the charity of others, to get people to feel sorry for him, to avoid work and relationships. I guess he'd suffered enough the day Jesus walked by and was finally ready, but he still couldn't do it himself. He needed the power of God and he got it! How long have you been trying to heal yourself by your own efforts? How long had I? Thirty-eight years for me wasn't far off! Get as close to the healing pool as you can, then become willing to allow God to take you in!

Here is one more non-Biblical example. Arguably my favorite movie of all time is *Shawshank Redemption* with Tim Robbins and Morgan Freeman. There is a scene in the movie where one of the inmates, Brooks Hatlen, is finally paroled after fifty years in Shawshank Prison. He tries to cut another inmate's throat when he hears the news, hoping the act will keep him in prison. It doesn't work, and he's paroled and released anyway. He quickly realizes he can't make it on the outside and spends all his time thinking about ways to break his parole so he can be sent back to prison. Prison is all he knows. Being a free man and functioning on "the outside" and in the free world is too frightening for him. He lasts a few months, then hangs himself. Even though Brooks was in Shawshank Prison (a metaphor for a defect) for nearly fifty years, he wasn't willing to give that life up because prison offered him a comfortable and known routine, three meals a day, and a position in life (albeit behind bars). It kept him from having to function in the real world and from being responsible for working toward a new and better life. Prison, as horrible as it was, was all he knew. He wasn't willing to let go of that for something infinitely better—freedom, a new life, and new experiences. He had a chance to make a positive difference in the world and in other people's lives. Brooks Hatlen is an extreme example of unwillingness. He would rather take his own life than let go of the "defects" of a prison that was serving his purpose by allowing him to feel safe in an environment he knew, was a part of, needed at some level, and that was in his comfort zone.

If I could sum this entire book up in one word, it would be "willingness." Or maybe better said, "unwillingness." Unwillingness is the point at which God is no longer able to help us, to heal us, to allow us to grow. It is the final and most difficult door we must open. When we do, however, God is waiting with open arms to carry us across the threshold, joyously waiting to love us, forgive us, and change us.

When your Dr. Jekyll and Mr. Hyde reach that same doorway, only one man walks through and lives. The other stays behind and dies. The choice of willingness is yours.

CHAPTER 20

TAKE THEM AWAY, PLEASE!

Those personal defects discussed thus far are the static on your communication lines to God. They are the problem. They are YOUR "Mr. Hyde," things about the person "you have been," and they are blocking you from being able to hear what God is trying to tell you and are preventing you from becoming the person you CAN be. The person God says you are! They are the same blocks keeping God from hearing your prayers. Our character defects become the "ice" on those transmission lines that we can only "willing" melt, but God can and will thaw them, if we will only ask. Matthew 7:7 says, "Knock and the door will be opened to you, seek and you will find, ASK and it will be given to you." Wait? Could it be that simple? We just have to ASK God to remove our character defects. Yeah! It's actually that simple! It's called a prayer. "God, please take away my arrogance and give me humility." Just like that and "poof" it's gone! Well not quite. You see, God's time is different from our time.

Unfortunately, we live in a world that demands instant satisfaction. Geico can save you 15 percent in fifteen minutes. Dominos will deliver your pizza in thirty minutes or less. We have Jiffy Lube, Speedy Mart, QuikTrip, Fast Cash, Instant Approval Loans, priority this and priority that, from mail and package delivery to express amusement park ride lines. Blockbuster video was too slow, and we didn't want to take the time to stop in, browse around, and pick a movie, so Netflix stepped in and allowed us to pick a flick in seconds before our one-minute rice and instant potatoes were ready. The bookstore is a waste of time, so we instantly download books, magazines, newspapers, and games on our Kindles and Nooks! We have "on demand" TV, same day delivery, and for heaven's sake, Amazon is testing miniature drones so we can get that new pitching wedge by Friday (like it's really going to improve our game on Saturday!). We've grown accustomed to, learned to expect, and frankly demand instant gratification and results. Tragically, that impatience, that need for instant results and instant relief, also shows up in matters of the mind and spirit. "I'm depressed, anxious, dealing with a past trauma, stressed, uptight, or having some anger issues and don't have time to work it out with a counselor, friend, family member, or through prayer. Just give me a pill that works fast, Doc!" Maybe your doctor isn't so cooperative. Not a problem, one can easily find instant relief and gratification on the street with a "hit," a snort, a shot, a smoke, or from the nearest liquor store. We want it now! We demand it now! Veruca from *Willie Wonka and the Chocolate Factory* may have said it best. "Daddy, I want an Oompa Loompa and I want it now." That's not how God works.

Have you ever seen that movie with Jim Carrey called *Bruce Almighty* where Morgan Freeman (what is it with me and Morgan

Freeman?), playing God, hands over his power to Bruce Nolan, played by Carrey? Bruce is hearing millions and millions of prayers, and he's granting everyone what they pray for with a "yes!" In doing so, one catastrophe after another begins to happen, and Bruce realizes that saying "yes" to everyone didn't lead to all good things. For instance, to everyone that prayed to win the lottery, he granted all their prayer requests, and 10 million people had the winning numbers, which meant each of their take of the mega millions jackpot was about seventeen bucks! Then forty-five people praying to get the same job all showed up for work the next day and chaos ensued. When it comes to prayer, God knows best. Garth Brooks sings about it in one of his famous songs: "Some of God's greatest gifts are often unanswered prayers." This is especially true when it comes to asking God to remove your defects of character. Some of them God will remove immediately, some of them He will tone down, and some of them, well, you just have to wait, because God's not ready to remove them from you quite yet. Maybe you're not ready either?

I recall my first experience with preparing myself to identify my defects of character and the blockage that existed between God and me. It was the point in my recovery where I was finally able to arrive at a place of self-awareness and willingness. I had gone through the exhaustive process of taking a life's worth of inventory we talked about back in Chapter Fifteen. Looking back on that initiative, I realize now, especially when talking others through it, what a daunting assignment it really is. I had the luxury of being in a long-term treatment center where I could solely focus on completing a personal inventory, and it still took me two months to accomplish. I can't imagine how long it would have taken had I been back here in the real world, with a job, a family, and other responsibilities to distract me. To do it right, to do it as thoroughly as possible, it could easily take six months or so. I suppose that timeframe varies widely depending on how old you are and how much you've screwed up your life. So let's call it two to six months! I can certainly empathize with the many other addicts and alcoholics I work with when they're up against this task. Most of them fizzle out and stop the process at this point. This personal inventory task, the assignment that helps you identify your defects of character and forces one to take a "hard look" at who they've really been, is mountainous. Forget about the fact that it's an emotionally painful assignment, an unpleasant look at yourself, or that it's humbling (to say the least); it's simply just a ton of work.

Anyway, I was lucky enough and willing enough to finally work through the inventory. The process became so distasteful at times that I simply had to walk away. The best I could do most of the time was to finish a resentment or piece of inventory, try to forget it, and move on to the next one. I became very depressed through the journey; was filled with regret, remorse, and shame; and was often stuck in morbid reflection. I pushed on however, because I wanted to get better, and after finally finishing, I was mentally, emotionally, and physically exhausted. I recall finally completing the task and letting the treatment center director know I was ready to share it with someone, to make my confession if you will, like we talked about in Chapter Eighteen. As we walked together from his office back toward the common area of the facility, he stopped suddenly, turned to me with a serious look and said, "Mike, are you absolutely SURE you got everything? Did you leave ANYTHING out? If you've held back one thing, you may never get better and you'll be right back where you were before you walked through our front doors in no time at all." As I looked into his concentrated, concerned, and deliberate eyes, I was struck with a wave of doubt, a rush of panic, and I just broke down and wept. Some of that emotion came from the fact that I was so spent from the process, but most of it came because I felt so broken and afraid of returning to the hell of active addiction. I just couldn't think of anything I might have possibly left out, so he gave me a hug, assured me I was ready to move on, and I spent most of the night searching my embattled memory for any last resentment or demon I might be hanging on to.

The next morning we scheduled a meeting with my local sponsor in Austin, and the following day he picked me up and we drove to a nearby lake. My sponsor parked, and we climbed a bluff with my two large notebooks full of painful self-examination. Once we found a big rock that overlooked the water, we sat down and started what ended up being a five-hour process of going through my notebooks. I shared the dark corners of my life, nooks and crannies, and confessed to another human being the things that I had done and about the person I used to be. Tears came, went, then came again over this long afternoon, and together we opened up my sinful vault and released the baggage that had been keeping me sick for years. I was there, listening to myself; he was there confirming my admissions; and I felt God there listening in and watching over as well. There is just something about sharing your deepest, darkest secrets with another human being that makes them so real. As we talked through each one, my friend initially would ask, "What is your character defect in this one?" At first I wasn't sure, and he'd say, "In this one it sounds like you manipulate others to get what you want." I'd say, "Ya, that sounds right." He'd say, "Write that down, then." Before long, the personal character defects I discovered in each piece of inventory became obvious to me, and I wrote every one down. When we were finished, I had approximately eighty different defects of character. Ouch! That's a lot of static!

We finally finished the process near the end of the day, and my friend prayed for me as we watched the sun slowly sink beyond the bluff across the lake. As we trudged back down the rocky trail to his car, I was overcome with a sorrowful sense of peace for the first time in my life, but felt emotionally unburdened and spiritually cleansed. On the drive back, I stared out the window, tears rolling down my sun-burned cheeks, and finally realized what the word humility actually meant. I was truly humbled in front of my friend, but more impor-tantly in front of God. Reviewing in detail the person I had been, and having had it confirmed by another human being, I found I had reached a true point of willingness. There was a real desire to change, to kill my "Mr. Hyde," and to become the person God intended for me to be. I deeply wanted to become the opposite of who I'd become, and to strive for the inverse of my character defects. I'd always hated myself on some level, but was never quite sure why. I could never put a finger on it until that day, but it was right there in black and white, eighty very specific reasons why I was broken! Now that I knew what I despised about myself, I knew exactly what needed to be changed. This is where God comes into the picture. We are not capable of changing ourselves. Just like in nearly everything else we do in life, we need God's permission, God's help, God's power, and God's strength.

My friend eventually dropped me off at the treatment center, along with my list of eighty defects, and asked me to go directly to my room and begin asking God, defect by defect, to remove each and every one of them. After finishing the most humble prayer I've ever said, I fell into a deep sleep and did not awake until the following morning, tucked in exactly the same position I had fallen asleep in, clothes, shoes, and all. I opened my eyes and saw a brand new world. The rocks I had been carrying around my entire life were left back on that high bluff overlooking Lake Austin. It was the happiest and most free I'd ever felt. I was an entirely different person, and the remembrances of the old me seemed a lifetime ago. The work, however, was just beginning. Every rock I left back on that bluff represented someone I'd hurt along the journey of my life—someone I had wronged, treated badly, cheated, ignored, disappointed, or failed. That work, however, would come much later, and we'll discuss it in a few chapters. For now, my goal was to recognize, understand, and accept my eighty shortcomings, to be willing to allow God to take them away and make my heartfelt request. You see, it doesn't do any good, as we'll see shortly, to go back to that unsightly pile of rocks, that highway littered with other human beings you've wronged, and try to set things right, if you haven't changed yourself first. Making those amends is a hollow process, wholly unaccepted by those you're seeking forgiveness from, if you're just going to continue acting like the same person you were before. Albert Einstein said "that significant problems cannot be solved at the same level of thinking or acting that they were created at. Only by rising to a higher or deeper level can an ultimate, effective, and lasting solution be found." So I can't, for instance, go back to my coworker and say, "I was wrong to gossip about you with the rest of the staff; I was just trying to feel better about myself, and that was wrong. What can I do to make it right?" if three days later I'm standing with another group of coworkers who are character assassinating the same person and I don't stand up for him, now can I? All I'm doing then is feeling guilty about the situation, like I'm lying to or betraying my coworker, filled with anxiety over whether or not he is going to find out I've been participating in gossip about him again. Those are the beginnings of the "spiritual malady," and we all know where that lead us! If my friend does find out, I haven't solved a problem; I've created a larger one! I have to rise to a higher level of being able to solve that problem, like Einstein said. That graduation to a higher level of thinking, acting, and being comes from the removal of your character defects.

So I asked God to take each and every one of them away and found that some of the eighty were immediately removed. For me, the urge to lie was instantaneously taken away. I did not want to be known as the liar I once was. I wanted to be known as honest, even if it meant suffering some consequences. I immediately stopped blaming others for my problems, failures, and unhappiness. God just made it obvious, right then and there, that it was no one else's fault. Any problem, failure, or bit of unhappiness was most likely my own fault, and even if it wasn't, I'm responsible, myself alone (with God's help) for solving those issues. Blaming someone else does no good, so immediately I became a guy who took personal responsibility for everything that happened in his life. There were many other defects that, once I recognized and truly wanted to rid my life of, God just took them away, leaf, branch, root, and all!

For others that I asked God to take from me, I noticed they didn't disappear completely, but they did get toned down. For example, I have a defect that keeps me from communicating my wants and needs, and like everyone else, I have a lot of wants and needs. The reason I do that and the real character defect behind that behavior is that I want everyone to like me. So when I need some time alone to rest my soul, to re-center myself, I don't tell my significant other when she wants to sit down and talk, go for a walk, go to the store, or go out on the town. I go, am resentful, cranky, passive-aggressive, and just end up being a big jerk who hurts her feelings and leaves her wondering what she's done! Then I feel remorseful afterward, begin to feel bad about myself, and have yet another relational mess to clean up. Wouldn't I have been better off simply saying, "Honey, I'm a little tired and stressed and would love a few hours to just relax and be alone with myself. Do you mind? Maybe we can do something fun later tonight?" Of course that would have worked better, and she would have said, "Sure no problem!" This one God hasn't quite taken away from me yet, but He has toned it down. I'll find myself in that situation today, catch myself being resentful or passive-aggressive, and I'll just stop and nip it in the bud, right there on the spot, and say what I should have said from the start. Why didn't God take that one entirely away from me? I'm not entirely sure, but I think it's because God needs me to understand and recognize how important honest communication is. Maybe there is a much larger test in front of me, and God knows I need to strengthen my defense around this defect through practice, recognition, and successful resolution on a smaller scale. He was right, because I found myself on a business trip sometime later, and while at dinner with a host of respected colleagues, wine was ordered, and I was asked if I'd prefer red or white. Wanting them to like me made me say "red, of course, I'm having the steak," when my real want, my real need was not to drink because of what it does to an alcoholic like me. God needed to show me, to teach me, and to strengthen me around that defect. So although I still have it, He has toned it down for me through self-recognition, and I am beginning to learn how better to address it through practice. As I am tested with that defect of wanting to please everyone, wanting them to like me by not expressing my needs and wants, I can see myself getting stronger, becoming more humble and more confident in the truth that it only matters what God thinks about me and what I think about myself, not what others think of me. I'm learning that the only person I'm trying to impress is God; the most important person that should like me is me! Every week, every month, every year, that defect continues to be toned down by God, and eventually it will go away completely; but for now, God and I still have a little work to do around it.

Finally, God doesn't remove other defects at all. He will, eventually, but in His time. For example, I avoid other people because I am afraid that they are going to hurt me, embarrass me, or want something from me that I won't be able to say "no" to! The real defects behind these characteristics are rooted in pride and selfishness. My pride is still so overpowering and fragile that I can't handle being embarrassed, humiliated, or made to look bad. The false sense of self I present to the world is a thin and vulnerable shell that is easily crushed, and avoiding others helps protect that. Fear of what others may ask of me is a function of selfishness that comes from not wanting to be inconvenienced from a financial, time, responsibility, or open, honest intimacy standpoint. I haven't been able to overcome this yet. God has not yet removed these personal shortcomings from me. Why? The real reason I'm finding is that although I said I didn't like that about myself, I'm not yet "willing" to give that up. If I'm honest with myself, I have to admit that. God knows it. So by not removing that defect,

I have to live with it until I do finally get to the point of enough willingness to let God have it. Until I'm willing to surrender my pride and my selfishness, God doesn't want to remove this defect from me. Unfortunately, that means I have some more hard lessons to learn about it, ones that will hopefully bring me a fork where I deeply want to rid myself of personal pride and selfishness. God has his reasons and His time. My responsibility is to just keep asking. "God, please take away my foolish pride and give me great humility. God please take away my selfishness and make me a giving, caring, open, and honest person." Sooner, rather than later, if you don't mind!

One effective tool I picked up in treatment that helped me eliminate some of my character defects was the act of "calling out or confronting" someone else on the same defects of character that I exhibit. It's an unbelievably frightening proposition, but it works, and almost immediately. I like to flirt, even to the point of inappropriateness. There's a BIG character defect in that. I don't have any intention of allowing my flirting to lead anywhere, but I do it because if I can get a woman to respond favorably, it feeds my ego and makes me feel better about myself. I struggle to find happiness in loving myself and use other people to make me feel good, rather than relying on the love that God has for me. I try to find comfort from the external rather than generating my own spiritual and emotional comfort from the inside, from a relationship with Christ. So there was a cute girl in rehab who has the same problem. She was flirting with me to get a response that would make her feel secure, and I was flirting with her to elicit the same response. Neither one of us particularly cared for the other, no relationship was going to form, and nothing was going to happen. We were just using each other to feed our own fragile and starving egos. My counselor said, "You need to confront her on this issue in front of the community tomorrow morning." What? Every morning the entire patient community, about thirty of us, would get together in a room and have this exercise called "confrontations." We would each be required to issue three confrontations to someone else in the community, to call them out for some behavior they had been exhibiting that offended or affected us in some way. "Call her out on it, man!" "No way," I said. "I can't, because I'm doing the same thing she is. She'll be pissed, and I'll feel like a hypocrite." He said, "I don't care; just do it and we're not leaving that group until you do!" I didn't sleep a wink that night thinking about it and the backlash it was going to cause. The next morning, however, as my counselor stared at me the entire session of "confrontations," I finally blurted out, "Stacey, when you continue to flirt with me, it makes me uncomfortable and fearful." The shock in her now wide open eyes, the look of contempt for me, was unbearable. She was angry, but our rule was that you couldn't confront the same person that confronted you that day, so she had to sit there, steaming, in silence. I felt awful, but you know what? It worked! I never flirted with her again, she never flirted with me again, and I never flirted with any other women my entire rehab "vacation!" By confronting her for the same behaviors I was exhibiting, it held me to a new standard, and that defect, at least with that community, completely went away. It was removed for my time there, but unfortunately only "toned down" by God as it crept back into my life when I was introduced back into the non-rehab world, where I'd have to do the same thing again. Not gone, but I'm getting better!

What we're talking about in this chapter is all about "real" changes in behavior. Our character defects clutter the road out of our past.

They block our lines of communication with Christ. In Isaiah 57, verses 14-15, God says, "Clear away the rocks and stones my people so (you) can return from captivity." Our captivity can be our own unhappiness, our self-made prisons, or a locked cell, of which we hold the key! In Jeremiah 18: 3-6, God told Jeremiah to go to the potter's shop to learn a lesson. He did, found the potter working at his wheel, but the jar he was making did not turn out like he had hoped, so he crushed it into a lump of clay and started again. God says, "Can I not do the same to you as the potter has done to his clay? You are in my hands. I can crush you and rebuild you. The clay does not argue with the potter, why do you argue with me, instead of letting me reshape you into something valuable?"

When we put our lives in God's hands, he will reshape us as He sees fit. It is our humility, or lack thereof, that allows God to do his work. Our pride, my pride, keeps me from asking God, or anyone else for that matter, for help in changing. We have to let go of that when it comes to our defects of character. With pride, with lack of humility, God cannot change us. Shame is a form of pride that also prohibits God from helping us change. For such a long time I felt so much shame about my past, about the things I'd done, about the person I'd become, that I felt unworthy to approach God for help. My past sins made me feel cut off from God, and I was too embarrassed to seek His help. Why would he have compassion on a sinner like me? It would be like going to your parents and asking for some candy ten minutes after you'd just hit your sister, colored all over your bedroom walls, and spilled a glass of grape juice all over your mom's new white sofa. Yeah right, like I'm going to ask mom for a piece of candy right now! That would be insane! But God's not like that.

You can sin, be wrong, be bad, and if you're really remorseful, if you acknowledge your shortcomings, if you ask for forgiveness, if you're willing to change, to be different, you can walk right up to God's candy counter and He will joyously give you what your heart desires. God only sees you through His eyes. He only sees us as we will be when His work is done!

And it is ALL HIS WORK that effects change! You cannot wish away, will away, or white-knuckle away your character defects. You have to ASK God to remove them and He will, in his time and in his way. Your job in helping to open the lines of communication with God and becoming the person God intended for you to be is to first identify and gain an exact awareness of just what character defects you have, and then become WILLING to have God remove those defects. It's an enormous battle you cannot win on your own, but it can be won with God's help, and He will help if you'll only be humble enough to ASK. So figure out what your defects of character are, own them, grieve their loss, but know they do not define you. They are not how God sees you, and they are not how you should see yourself. Recognize what you used to be like, then forget the past, look forward to what lies ahead, press on to reach the end of the race, and realize your heavenly prize (Philippians 3:12).

CHAPTER 21

MAKING IT RIGHT

There's a right way and a wrong way to say "I'm sorry." There is also a right time and a wrong time. There is no option to "Never say you're sorry!" If we ever expect to get better, if we ever expect to be relieved of our addictions, our emotional troubles, or our spiritual maladies, we HAVE to make apologies, but more importantly, our amends. If we ever expect to grow closer to Christ, if we ever hope to open our lines of communication with God, apologies and amends clear that static. Leaving the wreckage of our past lives unresolved is one of the single biggest blocks standing between us and a real relationship with our Creator. That wreckage also represents a whole lot of land mines that, if not diffused or detonated, become very dangerous trip wires in our future. It's also just another heavy bag of rocks we've been carrying around that needs to be dropped for our own sake, for our own relief, and for our own personal freedom. As in everything else we've discussed in this book, the work we need to do here does help others, but if we do it and do it right, we end up being the greatest beneficiaries. This chapter is no different.

Back in Chapters Fifteen, Sixteen, and Seventeen we worked through our personal inventories, our fear inventory, and our sex inventory. From those exercises, we clearly identified the wreckage of our past, and from that work we should have been able to see, very specifically, the people that we hurt, wronged, or neglected, and exactly how we damaged them. For these specific wrongful actions, we owe acknowledgment, restitution, apologies, and most importantly amends.

Now! If you don't want to go through all of the work we discussed back in the personal inventory chapters (because I know most of you don't), you can take a little shortcut here, but you won't get the full picture, and you might miss something important that is still blocking you from having a crystal clear relationship with Christ. Doing the work will yield the best results, but taking the shortcut won't be the end of the world and will certainly help you clear a large portion of the wreckage you've strewn along life's highway. So, in lieu of doing the full personal, fear, and sex inventories, just take a few days and put some thought and effort into jotting down a list of everyone you can think of, throughout your entire life, and in all your relationships, you may have harmed or wronged. Search your soul for the things of the past that still bother you, things you feel bad about, things you feel guilty over, people you might owe apologies to, then write them down and we'll let you off the hook a little here. It'll be like drinking 2 percent milk instead of fatty whole milk, though. Better for you, but not as healthy as skim milk.

Before we get started, let's first take a look at the differences between apologies, amends, and restitution. Apologies are "I'm sorrys," and they don't really carry much weight and really shouldn't be used in most situations. An apology is great if you're walking through a crowded room and accidentally bump into someone. It's appropriate and proper to quickly say, "I'm so sorry, excuse me." You didn't intend to bump into that person, it was an innocent mistake, and both you and the person you bumped into know it's not going to happen again. If you inadvertently and unknowingly cut in front of someone in the checkout aisle and realize it, quickly saying, "I'm sorry. I didn't notice you and I cut right in front of you. Please go ahead," works too. But, if on the other hand, you show up late for work for the 147th time this year, "Sorry, I'm late" just isn't going to cut it. You see, "sorrys" are only effective if they're backed up by consistent actions that support your apology. Getting really drunk and apologizing to my wife worked the first time or two it happened, because I hadn't developed a pattern (yet) of getting drunk all the time. After the fifth or sixth staggering home drunk episode, that "I'm sorry, it won't happen again" tactic was no longer believable. It carried no weight, and it did not rate forgiveness or satisfaction to the person I had offended or hurt. So pretty much forget about "the sorrys" unless you've just backed up your in-law's toilet and flooded the bathroom floor. Sorrys are NOT an effective tool in helping truly clean up the past and people you've hurt in it.

This is where "amends" come in. An amend is making compensation for an injury caused by you. It means to correct a mistake you've made, especially in behavior. It's something given or done to make up for damage you've caused. A simple "sorry" does not compensate anyone, it doesn't require a change in behavior, and it doesn't come attached with an action. An example would be hurting your employer by being late 147 days in a row but making "amends" for that by being on time or better yet early for the next 365 days. That carries weight! Your employer can see that you've changed, and you have some good history (365 days) that says you mean it. Only going to the strip joint one night a week instead of three, if you're married, is NOT an amends because your behavior is not changing, and your wife is not going to feel very well compensated by the fact that you're spending less time at "Million Dollar Babes." She will continue to be hurt by the fact that you're still going at all. Telling my kids "I'm sober" and ready to be a new dad after I've been dry for sixty days and have attended a few AA meetings is NOT an amends. They've heard me say, "That was the last time; I'm going to stay sober for good," only to watch me relapse time and time again. They were getting very little satisfaction and felt very little recompense after a lousy sixty days of sobriety considering my history. Making an amend is not a simple "sorry" and some shallow promises to do better, it's actually taking some action to do better, making a real permanent change, and it can take significant time and effort.

Restitution is "giving back to the rightful owner something that has been lost or taken away from them. It's a reimbursement intended to get someone back to a former condition or situation. When you've lost someone's trust, you can't give that back to them with an apology, with a single action, or with a small amount of effort over a short period of time. It takes much more to make restitution for lost trust. When your past behaviors have made someone you love feel insecure, belittled, or hurt, a couple of affirming words aren't going to restore them to their previous condition. It takes a lot of positive consistent behavior to make restitution for those kinds of things. A great analogy would be a bathtub full of warm water that represents a relationship full of trust, love, and security. If you go out and hurt someone by getting drunk, having an affair, or damaging them emotionally or physically, you've just pulled the plug on that entire warm bath, and it all goes down the drain in an instant. Restitution comes through filling that tub back up to its previous level one eyedropper of water at a time.

So, let's throw sorry out the door, consider restitution a subcategory to amends for now, and spend some time talking about how life-changing amends should be made. First let's talk about when, or the "right time." We have to refer back to Chapter Fifteen again when we made our personal inventories. From there, we were able to identify all of our defects of character, then share and validate them with another human being. After that, we had to get ourselves to a place of willingness to let them go and have God remove them, even though they still had some value to us. Finally we have to ask God to remove them. Once they have been removed, or at least toned down, we are then ready to make our amends, but not before. For example, I've got the character defect of not considering the impact on or the feelings of others in my actions. If I haven't been willing to give that up (because it serves me based on the fact that I get what I want), or even if I have become willing to give it up, but God hasn't removed it yet (because He's still trying to teach me something) and I'm still doing it, I'm not in a position or at the right time to make an amends to someone I've hurt with that character defect. For instance, I used to enjoy gambling and knew it really bothered my wife. It made her angry and insecure, and rightly so; she felt like financial decisions in a marriage should be joint decisions. I thought it was fun, wanted to do it, and expected to win money (yeah, right!), so I didn't bother considering how it impacted her or her feelings. I wasn't ready to quit doing it, so making some amends like, "I was wrong not to consider your feelings around gambling and making financial decisions jointly. So I have closed all my online sports betting accounts, I am not going to the casinos anymore, and I would like you to handle 100 percent of the money that flows through our household until you are comfortable that I am no longer going to waste money on gambling," just wasn't going to work. In fact, making that amends, then continuing to go out and gamble, would have made the situation worse. I would have been a liar and someone who didn't keep my word, or worse yet, someone who was hiding things from his wife. Not a factor considered to be conducive to a healthy marriage!

On the other hand, the right time to schedule an amend is when one has identified a character defect and become willing to have God remove it. You're ready when God has heard your prayer and taken that defect away from you. I used to have a character defect of putting blame on others for the mistakes I'd made. I was willing, and God removed that one from me altogether. When identifying this defect, I was reminded of the start-up of my business "eMarket." I had hired an advertising guy named John to design the logo, promotional materials, and to develop an advertising campaign. I signed his contract, agreed to his terms, and took the logo he designed for me and used it. I then got his bill. It was much higher than I expected it to be, and I refused to pay him. I blamed him for not doing the work we agreed to, overcharging me, and not taking the time to understand what I really wanted or could afford. I was the one who signed his contract. I was the one who had the opportunity to communicate to him what we wanted and what our budget was, but I decided to stiff him! Since

God removed this defect from me, and no longer being a person who blamed others for my past mistakes, it was important to make an amends to John to clear this past wreckage from my life. I was ready.

When it comes to "amends time," however, there is one more step. You don't just run out and do it. You ask God to help you, to come with you, to present you with the right opportunity and time, and then you wait, watch, and prepare yourself for it. He will, and it won't be long. Many years went by on this one, most of it spent drunk, and some of it in unwillingness to let that defect go, but after I got sober, identified it, and both God and I allowed it to go, the most amazing thing happened. I decided to start a recovery group out of LifeChurch and posted it on the church bulletin board. I hadn't seen John in ten years, but he showed up at our first meeting! I didn't even know he went to LifeChurch, and I was shocked to see him. I knew God had a hand in this moment, and after the meeting I pulled him aside. "John, I owe you an apology for getting angry with you about the eMarket advertising campaign and refusing to pay your invoice. I was wrong, and I want to know what I can do to make it right." There are three things you ALWAYS do when making an amends. First, you admit that you were wrong and explain exactly how you were wrong. Second, you ask the person what you can do to make it right, and third, you come prepared with suggestions of how you can make it right just in case they can't come up with an answer. Your goal is to get that person back to the place they were before you hurt them. I had already decided that 1) I was going to pay him the money I owed him (restitution), and 2) I was going to call his wife who was also involved and tell her that I was wrong, I was at fault, and she, John, and their company had done everything that I had asked them to do and were in no way at fault.

As it turned out, he was incredibly gracious and refused to accept the money. He explained that he was hurt by the incident and confused about what he had done wrong. He was bothered by the fact that he might have upset a customer and that my apology was so good to hear. My amends had cleared up something that had bothered John for some time. My action, intended to restore him, made his day. He gladly forgave me and thanked me for my honesty and efforts, and we became instant friends. I can't explain to you the sense of relief I felt afterward.

So other than the relief, why make amends? It can best be explained from a workbook the Scientologists used as part of their curriculum when I attend the Narconon treatment facility. The recovery workbooks they used were huge! They were each about 2" thick and had about 300 pages in them. The funny thing about them, however, was that they were filled with full page line drawings of human interaction scenes and even larger text. They were like "Dick and Jane" books for alcoholics and addicts. The whole 300-page book probably didn't have 300 words in it, but it was filled with sequential situational drawings. The particular one that comes to mind was a picture of a young man stealing $20 out of his dad's wallet, while another drawing showed his old man sitting quietly in an easy chair in the next room reading his newspaper. The young man left and went to buy drugs with the $20, and a few weeks later, he ran into his dad at the hardware store checkout counter and saw him pulling out his wallet to pay for a wrench or something. The young man had a pained and sad look on his face, and above his head in one of those "caption bubbles" was a smaller drawing of him stealing the $20 we saw in the first scene. The point was, seeing his dad reminded him of the bad thing he did by stealing money from his father. He was filled with guilt, shame, and remorse. Narconon called those feelings "emotional discomforts." Discomforts demand relief, and so the young man ran off and got drunk and high to make that emotional discomfort go away. The emotional discomfort originated from seeing his father and making the association to his theft. After the young man sobered up, he had a hangover, felt bad physically, and needed relief from that, so he got drunk again. The cycle continued until something or someone was able to stop him, like the police, an accident, or an institution. Once sober again, the young man realized that he needed to avoid his father so he wouldn't feel that "emotional discomfort" and have to seek relief for it with unhealthy behaviors. But the day arrived when he eventually did run into his father again, and the whole ridiculous scene commenced once again. To solve his problem and subsequently his addiction, the young man needed to confront his father about what he had done and offered to set things straight and all would be well. He would no longer avoid his father, and he would no longer have emotional discomfort from carrying around the guilt and shame of his thievery. The last scene in this "Drunken Dick and Mary Jane" drama showed the young man with a big smile on his face, handing his dad a $20 and shaking his dad's hand.

It sounds absolutely ridiculous! But it's true and it works! I've felt exactly the same way. Every time I would see a casino, a little bubble would pop out above my head, and I would feel guilty about lying to my wife, ashamed of doing something I knew I shouldn't be doing and that she didn't approve of. I'd be in fear that she might find out how much I may have lost. A casino sign gave me much "emotional discomfort," and I really did seek out relief from that discomfort in the bottle, which then always kick started my cycle of addiction. The same thing used to happen every time I saw the "eMarket" sign above our building. It would remind me of John and how I'd screwed him, and all I wanted to do was make that feeling go away with a shot of whiskey. But lo and behold, the minute I approached John with an amends, acknowledged my mistake, and validated his long-standing concerns, the mess was cleaned up. The thought or the sight of that logo sign didn't bother me a bit; it actually reminded me of something positive I'd done. I was proud of cleaning up a wrong, happy that I'd given John some satisfaction and healing that he needed as well!

That's why we have to identify all those people in our past lives that we've hurt. If we don't, we'll go through life carrying a heavy bag of rocks with words like guilt, shame, regret, remorse, fear, anxiety, and sadness written on them. Those are the things that create our spiritual malady and require immediate relief, relief we seek without even the slightest notion of the consequences.

Amends are not all rainbows and butterflies though, and there are many important things you have to understand about the amends process before diving in. Not everyone is going to be like John. Not everyone is going to forgive you, show you grace, or even let you make it right through the restoration process. Some aren't even going to be willing to let you make your amends at all. They may refuse to meet you, talk to you, or may even slam a door in your face. It doesn't happen often, but it does happen. What you must be willing to accept is the fact that you cannot control other people. You cannot control how they may react to you. Your goal is simply to "clean up your side of the street." How they respond is up to them, and God will work in their lives, just as he has in yours, to get you to this point of amends. You have to walk into every amends without expectation of the outcome. As in pretty much everything I do, I had to learn that the hard way. I've walked into an amends "all proud of myself" with expectations that this person was just going to absolutely think the world of me after I was finished. When I didn't get the response I was looking for, I found myself angry, frustrated, defensive, and even turned the tables back on them and started pointing out their mistakes in our unresolved situation. That just made things worse!

The point is, people are not always going to forgive you. They are not always going to welcome your sincere admissions and offers to make things right. They may never trust you again. You should not concern yourself with their responses. Everyone is different. God is in charge of the outcome, so leave that to Him. You are in charge of your "right actions."

Don't miss this one, people. As I said earlier in this chapter, leaving wreckage from your past unresolved and unattended is blocking you from having an open line of communication to God. It is also keeping you sick, emotionally, psychologically, and often times physically for us alcoholics, drug addicts, and eating disorder peeps! So identify your defects of character, extract from this last exercise all the people you've hurt over the years by exhibiting those defects, and become willing to allow God to remove those defects from your personality. When we ask Him to remove them, and He does, be ready to break out your broom and sweep away all the debris you've created, because it will be the last time you have to do it. Don't go it alone though. Take God along with you. Ask him to give you the courage to make the approach, and pray for the right words to say. Talk to a trusted friend about it, and then allow God to set the scene for you, remembering that you are there only to tidy up your side of the situation. You are not to bring up any part the other party may have had in the situation, although in most cases, they do have some responsibility. That, however, is NOT your mission. You take care of your wrongdoings and let God take care of the rest, including the outcome.

If you do it right, you will feel a freedom that you didn't think existed. You'll find yourself walking taller, being able to look people in the eye, and will sleep like a baby when your head hits the pillow each night. Apologies and sorrys are for amateurs. Amends-makers are professional life-changers!

CHAPTER 22

MAINTENANCE REQUIRED

I've moved twenty-two times in my life (don't ask), and last year I moved into a new house, making it twenty-three. The first thing I always do when moving into a new place is to set up my office. Strike that, the first thing I do is make sure my cable is working. The second thing is to set up my office. The desk, computer, file cabinets all are set in place before anything else happens. Then I organize all my files, my paperwork, my books, reference guides, and even sort out and organize all my office supplies. I take inventory of everything I have, go through every item in my office, and determine the things that are worth keeping and the things that are useless, dated, or defective and throw them out. I even test all of my pens before sticking them back into my little pen basket. I organize my drawers, restock the printer with paper, check the ink cartridges, defragment my computer, and even blow the dust out of my keyboard with one of those awesome cans of forced air. I'm a little OCD like that, but my office is like the nerve center of my life, and when it's not organized, functional, and clutter free I can't think straight. Every time I move, there's a serious purge of all the things in my office that are worthless, defective, or are no longer pertinent or useful in helping keep the nerve center of my life operating effectively. It's amazing how much stuff I can discard over the course of a year or so, stuff that is taking up space, clogging up file cabinets, and getting in my way. Having a disorganized office renders me ineffective and distracts me from focusing on productive things. So with every move or at least once a year (for those rare periods when I don't move), I do a comprehensive home office reorganization. After cleaning up, I feel empowered, focused, efficient, effective, and ready to make some serious forward progress. I'm energized!

But as the days go by, I begin to get lazy, lose my diligence, get distracted, and just don't feel like staying on top of the flow of things that roll in and out of my office on a daily basis. A pen runs out of ink and rather than throw it away, I toss in back in my pen basket. When mail comes in, I open it up, and then pitch it in a small pile on my desk because I'm too tired to file it away properly. When I get an updated statement, I stick it in its proper file, but don't bother to take the expired statement out and trash it. I spill a little coffee on my desk and avoid cleaning it up. As I get calls, I jot numbers down on little Post-it notes, promising myself to transfer them to the computer or notebook later, but never do.

Before long, I find my file cabinets bursting at the seams and can't ever seem to find the file I'm looking for. I spend five minutes going through the pen basket until I finally find one that works. Papers, bills, and mail are scattered all over my desk and floor, and the task of sorting and filing them away becomes too daunting, so I leave them. I find myself buried in Post-it notes, filled with numbers and information, and can't remember who or what they belong to. My office is a mess, I can't accomplish anything in it, and I become completely unproductive and usually just walk away. The more I ignore it, the worse it gets, and in no time at all the nerve center of my life is in complete chaos, so I tell myself, "It's time to move again!"

If you haven't figured it out yet, this whole bit about my neurotic office obsession, although true, is just a big analogy for what we've been talking about in this book. The move represents the big change we've become willing to make in our lives. Purging the worthless and defective things in my office is a metaphor for identifying and discarding all of our personal character defects. Keeping my office organized so I can be effective and productive is synonymous with making progress by serving the purpose God has outlined for our lives. When we're done with this exercise, the result is a new and manageable spirit, a fresh reliance upon God, an organized personal inventory, and a wastebasket full of character defects, that with God's help we've "trashed." We find that we are caught up on our amends "to do" lists, and our lives are on the course that God has designed for us. With all of this organizational work behind us, we're ready to handle just about anything life throws at us and handle it effectively, just like I'm able to handle anything that rolls through my office when it's clean, organized, and up to date.

But just like my office looks after being neglected for some period of time, our lives can get the same way. They get cluttered and disorganized, we hang on to things that just bog us down, we stuff defective items into the corners of our souls, carry around heavy briefcases full of worthless shame, guilt, worry, and fears. (And sometimes vodka.)

Our drawers begin to overflow with regret, feelings of uselessness, and anxiety. Before we know it, we get so overwhelmed with the messiness of our souls that we lose our effectiveness as human beings, and we are at risk for going back to the place we just worked so hard to get out of. For me, that's a return to the hell of alcoholism; for you it could be bingeing again, depression, or being hooked on pornography. It might just mean that you're living in fear and worry again, or you find the old "character defects" you'd given up are creeping back into your life. It happens and usually so subtly that you don't even notice it. It's not one of those things that just occurs overnight either. It comes on slowly, a little bit at a time, just like my office, which starts out in "tip-top" condition, then begins to deteriorate, one piece of paper or Post-it note at a time. It happens because of a lack of daily maintenance that comes from not cleaning up life's little messes as you go, from not addressing your "spiritual maladies" as they present themselves, from not relying on God to direct your life, and from not staying focused on the responsibilities God has given you that require you to use your talents and experiences to help others.

You might as well just get used to the idea that Satan is always on the attack. In John 10:10 we read, "The thief (Satan) comes only to steal, kill, and destroy." Then in 1 Peter 5:8 we hear, "Be sober, be vigilant, be alert because your enemy, the devil, prowls around like a roaring lion, looking for someone to devour."

When we let "our guards" down and don't stay focused and diligent about maintaining our spiritual condition, we are unlocking that "lion's den" and letting Satan out where he will most certainly steal our sense of peace, kill our efforts to pursue God's will, and destroy our relationship with Christ.

So how do we keep our guards up? How do we keep our offices clean and organized at all times? God tells us in Ephesians 6:11: "Put on the full armor of God, so that you can stand against the devil's schemes." We must be ready, we must be diligent, and we must be on guard at all times. We can't afford to drift into apathy, laziness, self-will, or arrogance. For when we do, we have taken off the armor of God, and Satan comes creeping in.

I know, I know! You get it; don't let your guard down. That's vague and ambiguous, so let's firm it up and give you some practical tools and examples of how that will help you stay the course. The "AAs" call this a tenth step, and in its simplest form it just means cleaning things up in your life as you go. It means attending to and resolving mistakes you've made almost as quickly as you've created them. Even Dale Carnegie knew that when he said, "When you're wrong, admit it quickly and emphatically, then make it right."

Now that we've scoured our pasts, identified all the garbage in it, recognized our part in it, and cleaned up all our past mistakes, we have to work hard not to let it get all messy again, not to let it overwhelm us. It's no different than my office. When I begin to let things pile up on me, I'm in big trouble. I have to keep it clean as I go. Which means filing those new statements when they come in and throwing out the ones I don't need any longer. It means trashing the defective pens, so everyone I reach for will be one I can put to good use. It means addressing each item that comes into my office and handling it before it festers and eventually becomes a problem, a past due bill, a forgotten appointment, or a missed opportunity.

In our lives, that means taking care of our missteps immediately. Easier said than done, however. Some mistakes are easy to spot, others not so much. For example, just the other day I barked at some poor kid at Jiffy Lube who was trying to talk me into buying a new air filter. I was annoyed because they always seem to do that, whether you need one or not. After I curtly told him, "No, it's not even dirty, just put it back in my car," I immediately felt guilty about being short with him. I was emotionally disturbed, and here's the deal. When you are emotionally disturbed, you've just done something that is YOUR FAULT! So I thought to myself, "Is this my fault?" and I quickly realized it was. My character defect of not trusting people because all they're trying to do is hurt me was shining through. It was subsidized by two of my other character defects—that I always know what's best, and I don't listen to other people. After I'd considered this, I had to admit that I wouldn't know the difference between a clean or a dirty air filter, and maybe this kid was trying to do me a favor. At the very least, he was just trying to do his job of trying to sell me an air filter. He didn't need my attitude, and I didn't need to go home feeling guilt and anger, both spiritual maladies that make me want some relief that a guy like me just might find in the bottle. So I walked back inside and said, "I owe you an apology for being short. I wrongly assumed you were trying to sell me something I didn't need. Can you take a few minutes and tell me about air filters, show me the difference between a good one and a bad one that needs to be replaced?" He did, we looked at my air filter again, and he agreed that it wasn't too bad and we'd check it again the next time I came in. I left feeling resolved, and he went back to work feeling like he'd really provided some great customer service, and he had!

Other times the self-examination is a little more difficult, and you have to think a little deeper. At Narconon, we learned the ten behaviors of an antisocial person. One of them is: "He habitually selects the wrong target." This means we're upset about something, but we take it out on the wrong person. I've heard it referred to as "kicking the dog" as well! Was that me with the Jiffy Lube guy? Yep! I thought about it for a minute and was required to ask myself, "Was I mad at something else and taking it out on this poor Jiffy Lube guy?" The answer was yes. I was a little bent that my son's insurance premiums just went up after a little fender bender he had, that I had to shell out $1,200 for repairs on his vehicle, and that my sixteen-year-old daughter was just added to my policy. We all know how much insurance costs for a teen. Add to that my annoyance of feeling like every time I turned around I was having to fill up another car with $4-a-gallon gas, and I was having serious auto-anger issues! Looking deeper, it was something even one more removed from that. I had been asking both my son and daughter to get me their school report cards and their driving school and defensive-driving certificates so I could get roughly a 35 percent discount on their collective car insurances. They weren't responding or coming through with the information after repeated calls, texts, and e-mails, and I was frustrated. It wasn't important to them, and I was mad because it was costing me money. It was all exacerbated by a short (insert double meaning for "short") e-mail from my ex-wife saying she was too busy and didn't have time to deal with my son's car wreck, followed by a comment that I needed to take care of it. I read into that e-mail and (wrongly) determined that what it really said was, "I do everything for these kids because you're an irresponsible and selfish drunk; I'm sick of having to take responsibility for the kids all the time. Why don't you stand up and try to be the good and responsible father that you're not?" Steven Furtick calls this the "chatterbox," if you've ever read his book titled the same. The chatterbox inside my own head started telling me that I am a bad father, my kids don't respect or care for me, and my "ex" was right, I'm worthless. Overwhelmed with guilt, anger, and self-doubt, I lashed out at the wrong target, a Jiffy Lube employee! Maybe I should have explained all this to him? He might have just given me a free air filter to get me out of there!

If we let all our "junk" pile up on our spiritual desks, we're in trouble, so it is crucial to clean it up in the moment. I was feeling angry, hurt, guilty, "less than," and that the whole thing was MY FAULT. Okay, so how do I resolve and clean it up? I take it head-on and immediately. I think about my kids and quickly realize that I've been acting like the world revolved around me. Then I remember how many times I let them down, how many times I didn't respond to their needs, and how many times I thought I had more important things to take care of than their petty requests. How could I be angry with them when I had behaved in exactly the same way on numerous occasions, and in a lot more serious ways than some dumb insurance discount? I immediately called them both, told them I knew they were busy, explained to them in a kind tone the purpose and the importance of getting their transcripts and certificates, and then asked if there was anything I could do to help them secure the required documents. I finally apologized for being pushy and irritable. They also apologized for the delay, did ask for a little assistance, which I gladly gave, and I had all the information twenty-four hours later. My malady was gone, and they were just relieved I wasn't bugging them anymore! The other character defect I realized I was exhibiting was that I expect people to know what I want without effectively communicating my needs to them. Why was I angry? I was the one who wasn't specific in my communication!

To clear up the issue around my ex-wife's e-mail, I had to admit that I most likely read too much into it, and even if I hadn't, she had, in fact, assumed a majority of the responsibility for the children, and I was a bad and irresponsible father and husband for many years. She had a right to feel that way. Cleaning up that little e-mail and making a quick amends around it did not require a call or an e-mail response. She had been listening to my excuses, empty promises, and my "BS" for years. It required "action," which meant resolving all the issues around the fender bender without looking for acknowledgment or appreciation for doing something that I not only owed her after a lifetime of letting her down, but it was my responsibility as a father as well.

Let me try to make this "daily soul maintenance" exercise a little more formal, because it's not always practical or obvious during the day to recognize when we may have stepped out of bounds. It's not always appropriate either to spontaneously jump into an "on the spot" amends before having some time to think through what the real issues are behind what caused you to get upset. It's fine to immediately tell a Jiffy Lube guy you're sorry for being rude right there on the spot, but as you just saw the deeper inner turmoil I was experiencing around my ex-wife and kids, you can imagine how that amends was going to require a little more thought, patience, and prayer. So here is the best habit to get into which will help you keep up with the daily maintenance of your soul.

At the end of EACH day (not just when you're feeling off), sit down in a quiet place for fifteen minutes and review your day. I usually do it in bed when I'm not distracted by all the stimuli around my house. It's best if you have a pen, a little pad of paper, a journal, or if you're fifteen, a clean spot on the underside of your forearm so you can jot a few things down. Writing things down helps make them clearer and more real. When we've quieted our mind, we simply review our day, from the moment we woke up until the very moment our day is ending. Recreate and walk through your entire day, including every detail, big or small, and ask yourself and God these questions. Where was I selfish today? Where did I cop a resentment? Was I dishonest anywhere in my day? Did I find myself afraid or in fear and worry? Was there someone I encountered in my day that I owe an apology to? Have I kept something to myself that should have been shared with a trusted friend or counselor? Was I kind and loving to everyone I encountered today? What could I have done better today? What little difference did I make in this world today?

The answers will come to you, and through this exercise you may discover that there is still a whole lot of work to do in your life! There are many days I'll come home feeling that it was a good day, and it usually was, but on reflection I'll realize there were many things that needed addressing. I was just looking back in my nightly journal and reading through a day that I had classified as a good day. I'll share it with you.

Notes from Mike's Nightly Review:

1) Where was I selfish?—A friend I know who is struggling with alcoholism called me twice and I didn't call him back because I was tired and wanted to go to the gym, and I was afraid I might have to go meet him.

2) Was I resentful today?—Yes. I was angry because someone at the office tattled on me for discussing a confidential transaction with another employee who really didn't need to be in the loop.

3) Was I dishonest today?—Nope. I can't think of anything dishonest I did today (not today, but I am always surprised at how many little dishonest things I do!).

4) Was I afraid or operating in fear today at any time?—Yes. The church was doing their annual background check on me since I lead some small groups, and I'm afraid they are going to find some things from my past that are going to embarrass and humiliate me.

5) Do I owe someone an apology?—Yes. I need to apologize to my friend who called twice for not returning his call.

6) Did I keep something to myself that was bothering me?—Yes. I'm a fifty-year-old man, but my mother keeps e-mailing me and telling me in a scolding way to take my Antabuse medication.

7) Was I kind and loving today?—Yes. I was kind and loving today! (This wasn't the Jiffy Lube day.)

8) What could I have done better?—I could have gotten up earlier and spent fifteen minutes with God. I should have called my alcoholic friend back. I should have checked in on a coworker whose daughter was just diagnosed with leukemia. I should have taken care of some work items that I decided to put off until tomorrow.

9) What difference did I make in this world today?—I sent an e-mail to a Christian coworker with a scripture verse I read that reminded me of how strong her faith was and what a good person she is. She replied and told me that made her day. I also caught a woman trying to lug a big box of files up a flight of stairs, and I took it from her and delivered it to her office. I praised and thanked some guys at work for their great efforts on a big deal we've been working on. I smiled at strangers.

There's a lot more that happens in a day than you think! Some good, some not so good. So now that I have my little daily review, I have to look at it seriously because, as insignificant as it sounds, there's some danger in it. There are a few "Post-it" notes and "bad pens" in there that I need to clean up before they become bigger problems. There are some little tadpoles of guilt, anger, resentment, and fear that, if not addressed, will turn into a big ugly frog before long.

So after making this little fifteen-minute review, I turn to prayer and I ask God to forgive me for the mistakes I've made today. I thank Him for the blessings of the day, then I ask Him to show me what corrective measures I need to take for the things that happened in my life today, and I jot them down on my "to do" list for the next day. So my prayer goes like this . . .

"God please forgive me for being selfish and not calling my friend today. Take away the resentments I have against my coworker who tattled, against my mother for reminding me to take my medication, and forgive me for not reaching out to my hurting coworker whose daughter has leukemia. Take away my fear around the background check and allow me to serve you through the church where you best see fit. God, I thank you for keeping me sober today,

for my job, for my parents and family that love me, and for giving me a few small opportunities to allow others to see You in me.

Lord, please remove from me the negative emotions I experienced today, show me what corrective action I should take tomorrow, and provide me with an opening to take that action. Amen." Then I sleep like a baby!

The next morning, it all becomes obvious to me. I get up fifteen minutes early and spend some time in God's word. I know I have to call my friend, the struggling alcoholic, apologize for not getting back to him, and then meet whatever need he has. I have to approach my coworker and apologize for not being discreet about a confidential transaction. I need to send my mom an e-mail and tell her I am taking my meds and assuage her fears and worries over my possible relapse into the nightmare of alcoholism that I dragged her through. Finally, I make a point to carve out thirty minutes to talk to my coworker who's struggling over her daughter's battle, and I stand ready to offer help in any way she needs me.

Now that's a great daily plan, and I know when I accomplish these small tasks, my soul will feel clean and my spirit will rejoice! But guess what? The day happens, life happens, and today's corrections become tomorrow's "How was I kind and loving" and "What did I add to the stream of life?" Other things happen as well, that maybe aren't so positive, so . . . I do it all again tonight, because I want to keep my office and my life clean and organized, which will allow me to be as productive for God as possible.

Daily Maintenance Required!

CHAPTER 23

MY IMAGINARY FRIEND

My Grandma Dorothy was like that weird little kid with the imaginary friend except that she was ninety years old and still had one. She called him "Lord." Oftentimes I wondered if her senility wasn't getting the best of her. She was always carrying on a continuous and secondary conversation with this little friend she always referred to as Lord. No matter where she was, or who she was with, this guy always seemed to be right there with her, helping her through every moment of every day. "Who are you talking to, Grandma?" I used to always ask. She would raise the pitch of her voice with a little laugh and just say, "Oh, just the Lord." "Okay Grandma; well tell him it's time for him to go home so you can fix me a snack."

We all just kind of got used to the frequent conversations with her secret friend and never really put much more thought into what we considered to be just some little old lady's neurotic behavior. In hindsight, however, and years later, I realized that she was actually on to something important!

Grandma Dorothy would announce first thing in the morning, "Good morning Lord, how are you?" Then she'd mutter to herself, "Oh Lord, I hope there's some Earl Grey tea in the cupboard," and when there was, she'd say, "Oh thank you, Lord." She'd have her tea and then decide a trip to the grocery store was needed. After getting herself ready, she'd get in her car, leave her apartment complex, and drive to the first main intersection just down the road from where she lived and say, "Oh Lord, please give me an opening to make a left turn." One would open up, and she'd make the turn in her big Buick Riviera and say, "Thank you, Lord." Once the Lord had helped her find a good parking spot and she was inside the grocery store, she'd say with a nervous and worried laugh, "Oh goodness, Lord, please help me get a cart without a bad wheel." She would (and that's really a miracle), and follow it with a big proud smile and more nervous laughter. That dialogue would continue, helping her find the pie tins, the cocoa powder, and the Philadelphia cream cheese. It was the same routine on the way back to the retirement village. After putting away her groceries, she'd go down to the "old people common area" and chat it up with her friends. They would all swap stories about their days, their illnesses, and their grandkids. Every time she'd hear something good, she'd just blurt out, "Oh Lord, thank you for fixing Mamie's stopped up sink" or "for Dottie's new hip." When she heard bad news, she'd ask her imaginary friend for help right there on the spot. In the evenings she'd thank Lord for another day, tape up her beauty shop hair, and go to sleep.

A few years later and in her early nineties, she made a left turn into oncoming traffic, got broadsided, and was transported to a hospital where her soul eventually left, but body stayed behind. A year or so prior to the accident, she had resolved that due to the difficulty of making left turns into unyielding traffic, she was no longer going to make them. So from that point until the accident, every trip in that Buick consisted of right turns only. If the store was only half a mile down the street to the left, she wouldn't make that left, but would rather make four right turns (a total of four miles) to arrive at her destination safely. It made me laugh. Why on that particular day she decided to make a left turn, I can't say, other than that her friend, Lord, decided this was her day!

Before grandma died, I was fortunate enough to visit her in the hospital shortly after I had just returned from one of my early treatment center stints. She looked pretty rough (I suppose I did as well). I apologized for not having been in earlier to see her, but I'd been battling my own demons and hadn't been feeling too well. She grabbed my hand (she always wanted to hold your hand) and said, "I know honey; I've been talking to Lord about you a lot lately." It broke my heart. Here was this frail little old woman, hurting badly from a life-threatening accident, facing death, and all she was concerned about was my welfare. The "three" of us chatted for a while, and I could tell she knew it was her time. She wasn't scared in the least and was ready to go meet this Lord person she'd been living her life with for so many years. I would have been scared to death, but she knew this Lord fella so well that the transition and opportunity to meet him in person soon was actually exciting her. I suppose it's like the fear a kid has about getting transferred to a new school. He's frightened, unsure of what lies ahead, and anxious about the unknown. Then he makes a new best friend over the summer who's going to the same school in the fall, and he begins to feel safe, excited, and loses his fear because he'll be walking into the unknown with a friend. It just makes it easier to go when you know someone who's already there. My grandma knew someone already there.

I left the hospital feeling ashamed and unworthy to be her grandson. So I got drunk and stayed drunk until finally being sent off to yet another rehab. I wasn't there when she passed and missed the funeral, but for the first time in my life, I felt like I had a new friend up there who was watching over me, so I started talking to my imaginary friend, Dorothy, and am looking forward to seeing her again someday.

In the last chapter, we talked about daily maintenance of our spiritual condition and how to keep our lives clean and on the right track. Staying close to God dovetails into that and what this chapter is all about. So how do we stay close to God? We take a lesson from my Grandma Dorothy! We keep God on a "continuous loop" in our minds and in our lives, and we practice staying close and in contact with Him 24/7.

I struggle with arrogance and like to take credit for the good things in my life. It's very easy for me to "pat myself on the back," assuming all the blessings I have are a result of my own efforts. It's hard to need God, to seek God, and to communicate with God when you're taking all the glory for the successes in your life. So when I wake up every morning, I have to begin "humbling myself" before even pouring a first cup of coffee. That begins my conversation with God. "Lord, please take away my arrogance, my selfishness, my pride and ego. Help me understand that everything good in my life is a result of your blessings, and not of my own doing. Give me humility, Lord, so I can be of service to You today." Then I draw on my troubled past and begin to think about the people in this world who are less fortunate than me. I used to live in a cheap motel room, was sick, both mentally and physically, had no money, no healthy or positive relationships in my life, and no hope for the future. I've been locked in a jail, unemployed, had no health insurance, been in great debt, despised by many, and have even had to spend a few nights in my car because I had nowhere else to go. Then I think about what I have now: a great house; a paid-off car; an unbelievable job; cable TV; a pantry and a refrigerator stocked with good food; a warm bed to sleep in; two great kids who have allowed me back into their lives; a host of loving, caring, and supporting friends and family; and great hope for my future.

Did I do all of that? No way! There is no way a guy like me comes from the place I was in and into the place I am now without God's approval, God's blessing, and God's help. I didn't effectuate any of my blessings—God did. So rather than get caught up in taking credit for what good has become of my once miserable life, I get focused on asking God, "Why did you allow this transformation to happen to me? Why me, instead of someone else? For what reasons have you blessed someone so undeserving as me, Lord?" The answer is simple. God turned tragedy into triumph in my life so I could be an example to others in the same situation. It's hard to reach and convince a struggling alcoholic, whose life has completely fallen apart, that if you stay close to God, have faith, and work hard, God will turn it all around for you when you're still living in your car, can't stop drinking or using drugs, are unemployed, and separated from your family—and that it's all going to be all right. Your words don't support your current situation. People have to hear my story, especially the desperate and low parts of it, so they can relate. I have to be able to win their trust and credibly convince them that once I was in the same or worse shape than they are in now. Once they understand where I was in life compared to where I am now, only then do they become ready to allow God to help them through me. That's why God blessed me with the life I have today—to serve His purpose of helping others find that same victory through Christ. If I don't forward that purpose, God can take away all of my blessings just as easily as He gave them to me. I have to remind myself of that EVERYDAY and often times throughout the day.

So I ask God to humble me every morning, then I make a very generic request. I ask, "God please show me who you would have me help today. Make it obvious to me who that person is, and give me the courage and resources to do Your will today." That's it, and then I keep my eyes open and my mind aware of everything that is going on around me.

At Narconon, when you first arrive, you are assigned a counselor who pretty much spends the first week walking every square inch of the campus with you in tow. They do these ridiculous and weird little assignments as you're walking around the building, the campus, and the nearby lake. As you walk, the counselor will say, "See that chair over there," and you're supposed to look, see it, and say "yes," to which he responds, "good." Then he'll say, "See that picture on the wall?" "Yes." "Good." "See that fireplace, that window, that tree, that bird, that boat, that person, that car, that fence, that sign, that light fixture?" "Yes." "Good." "Yes." "Good." "Yes." "Good." (I thought to myself, this is the dumbest thing I've ever done.) After participating in this little exercise for an hour, three or four times a day, the counselor started another one that's similar. "See that wall over there? Go touch it." So you walk over and touch it. "Good." "See that tree? Go touch it." I do, then "Good." "See that chair, that railing, the flower, that mailbox?" "Touch it." "Good." "Touch it." "Good." "Touch it." "Good!" (I think to myself, I'm going to be crazier when I leave this place than when I came in.) What is the point of these bizarre exercises?

The point, and actually it's a good one, is that these exercises help us stay in the present, in the now, in reality. As human beings, we allow our minds to wander far away from where we are at this moment in time. We worry about our families, our jobs, our problems, our futures. We marinate on our pasts, our mistakes, our failures, and we get trapped in regret, remorse, and morbid reflection over decisions made or things done. We feverishly obsess over things that we have no control over at this moment in time, over things we cannot change. This exercise helps put the participant back into the present. Soon it becomes apparent that all you have is what is right in front of you—that chair, the wall, a person, and sunlight coming through the window. We can't do anything about the past; we can't worry or think our way into changing the future. All we have is the now. All we have is what is right in front of us these ten seconds, and that's exactly where God wants us all the time. When we're in this place, we have an awareness of what and who is in the "here and now," and since those are the only things we can affect, this becomes where God is asking us to be of service to others. When I was in rehab, my mind only wanted me to focus on broken relationships with my wife and kids, on fixing a failing business, on where I was going to live when I got out, what work I was going to find, and what messes I needed to clean up. But I couldn't do anything about those things at the moment. What I could do was talk to a struggling person sitting right in front of me, join a group of other alcoholics playing a board game and share a laugh, talk to the counselor standing right beside me, breathe in the fresh crisp air, and ponder the beauty of a calm lake or the turn of a golden oak tree. That's where God wanted me. That's where God needed me.

So when you're having this ongoing conversation with God, you're continually thanking Him for the blessings in your life, you're reminding yourself that you did nothing to deserve them, that these are gifts. You stay in gratitude for that. You continue to ask God to show you who you can help today, and you stay in the present, because that's the only place you'll be able to see the people God is trying to show you.

As you go through your day, keep talking to God, just like Grandma Dorothy did. My Pastor, Craig Groeschel, calls them "flare prayers." Scrap the "thees and the thous" and just toss up a quick one for everything that you encounter throughout the day. I walk into my office and whisper, "Okay God, help me be effective today. Let other people see You in me today." Then my phone will ring and I'll see it's such and such from such and such company and I know he's got a problem. I fire off a quick one to God, "Okay God, help me solve this man's problem." A while later I'm on a conference call with the executives from our firm, and I'll silently pray, "Lord, take away my nervousness and anxiety, keep me focused in this meeting, and help me make a contribution that helps the situation." After work, I'll thank God for a great day, ask Him if there is anything I can do for my family or friends that night, and if so, to please show it to me. I head off to the gym and thank God that I'm healthy, asking Him to show me anyone at the gym who He might want me to interact with. (It's amazing how many people God has thrown into the sauna with me!) Then I come home and ask God to keep me from vegging out on the sofa and watching mindless television, and to give me the energy and focus to do something productive that evening, like write this book, call someone who's been on my mind, or clean up my office!

That's what you call continual conscious contact or the "triple Cs." When you're staying close to God and doing His work, your life can be nothing other than a success. Your days are filled with peace, with joy, and with fulfillment. Your nightly reviews become more of a time for praise than a time for reflecting on where you may have been selfish, in fear, could have done better, or who you might have owed an apology to that day. When you stay close to God throughout the day, you'll find that you're not making those mistakes. When you don't make those mistakes, your life doesn't get messy, you don't generate spiritual maladies or discomforts that stack up on you, and you don't need to seek relief from them in destructive ways.

Most of us, myself included, usually just call on God and try to draw near Him when we're in trouble. When things are bad, or I'm going through a rough patch, it's amazing how close I can get to God. When things are good and life is running smoothly, I find myself falling away. That's usually why bad stuff happens to me! It's God's way of reminding me that I need to stay close to Him in good times and in bad. At some point we need to make that transition from only wanting to be close to God in order to relieve us of our difficulties into a place where we want to be near Him all of the time because of the joy we experience in His presence.

King David gives us a glimpse into his personal relationship with God in Psalms 27: 4-6 when he says, "The one thing I ask of you Lord, the one thing I seek most, is to live in the house of the Lord all my days." ALL OF MY DAYS, not just when he was in trouble. David realized that he was able to find great joy in life by continually improving his conscious contact with God. He recognized that God is ALWAYS there, but we are not always aware of his presence. Initially we learn that God is there when we have a desperate need, but from His intercession during our struggles, we can begin to see and trust that He can also bring us happiness in every aspect of our lives, both good and bad.

So we have to learn to "stop" being a part-time Christian and only calling on God when we "think" we need Him! God loves it when we come to Him with our burdens, but He loves it even more when we come to him with praise for all the blessings in our lives. I think about all the people I called upon for help when I was in the most active seasons of my disease. They were all glad that I reached out for help and for the most part were willing to come to my aid. Then I think about all the good times in my life. Did I call upon them then, to share my joys, my happiness, my victories? Did I remind them of my gratefulness for their help along the way? Did I praise their efforts and ask them how I could repay their compassion and kindness? No. No wonder people got tired of answering my desperate phone calls. The only time I ever called was when I was in trouble or needed something. God must feel the same way at times.

There is a saying: "Dance with the one who brought you to the party." That one is God. He brought you into this world. So stop dancing with other people who you think will bring you happiness and joy; stop dancing with the material possessions you think will bring you security; stop dancing by yourself and basking in the glory of your own accomplishments. Dance with Jesus. He brought you to the party, He is the one who will bring us the joy we are all seeking to find in this celebration called life, and at the end of the dance, He is the one who will take you home.

CHAPTER 24

WHERE DO I FIND THE HAPPINESS?

W hat is life all about? What is the goal? What are we all trying to find? Just ask anyone and they'll mostly likely answer "Happiness." Isn't that all we really want? What is the end goal of our every action, our every decision? Isn't every effort we make in this life an exercise in trying to find personal joy and fulfillment? Sometimes it's masked or framed up in different ways, but the underlying drive is the pursuit of happiness.

Sometimes, however, we're a little misguided in this drive to find it. Sometimes we think we know what will make us happy when we don't. So many people go through a lifetime process of trial and error in search of it. Our motives are good, our search for joy, comfort, rest, fulfillment, satisfaction, and happiness are all worthwhile human endeavors. It's just our ideas and notions of how to get it that can be flawed. Mine certainly were. For example, we think to ourselves, if I only had more money, I'd be happy. So we go out and work hard, work smart, play the game, compromise our families, our physical and mental health, ourselves and oftentimes, our integrity to get the thing—money—that we think will make us happy. If and when we do get it, we realize that it didn't bring us any more happiness. I've been rich before and can tell you firsthand, it didn't make me one ounce happier. As a matter of fact, it made me less happy because it caused me to buy a bigger house, a nicer car, to take grander vacations, join country clubs, and to frivolously spend on all kinds of things I didn't need. The more stuff I bought, the more stress I experienced, the higher my anxiety levels became, and the more responsibility I had to take on. My feelings of guilt increased, I became possessive of my stuff, was jealous of people who had more or better stuff, and my selfishness meter was off the charts! I didn't own my stuff; my stuff owned me! My quest for riches didn't free me and provide me with the happiness I expected; it imprisoned me and actually made me unhappy.

When looking back, the happiest time of my life was when I was flat broke. The year my ex-wife and I got married, we lived in a small apartment, had a used car, ate ramen noodles, woke up smiling, and went to bed laughing every night. We were truly happy, and it had nothing to do with money or possessions. I got a chance to do that again a few years ago coming out of long-term rehab. I was busted. I had no place to live, no vehicle, no job, no health insurance, no savings account, and only a few bucks in my checking account. I was able to get a small apartment, a used truck, a refrigerator full of groceries, and have a cupboard stocked with ramen noodles again! It was the greatest apartment in the world, and I felt like Eloise at the Plaza! My life was simple, and I was genuinely happy. All I was trying to find before with money was happiness, but it wasn't there.

Where Do I find the Happiness?

Why do we spend so much time looking for happiness in all the wrong places? (Hey! Isn't that a song? Or was it love?) I was certain that a good job would bring me happiness. Feeling a part of a productive organization, making a contribution to the business efforts, finding identity through work, and gaining the respect and admiration of my colleagues will bring me happiness. Yes, that's the secret. So I worked hard, I stepped over and on top of people, I cheated, lied, and manipulated in an effort to stake my claim, gain my position in the business world. But that brought its own bag of stresses, frustrations, sleepless nights, worry, disappointments, and responsibilities that weren't worth the tradeoffs. No. A good job never made me happy. Wait! Let me think about this? Maybe it did? Looking back, I remember opening our first gourmet coffee shop. We weren't making any money, my executive friends were less than impressed with a Wall Street trader turned barista, but that job made me happy. Why? It wasn't the money, the prestige, the success. It was because I got to make coffee, cappuccinos, lattes, and watch customer's faces light up as I handed them the beverage that started their day. I got a chance to smile at them, say something positive, and be the guy who had the power to start their every morning off with a little positive energy. The guy who could "pick them up" at the end of the day, give them a moment or two of my time, and make them feel good about themselves, brighten them up with a little joke or a jab. I got to encourage people who were down, cheer up cranky or crying kids with a little sweet or a cookie. My job didn't make me happy, the money (or lack thereof) the business generated didn't make me happy, and the reputation of being a coffee store retail worker didn't make me happy. What made me happy was making other people happy! Hmmmm . . .

In our search for happiness, oftentimes we think other people can make us happy. We think, if I only had a cute girlfriend or boyfriend. If I could only find the perfect person to marry I'd be happy. Then we find that little hottie and dive headfirst into that relationship, and guess what? We don't find happiness there either. Maybe we even take it a step farther and get married, because married people are so happy because of each other! Wrong! And that route, by the way, can get a little expensive! (But you don't want money anyway, because it didn't make you happy!) No, happiness isn't there either. Why not? The answer is because we're trying to use other people to make us happy, and that just doesn't work. It's actually really selfish on our part. The happiest people I know in relationships are not in them for themselves, they're in them because they've found someone that they can make happy. They find their joy and their contentment in the happiness that they can give away! When both partners have that kind of attitude, marriages are unbreakable!

So we keep looking . . . Maybe if I lost twenty pounds, won an award, shot an even par round, met someone famous, had a clean house, disposed of my credit card debt, had children who behaved better, won lawn of the month, hit the lottery, got a promotion, some braces, a new hairstyle, or published a book, I'd be happy.

Sorry, none of that will work, either. The only true happiness you will ever find for yourself comes from two things. The first way comes by bringing joy, happiness, comfort, and peace to other human beings. The second is through obtaining God's approval by serving the purpose that He has outlined for your life. Let's start with a simple example. What made you happier at Christmas, watching the excitement of your children as they opened up the gift they'd been dreaming about all year, or opening up your gift from them? Bringing THEM joy through the gift you had given, of course, made you happier. They may not have known it, but they felt exactly the same way. I remember how elated and giddy my kids became as they presented me with the gift they had bought for me. They couldn't wait to give it to me. They nuzzled up beside me, screaming, "Open it, open it Daddy!" The "Sounds of the '70s" CD didn't make me all that happy, but giving it to me sure made them happy! When my friend, Chris, died in that helicopter crash and I sat alone on the sofa weeping for the loss, my wife sat down, put her arm around me, and consoled me with great empathy. That didn't make me happy, but it made her happy because she had the opportunity to comfort me. It brought her joy to know that I needed a shoulder to cry on, a hug that told me "everything was going to be all right." She got to give away something that someone else needed and only she could provide. When my brother reached out to help me when I was at my lowest, I wasn't filled with joy for his help, but he felt great contentment by making a sacrifice that only he was willing and capable to make for a brother whom he loved very much. His words of encouragement, his physical and financial support, his love and understanding, were things I was in desperate need of, and he found joy in giving me what only he could. The host of other friends who helped me felt exactly the same joy, as did my other siblings. In all of these examples, the giver, the sacrificer, the empathic one are the real benefactors. They are the ones who derive true happiness, not the recipient. Giving brings happiness, not getting! I think we all knew that though.

Believe it or not, however, there is a wrong way, a wrong place, and a wrong time to bring joy, happiness, peace, and comfort to another in need. God has specially designed each one of us. We each have unique gifts, talents, personality traits, and possessions, all given to us by God. We aren't equipped to help everyone. We are not made to solve every problem, dry every tear, or bring peace to every situation, and that fact is critical in using what God has given us to help others. If you're flat broke and you see a large financial need, give the last of your measly savings to someone, but then can't make your own rent payment on the first of the month, you're probably not going to feel real happy. God didn't bless you with abundant finances, so he doesn't expect you to step up and meet that need when it arises, and you shouldn't. If you're an introvert and have high anxiety in large, unfamiliar crowds, walking into a homeless shelter or a nursing home to lift up and encourage lonely people through proactive conversation isn't going to make you happy—it's going to give you anxiety and fill you with dread about having to go back a week later. God didn't design you for that. If you don't have the gift of being able to relate to kids, you won't find much joy in volunteering to take the youth group on a camping trip. If you do and are disappointed, God will tell you, "That's not your thang!" If you're frightened of prisons, taking an AA meeting to the penitentiary is most likely not going to leave you on cloud nine when the cell doors crash closed upon your arrival. If you've never had a child die, lost a parent at a young age, been sexually abused, survived cancer, been through a divorce, or had a problem with drugs or alcohol, I highly doubt you'll find a lot of satisfaction trying to empathize, relate, or give advice to someone who is going through one of those exact trials. God didn't give you any of those experiences, so you have nothing to "give away" in those areas.

On the other hand, if God made you a person who has a "take charge" personality and you "step up" in a situation that has gotten out of control, calm tempers, bring peace, and establish orderly direction that results in a positive outcome for all, then you walk out of that meeting one happy and proud camper. If God has given you the gift of empathy, compassion, and the ability to listen and understand and you're approached by someone who is going through a tough time in life, is lonely, and needs to unload, then you're the man for the job. When you see the relief and gratitude from the person who simply needed some understanding and a sympathetic ear, you'll fall asleep with a smile on your face that night knowing you made a difference. If you've had the experience of being fired from a job or being unemployed for months on end, when a friend is experiencing the same thing and is down in the dumps, you get to share your experience, strength, and hope that lets this person know he's not alone in his struggles. You get to be his encouragement, his example of how to pull out of it, and when he does, and lands that job, who is happier? If God has blessed you with material wealth and you see a real financial need and meet it, hopefully anonymously, who feels the joy? You do! Because you were able to use the experiences and talents God entrusted to you to help others.

Genuine happiness in life comes from helping others, and the great news is that achieving it should be easy for you. If helping others is NOT easy for you, you're not helping where God designed you to help. No football team ever calls a play where the center goes out for the "long bomb" on two. The center is slow and has clumsy hands. He'll never outmaneuver or outrun a defensive back, and he'll never make a diving catch. He wasn't designed to help the team in that way, and neither he nor the team will find any happiness as long as he's trying to be the primary receiver!

The same holds true for each of us. God gave each one of us very specific talents and very specific experiences in life. Those and those alone are the tools you use to help others, to bring them happiness, joy, and peace. When your number is called and you respond by doing exactly what God created you to do, then and only then will you find happiness.

Let me give you some of my own examples. One Christmas our family decided we would adopt a struggling and needy family and buy their Christmas. God had certainly blessed us financially, and spending $1,000 did not put us in any kind of financial tight spot. So I thought to myself, "Yes, God has given me possessions, and I'm qualified to help in this way. That will make me happy." What I didn't realize was that part of the program required us to take the holiday "mother lode" over to their less-than-modest home, deliver the presents, food, gift cards, and decorations, and spend the evening with them while they and their children opened our gifts. I'd never been in need my whole life, I didn't have any friends who lived below the poverty level, I didn't have anything in common with these folks, and I wasn't in a position to relate to them, their needs, or their struggles. It turned out to be an incredibly uncomfortable evening. I could tell the father was ashamed that he couldn't provide a Christmas for his family, the kids were shy and skeptical, and the mother was grateful, but embarrassed. My anxiety levels exploded, I couldn't think of anything to say, make a connection, offer any hope or comfort. My awkwardness was just making everyone feel worse. We left, and I was filled with regret, guilt, and shame for what we had and they did not, and for how I must have made that father feel. My intentions were good, but God didn't design me for that task. What he designed me for in that situation was to make an anonymous contribution to that family, or go out and buy all the gifts and let someone else deliver them who could relate to their situation and give them more than just "stuff." They needed someone who could give them hope.

At another time, I thought volunteering to help out in the pre-school class at church would be a giving contribution that might bring me some joy. It turned out I wasn't overly fond of other people's kids, panicked when I detected a dirty diaper, scared some of the kids, made others cry, and was looking at my watch every five minutes wondering why this sixty-minute volunteer gig felt like a full day's work in a rock quarry. I was an overly stressed out basket case by the time church was over and the parents were picking up their little loved ones! I did NOT find any joy in that little endeavor that God clearly had not designed me for!

On the other hand, when I was asked to lead a small group of men through a program designed to identify the defects in our lives that were keeping us from being the spiritual leaders of our families, I left our meetings every Thursday night feeling happy, contented, close to God, and fulfilled. Why? Because God gave me many relative experiences of my own that could be shared with and related to this group of men. He gave me the kind of personality that allows me to disarm the skeptical, the untrusting, and the fearful. He gave me a self-deprecating sense of humor that comes off as humility. He gave me a friendly face and smile that made others lower their guards, open up, and not feel threatened around me. I have the gift of knowing how to build people up, how to encourage them, how to get them excited and engaged. I used my personal God-given talents and the experiences of my life that God allowed me to have and was able to use them to help others. When you find those times to touch someone's life, to effectuate a positive change in their lives, an opportunity to help lead them out of darkness and into the light of Christ, that is where you find some real happiness!

The other secret in finding genuine joy in this life comes from developing a meaningful relationship with Christ. There is only one person in this world who you should be trying to impress, and that's God. You find your happiness in what God thinks about you, not what others think about you. You find your happiness when you're doing what you know God wants you to do, even if it's not popular with all these difficult humans we have to live with. When God can say to you, "Well done, my good and faithful servant," that's the day you find a personal happiness you never thought existed.

CHAPTER 25

MY LIFE TODAY

What is my life like today? That's a tough question. If I had to sum it up in a sentence, I would have to say my life today is a "not-so-perfect miracle!" I was talking to my dad the other day and think he "called it what it was" when he said, "You know Mike, I've been alive for seventy-seven years and honestly don't think I have ever seen a miracle until now." I hadn't considered it much, but if a Christian guy tells you he's been on this earth for seventy-seven years and has never seen a miracle until he considers your situation, then you had better put some stock in it! He was obviously talking about my recovery from a hopeless state of alcoholism. He and mom had watched me disintegrate from a great son, loving husband and father, responsible businessman, and healthy middle-aged man, into a pathetic, hopeless human being trapped in an unstoppable death spiral that no earthly power could reverse. They had given up on me and were ready for, and fully expected, me to die. When your parents finally give up on you, you know it's the end, because parents never give up on their children, but that's how emotionally exhausted they were. I'd lost my wife, my kids, my business, my money, my self-respect, my health, and my mind. A shot to the head may have been preferable to everyone involved, rather than having to endure a slow and tortuous alcoholic death that seemed imminent, but one way or another I was a goner and everyone knew it.

Ten months later, I was sober, leading a recovery group of other addicts and alcoholics, back involved in the church, had begun to restore broken relationships with my children, family, and ex-wife, and replace them with forgiving, loving, and healthy attitudes. I had landed a great job back in the energy business, was back in great shape, met someone special, and even bought a house. I don't know what else you can call that except a miracle. Everyone figured, myself included, that at best I'd struggle to regain any semblance of financial security and would spend a lifetime toiling to mend broken relationships, reputation, and position. Every day, I wake up and look at my life and thank God for pulling me back from the gates of hell, scooping me up from the human trash heap I was lying in, and for giving me yet another opportunity to serve the purpose he has outlined for my life. I couldn't have done that on my own, and as hard as they tried, friends and family couldn't have done it either. There is only one explanation, only one plausible answer for how that could have happened, and that is that it was a miracle that comes from the all-powerful grace of God. For that I feel unbelievably blessed and special, but I also feel great responsibility for having been given another "kick at the kitty," as my sponsor used to say.

With that said, my life is far from perfect. I still find myself vacillating between inflated ego and humility, toggling between my own will and God's will for me, and volleying between regret over the past and staying focused on the future. I struggle with anxiety, loneliness, fear, and resentment. I still make a lot of mistakes. I find myself, at times, feeling very close to God, and other times far away from Him. That's all just a reality of the human condition. It doesn't go away. What changes, and what changed in me, was the ability to recognize it for what it was and to use the things I've learned, the things we've talked about in this book, to deal with it.

I'm glad I have those tools, because unfortunately my Mr. Hyde's not totally dead yet. He's in remission right now, and someday God may help me eradicate him completely, but for now I wait patiently. But my Mr. Hyde also waits patiently, lurking, haunting, scheming, keeping me on my toes, and awaiting the moment I wander from God without my protection so he can attack me again. In 1st Peter 5:8, God tells me to "Be sober, be watchful, your adversary the devil walks about seeking whom he may devour." I pray to be always ready and never overconfident, or the man I used to be will rise up in me again.

Just the other day I was watching an old home movie of my siblings and me as little kids. We were squinting and waving into that 8mm camera with the eye-damaging giant light bulb affixed to the top. We were laughing and playing with not a care in the world. As I watched the "little me" from some forty years ago, I began to weep and wished I could go back and talk some sense into that kid. Tell him about the pitfalls ahead. Spare him from a lot of pain that I knew now lay ahead. But I couldn't, so I just wept for how innocent, how pure, and how protected from the world he was. He had his whole life ahead of him, and I wondered what was going through his little undeveloped mind. I'm sure it wasn't the thought that someday he'd be an alcoholic that hurt everyone who crossed his path. That someday he'd put his own kids through hell, that someday he'd end up a fragile basket case lying on the floor of a cheap motel room in a pool of blood and vomit. The remorse and regret was overwhelming for me, so I just cried and grieved that loss. Then it was over. The old me would have watched that video, then gone out and bought a bottle of vodka from the sadness it invoked, then watched it over and over until finally passing out. The new me recognized it for what it was. The past. A past I can't change, but have to learn from. I can look at that boy though and take a page from his book and know still that I have an opportunity to be a fifty-year-old little boy who laughs and plays, who doesn't have a care in the world and can be as innocent as I choose to be from this day forward.

The truth is, I don't want to go back. My life has turned out exactly like it was supposed to. Not a path I would have picked, nor would anyone near me have probably chosen for me, but it was the path designed for me, or at least allowed by God for me. Without all of those experiences, both good and bad, I wouldn't be the person I am today. I wouldn't have the "life tools" that God intended for me to have to serve my purpose. So having had these experiences, having had a spiritual awakening, a watershed of self-awareness, and a reunion with Christ, "How has my life changed?"

For starters, I wouldn't really call it a change, it was more like the "old me" was just gone. I'm not that person anymore; I'm someone completely different than I was just a few short years ago. A very large part of me died, and I've become a new human entity who has begun the process of human development again. The finished product is still under construction and will be for some time to come. The realization of who I used to be was clear, and I knew beyond a shadow of a doubt I no longer wanted to be that person. God is helping me destroy him for the most part, and through doing the work and seeing the person I had deteriorated into to, He gives me a very good outline and road map for who I'd like to inversely become. I can see it, I can claim it, and now I just have to earn it.

I can't get back the relationships I used to have, and frankly, I don't want them back "as they were." They were broken and defective, mostly from my own doing. My mind romanticizes a past time when I thought I had great relationships with my children and my wife, and I find myself wishing I could return to that happy place, just like I dreamed of returning to my childhood as I watched the old 8mm films. But I can't go back, real or imagined. That time has passed, and I can drive myself to the gates of insanity trying to return to a moment or place in time that no longer exists. Everything has changed, and all I can do from today forward is to write a new story, my new story. I like that, because I don't want to be the father I used to be to my children. I don't want to be the kind of husband I used to be with my ex-wife. I want to be better, I want to be different. I want to design healthier relationships that are infinitely more rewarding than the ones I used to know in the past. That requires a paradigm shift.

It means going from ex-husband in a romantic relationship to a kind and caring friend, supportive co-parent, encourager, cheerleader, responsible family member, and a promoter of Lori's happiness. It means to be an assistor of her life's goals and dreams and a contributor to her peace and happiness in any way that she will allow me to contribute. It means shifting from the notion of traditional family "dad" to self-sacrificing, loving, stand-up, responsible dad who meets the needs of his children as they exist today. It means to be a new and different kind of "rock" for them, to be a leader through positive action and example. To be a beacon of hope, faith, and strength they can call on when times get rough for them. I can be their mentor, their friend, and their unwavering lighthouse of stability. That's one way my life is different. I'm not holding on to the past; I'm forging a new future with my ex-wife and children.

My life is different with my parents, siblings, and friends as well. I no longer use them to get what I want. I used to take advantage of their kindness and responsible hearts to secure money, resources, shelter, pity, empathy, and cover for responsibilities I should have been taking myself. I used to inconvenience them at will with no regard for their lives. I used to fill them with worry, anxiety, and fear with no consideration of how they may feel. I'm not that guy anymore. Today, I try my best to think about their needs, their feelings, their hopes and dreams and how I can assist them; how I can return the love and compassion they've shown me. I do my best not to do anything that would cause them worry and fear, and I try to pitch in on more than my share of family responsibilities. I try to be someone they can count on, someone they can trust, and someone they can be proud of. That's how I'm different.

My paradigms of what the "good life" is have changed as well. I've had to relearn how to have fun, to be entertained, to enjoy activities, and to find different ways of extracting joy out of life. Everything used to revolve around drinking. I used to love spending all day Sunday watching NFL football and drinking myself in and out of naps. When I quit drinking, I would complain that Sundays just weren't fun anymore, that watching the NFL just wasn't enjoyable without beer. I'd feel sorry for myself and opine for a chance to have a few beers, catch a buzz, and watch the games. What I realized is that I don't really like sitting around wasting an entire day watching a bunch of teams I could care less about. It was the drink I was after; the game was just an excuse. It's like cold shrimp! Do you like to eat cold shrimp by themselves? I don't; they're gross tasteless little crustaceans with a disgusting vein full of something in them! But give me some cocktail sauce and I love chilled shrimp! What I'm saying is that I really just love the cocktail sauce! So I realized a lot of things about what I like and what I don't. Football marathons are not one of them. So when football season rolls around, I usually pass on most games, and when I do watch them, they're the shrimp, and the cocktail sauce I throw on them is the enjoyment of having friends and family around to watch them with. The joy in my life is having a relaxing and fun afternoon with my kids; the football is secondary.

I went to a bar the other day (not to drink) and realized I can't stand loud, smoky bars, crowded with drunk people and dirty everything. Hanging out in them used to be my most coveted pastime. I've changed and would much rather take a walk or a bike ride, watch a movie, or play a board game with someone I love. I'm not interested in glad handing with muckety-mucks from high society, but would rather have open, honest, and vulnerable conversations with people of faith or commonality. I'm learning to enjoy a cup of coffee on the back patio as the sun rises, breathing in the fresh air, and resting my soul as I think about the day ahead. My mornings used to consist of knocking the cobwebs out of my head, fretting over what the day would bring, and being preoccupied with when I was going to be able to get that next drink. I'd spend the early morning planning hours figuring out what I could take out of life; now I spend my mornings figuring out what I can give back to it.

I'm like the person who's suffered a major brain injury. I've got to teach myself how to walk again, to talk again. I can't go back to my old way of doing things, and as much as I miss it sometimes, I have to grieve its loss, let it go, and create a new life for myself. I can't go out and drink a few beers with my friends after golf, mellow out with a glass of wine in front of a roaring fire, or be the life of the party after a few cocktails. I'm not that person, so I struggle to find who I am and how to rebuild a different life. It's frightening because I don't know anything else, but it's exciting because I have the opportunity to be the man I've always wanted to be, the man God designed me to be.

I find my mind more than ever in the present, instead of stuck in the past or worried about the future. I'm in the moment more often when my kids are around, when I'm with friends or family. My full attention is normally on who I'm with and where I'm at, rather than a million miles away.

I have a lot more conversations with God than I used to, and that's a big change. They're different kinds of conversations as well. I'm not asking God to get me out of this jam or that pickle; I'm spending my time thanking Him for the blessings in my life and asking him to show me how I can help other people. That's a big change!

I no longer spend my workdays figuring out what I can extract from my employer. I go to work with a little prayer to God asking Him to allow me to be the best example I can be of a Christian in the workplace, and then I spend my days thinking about how I can add value to my company, how I can be of help to others around, instead of trying to undermine their efforts. And I do my best to hold up my end of the employment bargain, which is a full day's work for full day's pay.

I spend a lot more time these days watching, observing, and marveling at the greatness of God that surrounds my world. I notice people, I listen a lot more than I talk, and I take in and appreciate the sun, the rain, the wind, and the snow. I love the fall more than any other season, and I recognize that I am in the "fall" of my own life and love it just as much, but I can still appreciate the things I've learned from spring and summer, and I look forward to the winter. I'm aware.

Something else that's different about me is my approach to life. Before having this awakening, I was a reactive creature, responding to the whims of the world and the people in it. The wind dictated the direction of my life, and it didn't always blow me toward warm and calm waters. In fact, it rarely did. One of my great transformations came from the removal of two of my character defects, "always blaming others and playing the victim." Once I recognized those, asked and had God remove them, I became a person who now takes responsibility for himself. A large part of taking responsibility for yourself and one attribute I gained from this process was becoming proactive in everything I do. I do not let others deter me from the path I believe God is leading me down any longer. I am responsible for everything that happens to me and for me. That means I have to be aware of all the distracting stimuli around me and diligent about protecting my course and my purity with Christ. My armor is on, my shield is up, and my own actions yield my own results. God leads my way, and I am proactively treading the path He has laid out for me.

Part of that proactive approach to life revolves around knowing what weakens me and what strengthens me. I now choose who I associate with, where I go, what I listen to, what I put into my body, and how I allocate my time. I am responsible for myself, and I've realized that when you're not, the world will take advantage of you, and you'll end up someplace you never intended to be, wondering to yourself, "How'd I get here?" Here's a great example. Every other radio station in Tulsa plays country music, so no matter where I scanned, I always got country radio, so I just resigned myself to that genre and started to get used to it. I began to get brainwashed with the likes of such country greats as "Drink a Beer," "Bottoms Up," "Save Water, Drink Beer," "Drunk on a Plane," "Whiskey and Water," "Cold One," "Hey Bartender," "Drinks after Work," "Drunk Last Night," and the list goes on! Why is an alcoholic feeding his brain with song after song that glorifies getting drunk? Before long, I was singing along and thinking to myself, "Those cowboys have got it right. I just need to go out and drink my problems away!" I don't need to feed my mind with that kind of garbage; I'm an alcoholic for God's sake!

I did the same thing with mouthwash. I just got in the habit of buying Scope because that's what the advertisement told me to do and it's what I've always recognized on the grocery store shelves. I didn't even consider the fact that it was 15 percent alcohol. (It's not like I was drinking the stuff, but I have tried it before when I was desperate.) So when you have a disease of the body as well as the mind, even a rinse with 15 percent alcohol sets off a physical craving that can be hard to overcome for an alcoholic. So I CHOOSE to use alcohol-free mouthwash these days. Upon a comprehensive review of my actions, I found the list of reactive behaviors I was exhibiting quite overwhelming as I began to uncover each one. Recognizing them helped make my life different. Now God and I are in charge of my life, not what the world parades in front of me!

I would have to say, however, that the biggest change in me, the best part of my new life, is that I'm getting comfortable with just being me. I don't miss the days of having a split personality, not just the Jekyll and Hyde part that came from drinking, but from living a double life of exhausting myself by trying to be whom I thought I needed to be in every situation. I used to pride myself on being such a chameleon and with my ability to adapt to any social situation, but I've realized the luster was really just a two-faced facade, a disingenuous fraud, and a sickening fake front I spent most of my life trying to desperately maintain. That shine is gone, and it was a thin cover anyway. My secrets are out, and I don't have to hide anymore. My friend was right when he said, "So what if everyone finds out, then what?" Well, nothing! I don't care what they think anymore anyway. I have to humble myself every day, face my fears by trusting in God, and only care about what He thinks. I'm different because I spend most of my time trying to impress God instead of other people. So then what? God is proud of you!

Finally, when I think about what my life is like today, the word "peace" comes to mind. I've never had peace before! I had no idea what that might look or feel like, but now that I've been able to experience a little bit of it, I can't believe what I was missing! I'm hooked. So where does this new sense of peace come from? I'll tell you, but its best described in a movie called *The Horse Whisperer* with Robert Redford and Kristen Scott Thomas. Thomas asked Redford where he finds his peace and he responds, "Getting up every morning and knowing what I have to do that day, I suppose, is where I find my peace."

That's where I've found my peace as well. Embracing my life's past experiences, identifying the talents that God has given me as an individual, and using those experiences combined with my talents to know my purpose. Knowing what my purpose is, knowing how God wants to use me, allows me to wake up every morning knowing what I have to do that day, and just like Redford, that gives me peace.

To summarize what my life is like today . . . It's a beautiful mess, but it's a miracle. It's far from perfect, but progress is perfection in God's eyes, and just so you pop country folks don't think I'm picking on your music, I'm going to end this chapter with a pop country lyric that best describes what my life is like today. Tim McGraw says it best, "I ain't as good as I'm gonna get, but I'm better than I used to be." (See, they're not all about drinking!) You know what, that song is so "spot on" I'm going to print the whole thing.

"Better Than I Used To Be"

I know how to hold a grudge
I can send a bridge up in smoke
And I can't count the people I've let down, the hearts I've broke
You ain't gotta dig too deep
If you wanna find some dirt on me
I'm learning who you've been
Ain't who you've got to be
It's gonna be an uphill climb
Aww honey I won't lie

My Life Today

I ain't no angel
I still got a few more dances with the devil
I'm cleaning up my act little by little
I'm getting there
I can finally stand the man in the mirror I see
I ain't as good as I'm gonna get
But I'm better than I used to be

I've pinned a lot of demons to the ground
I've got a few old habits left
But there's still one or two I might need you to help me get
Standing in the rain so long has left me with a little rust
But put some faith in me
And someday you'll see
There's a diamond under all this dust

I ain't no angel
I still got a few more dances with the devil
I'm cleaning up my act little by little
I'm getting there
I can finally stand the man in the mirror I see
I ain't as good as I'm gonna get
But I'm better than I used to be

I ain't no angel
I still got a few more dances with the devil
But I'm cleaning up my act little by little
I'm getting there
I can finally stand the man in the mirror I see

Killing Mr. Hyde

I ain't as good as I'm gonna get
But I'm better than I used to be

CHAPTER 26

RELAPSE!

It has always been a widely held belief that all great art, or in my case writing, comes from pain. Van Gogh painted *The Starry Night* while in emotional torment, then later decided to cut off his own ear. I am supposing because he couldn't think of anything else to paint or just ran out of red paint. (Okay, that was inappropriate.) Milton penned *Paradise Lost* after losing his wife, his daughter, and his eyesight. Hemingway was tortured by drink and depression, but wrote some of the world's most classic books. These artists chose not to recoil in passive suffering, but instead turned their pain and their adversity into something valuable.

Art, literature, and personal inspiration that can manifest itself in many forms of expression, are simply reflections of humanity, and humanity's greatest challenge has always been to overcome adversity. Adversity inspires art, literary works, and an encyclopedia full of positive action, benefit, and victory over the human condition. Suffering and failure do not have to happen in vain; they can and almost always do have a silver lining inspiration with a purpose.

I'd like to say that is why last year I chose to have a massive relapse, spend three days back in hell and three more days recovering only to tear down all the personal, emotional, and spiritual progress I'd made over the last several years. It was because I needed some creative insight, I had writer's block and couldn't quite get this book finished, but that's not the truth. I'm also hardly comparing myself to a Van Gogh or Hemingway either, as you can tell from my writing style. I just flat out relapsed. I went on a bender to end all benders, and I can tell you those AAs are right when they say it's a progressive disease, because not only did I drink an unbelievable amount of alcohol, but I think I set a lifetime consumption record after being completely sober for nearly three years!

The truth is, I can't tell you why. There is very little defense against the first drink, the first hit, the first chocolate donut, the first purchase at Macy's, or the first look at porn on the Internet. What I can tell you for many of us in this category, once that decision is made, that action taken, it becomes nearly impossible to stop yourself, and you must be stopped by some other force, like the police, an institution, possibly another person (but only in rare cases), or the ultimate halting mechanism, death. I can tell you I've been intervened on by three in the past and almost the fourth on a handful of occasions.

There's not a lot of gory details I can give you on this one, primarily because I don't remember much of it (that's both the beauty and the horror of a blackout). I do know that prior to the relapse, I was feeling extremely overwhelmed and stressed at work, had had a verbal altercation with someone, and had put myself in an awkward position during a "drink-filled" business outing. I was also bothered by the fact that I was about to turn fifty, was feeling lonely and regretful about a broken relationship from a few months earlier, and was dealing with some issues associated with the kids. I was definitely in a funk and experiencing a wide range of negative emotions from anger to fear to depression. No one catalyst was that unmanageable, but roll them into the perfect emotional storm and I was in need of immediate relief. I became a perfect case study of the "cycle of addiction" we talked about back in Chapter Eleven, and the threefold illness kicked in with a vengeance.

I was most definitely suffering from the emotional and "spiritual" malady we have discussed, wanted quick relief from that uncomfortableness, and allowed the "mental" component of the disease to kick in and begin to tell me lies. I said to myself, "I just need to get away for a few hours, decompress, and forget about everything. I'll just get one bottle of wine, unwind tonight at home, and tackle the issues tomorrow." My sobriety, most of us alcoholics' sobriety, is that fragile. It always boils down to one seemingly harmless thought and one defining, yet vulnerable and careless moment. I didn't hesitate on my way home from work pulling into that liquor store, and before I knew it, I was walking out the front door with not one, but two bottles of wine. A couple of hours later the fog had settled in and the "physical" part of the disease had taken over. From there, most of it is still a blur. I have truncated memories of going back out for more alcohol, but most of the proof was later found scattered around the house and garage in the form of empty whiskey bottles and a recycling bin full of enough aluminum to build a new Ford F-150. I was still finding remnants weeks later. There are thinly painted recollections of AA friends and other friends, including my brother, coming and going, as well as trips from one friend's house to another and then back.

I'm later told my helpers became my providers, as they continued to supply me with beer for fear I might suffer from a seizure. Several days, unknown to me, passed by and the first real moment of gravity comprehended found me lying in bed, shaking, sweating, withdrawing, and wondering what just happened.

I can imagine you're asking yourself if you've gotten this far in the book, "Has what this guy been telling us just been a load of crap? He can't even stay sober himself long enough to finish a book on how to stay sober!" It would be a fair question, but this book isn't about staying sober, or pure, or eliminating porn, or purging. It's about identifying the things that are blocking you from God. It's about learning how to hear God's voice, his purpose for your life, killing the "Mr. Hyde" in you, and learning how to become the person God intended for you to be. Life is a war with many battles. Satan is always on a mission to steal, kill, and destroy your soul. I lost a battle and you will too, but God always wins the war, and if you've got him on your side, you'll win the war as well. So will I.

In every relapse, in every lost battle, there are always truths, insights, revelations, and new inspirations. It's just God's way of redirecting you from a wrong turn you've made on the way toward His Kingdom. In the Civil War, had General Meade pursued General Lee after his retreat at Gettysburg, the war would have surely ended. Lee had lost the battle but had not yet lost the war. On second thought, that's probably not the best example, because eventually the South and Lee did lose the war. Maybe a better one would be the fact that George Washington lost more battles than he won, but his persistence, his courage, his faith, his determination, and his belief in what he was fighting for eventually handed him a Revolutionary War victory and complete independence for a United States of America. My apologies if there are any Europeans reading this book! You didn't want us anyway.

The "truths" in my recent lost battle were that I failed to take my own advice. I failed to continue to rely on God, I failed to continue to enlarge my spiritual life. The spiritual maladies we've talked about over and over in this book began to pile up on me. I allowed fear to creep back into my mind, and allowed anxiety, depression, jealousy, anger, and insecurity to join the party. I didn't take them to God, I didn't discuss them with a trusted friend or confidant, and I didn't allow myself to turn my thoughts to helping someone else so I could get out of my own self and out of my own self-centered selfishness. Instead my weak mind and my weak will looked for the easiest thing I could find to relieve my internal and emotional discomfort. In my case, that's a bottle of Jack Daniels and an eighteen-pack of Natural Light! Sure, they worked and worked well for a little while, but before long the things that provide you immediate comfort and relief boomerang on you and leave you incomprehensibly demoralized. They wreck your soul, deflate your hope, and amplify, times ten, the unmanageable "spiritual maladies" that kicked off the entire process in the first place. Never a good risk/reward proposition, but we don't care when we're feeling emotionally low. We've already let those "lines of communication" with God become caked with ice again, and that's exactly what I did. By not taking care of my emotional and spiritual well being, I allowed my best personal defects to resurface. My pride and ego swelled, I lost all humility, I started blaming others, I shirked responsibility, and I got greedy and selfish. I stopped caring about others, stopped thinking about how I could be of service to God, and began to think only of myself again. A common human problem, but that doesn't make it right. That is not the person I want to be. That is not the person God intended for me to be. That is not the person that God says I am, but we can't live this life on our own. We need God's power, God's strength, and God's direction, and if we're smart enough to ask for it, He gives it to us. I'm not that smart and continue to prove that pain is a better motivator for me than insightfulness, reliance on others, and prayer! I left that beautiful green pasture, it then started to rain on me a bit, then a little harder, and before long it got very dark and windy. Did I turn around and head back toward my Shepherd? Nope! I headed for the electric fence, got shocked and stabbed with barbed wire, and went through enough pain again to head back to the safety of the herd. Hopefully you'll be smarter when one of life's storms begins to rain down on your soul.

So now I search for silver linings. I search for lessons. I search for what God was trying to tell me. I search for that narrow path He is asking me to tread. Maybe I should stop searching and start asking God for the answers. If I remember correctly from an earlier chapter, God will speak to me through His word, through circumstance, through other people, and through my own thoughts and intuitions. So I open my Bible (well, first I check the Internet for God's word on straying from the path he has outlined for us) and I find Isaiah 53: versus 6-12. I'll paraphrase, but it says, "All of us have strayed away like sheep. We have left God's path to follow our own. Yet the Lord laid on him the guilt and sin of us all. He was oppressed and treated harshly, yet he never said a word. He was led as a lamb to slaughter. And as a sheep is silent before the shearers, he did not open his mouth. But it was the good Lord's plan to crush him and fill him with grief. When he sees all that is accomplished by his anguish, he will be satisfied. Because of what he has experienced, my righteous servant will make it possible for many to be counted as righteous." In Proverbs, chapter 1, verse 33, it says, "But all who listen to Me will live in peace and safety, unafraid of harm." In Jeremiah 15:19, God says, "If you return, then I will restore you. Before Me you will stand, and if you will extract the precious from the worthless, I will make you my spokesman."

That's a pretty good answer, don't you think? I strayed like a clueless sheep. God laid on me the guilt of what I was doing and helped me recognize that I was "off His path" and sinning again. I was silent before God and did not open up my mouth to Him or any other trusted friend. So the Lord crushed me and filled me with grief through a relapse. But now I see that if I will just listen to God, if I will return to His path, he will restore me. I will be able to see what has been accomplished through my anguish over the relapse. And if I stand before God with repentance in my heart, He will allow me to see the precious from the worthless, and God will make me his spokesman! Wow! Right there in black and white. So I did. I asked God for his forgiveness; I returned to the path He has designed for me. I "opened my mouth" and talked to friends about my troubles and the darkness that led up to my slip, and now I can take the precious and valuable lessons from this worthless relapse experience and once again become God's spokesman in an effort to lead others to Christ and sharpen existing Christians. As God says in Proverbs 27:17, "Iron sharpens iron."

So what precious lessons have I learned about myself that I can share with others? What great insights and revelations have I had that have become valuable tools I can use to lead others closer to Christ? What inspiration has come from this lost battle? The first thing I realized was that I and I alone was responsible for myself. I don't want to say that no one else cared, because they did. No one else, however, could help me. I had to be "willing" to help myself. I wasn't at that place during the relapse. I was reaching out to people like a drowning man, desperately searching for something or someone to grab on to. Someone I would probably have just taken down with me. Someone other than God to save me, take responsibility for me, fix my problems. That character defect of "not wanting to take responsibility for myself" reared its ugly head. I realized that I'm really in this alone when it comes to the world and the people in it, BUT I don't have to be alone if I choose to engage God. I realized that I had lost a significant amount of humility over the last few years, that I'd grown arrogant again, cocky, and was living way more in my own will than in God's. I realized that although I'd been spending two days a week trying to help others in recovery, I'd let my own personal diligence lapse in relation to sobriety. I understood that I am no good to others unless I am good to myself, the same reason the airlines tell you to put your own oxygen mask on first before you put one on the child sitting next to you. If you pass out while trying to help someone next to you, you're both dead!

I also came to the realization that we all fail, and it was hard for me to believe, but even I can fail! Can you imagine that? With that said, I shouldn't, you shouldn't use that as an excuse. I've done that in the past as well. "Well, we all fail, so I might as well go ahead and get good and drunk." I'm not saying that at all. What I'm saying is that even among our best efforts in life, there are times we will fail, and when we do, we are faced, yet again, with another choice. A choice that says we can wallow in our misery, be depressed, be downtrodden, be the victim, and lose all hope. OR we can keep our chin up and say, "God, okay, I just failed. What happened? Where did I go wrong? What are you trying to teach me here? How can I use this experience to fulfill the purpose you have for me? God, I am sorry that I have turned away and gone the wrong direction. Help me get back on Your path." As I've said over and over, God does not make terms too hard for those who seek Him. If you'll ask Him these things, He'll show you, and inside of floundering weakness, you'll be strengthened beyond the place you were before your struggle, in my case, the relapse. Failure has always been seen as a negative word, but it really should be one of the most positive and uplifting words in the English language! From failure comes the greatest things in life! Thomas Edison was fired from his first two jobs and told he was too stupid to learn anything. Henry Ford failed five times and went broke before he gave the world the automobile. R.H. Macy failed at business seven times before his famed Macy's stores finally took off. Babe Ruth held the record for most strikeouts before he set the record for home runs. Walt Disney was fired early in his career for "lack of imagination!" The list goes on and on. All of these people found strength in their failures and went on to do amazing things in this world.

So I failed. I moped around for a couple of days, got discouraged, decided to play the victim, refused to take responsibility, tried to figure out who to blame, and had anxiety attacks about what everyone else was going to think about me. Then I realized all those things were the very best of my character defects, the same ones I'd figured out about myself and asked God to remove. Obviously "not removed," but certainly "toned down," since I was at least able to recognize them after a couple of days of feeling sorry for myself. So I had a relapse! I'm not proud of it, I'm ashamed of it, I'm setback by it, and I'm disappointed by it, but I have a choice and so do you. I can stoke these negative emotions and allow them to become spiritual maladies again that require relief I might find in the bottle, or I can ask God to remove them, talk to a friend about my feelings, get some encouragement, and take what I've learned and ask God to show me someone I can be of service to. From that maybe I, too, can assist someone with the light bulb, the automobile, or the home run record of their life!

What else have I learned? That no one goes through life on an unwavering upward trajectory. Shooting stars always burn out. Life is about two steps forward and one step back. Sometimes you get lucky and you'll make five positive steps forward before you take a step back, and other times in life, you'll fall five steps behind before you can muster one small stride forward. The point is "progress, not perfection." The world demands perfection from us, and if we allow the things of this world to drive us, we will always be destined for failure and disappointment. It's all about you and God. Keep telling yourself that you're not perfect, but God is. Be content and proud with simply progress. Don't let "perfection" be your benchmark for happiness and success. It's a losing proposition.

Finally, I'm telling myself, but more importantly, I'm telling you, that "I'm not perfect." I'm merely trying to make progress in this journey called life, just like you are. I'm no authority on anything. I shouldn't be considered any "respected" teacher on life or how to best manage it; I'm simply sharing my experiences. You and I are exactly the same—we're both just trying to navigate our way through life the best we can. Sometimes by ourselves, under our own wills (which almost always ends in disaster), sometimes as co-CEO with God (which isn't disastrous, but certainly never ends up being overly successful), and sometimes, when the ice has been cleared off those lines of communication and we're walking and talking closely to God, we get these rare moments where we get to feel a fraction of the joy, happiness, and peace I imagine we'll feel someday in heaven.

So if you've failed, if you keep failing like I did and like I have and like I will continue to do, it's all right. There is victory in defeat, and if you'll ask God to show it to you, He will. Hang in there. I'm going to. We can hold each other up, and with God's help we're going to make it. You're going to make it. I'm going to make it, because if you're still breathing, there's a reason. God still wants you here. If he didn't, you'd be dead.

If I can quote my favorite movie again, I'll end this relapse chapter and leave it in the past, where it belongs, with this quote from the movie *Shawshank Redemption:* "Remember Red, hope is a good thing, maybe the best of things, and no good thing ever dies." So check yourself, and if you're not dead yet, then you must be a "good thing." I must be a good thing because I'm not either!

CHAPTER 27

GOODBYE
MR. HYDE

So what's the take-away from this book? I guess it just boils down to one question: Do you want to be someone different than you are today, someone better than you have been? Do you want to identify the worst parts of your character and have God remove them so you can be happy, joyous, and free? If you don't, then you just wasted $14.95 and several hours reading this book. If you do, then you have a choice. You can keep doing the same things you've been doing and continue getting the same disappointing results, or you can change what you've been doing by identifying exactly who your Mr. Hyde is. You can begin the process of exterminating that undesirable part of your being and work on bringing back to life the person who God intended you to be. Continuing to operate your life just like you've always operated it and expecting to get better results is the definition of insanity. Status quo behavior nourishes and strengthens your Mr. Hyde. We said we didn't want that in the first chapter of this book. I wanted something different, you wanted something different. We don't want to look back on our lives with regret knowing that we didn't fulfill our God-given potential and purpose. So I'm asking you to be different, God is asking you to be different, but you can't reach your full potential or achieve the purpose God has outlined for your life without a complete paradigm shift. God says in Matthew 16:25, "Whoever has a desire to keep his life safe will have it taken from him, and whosoever loses his life to Christ shall find it." If your life's a mess, your past mistakes haunt you, your spiritual life sucks, and you have no idea why God put you here on this earth, then you need to throw away everything you ever knew about how to live life and start over. It's never too late to start over, and it's never too late to turn around if you're going the wrong direction. If you feel that way, then join the club, you're normal. If you don't feel as if you have a connection with God and your communication efforts to heaven are broken, you're not alone. If you are always restless, irritable, and discontented, then take a number, because there are a bunch of us in line in front of you. The point is, we don't have to live like that any longer. Who would want to live that kind of life anyway? That's the life you want to lose, the Mr. Hyde you want to kill. Give the old you to Jesus, and take the new life He offers each and every one of us.

The only life that has genuine value is one that is directed by God anyway, but many of us don't know how to ask God for direction. Many of us can't hear or comprehend the messages God wants to share with us. Our lines of communication are blocked. They're blocked by our self-will, our yearnings for self-sufficiency, and our inability to humble ourselves to God and to others. The reception between us and our Maker has been drowned out with a pride that keeps us from asking God for help, an ego that says, "We can handle this on our own," and an unwillingness to admit that we are not in control and our lives and spirits are unmanageable. We refuse to give up control and trust God. Our faith is weak. We are tormented by our pasts and afraid of looking in the mirror to see the kind of people we have become. We find ourselves too ashamed to ask a loved one for help, too resentful to extend that olive branch of forgiveness, regardless of whether it is returned or not. We're too busy in this overstimulated world to focus on staying close to God, and we're too lazy to clean up life's little messes as we go. Most of all though, we're too selfish to sacrifice our own lives, our treasures, and our precious time to help others.

I'm guilty too. The world tells us to be strong and never show our weaknesses or vulnerability. The world rewards us for being independent and self-sufficient. We're told that "nice guys finish last" and that attitude and self-confidence are 80 percent of the secret to success. We're taught that if we give up control and are accommodating and kind, we'll just get "run over." Weaklings ask for help, and victory comes from getting the other party to capitulate and apologize first. A rolling stone gathers no moss in this world, and if you slow down, others will pass you by. The world tells us we have to step on a few people to get to the top; collateral damage is the price of success, and everyone knows the giver gets taken advantage of and is considered the "sucker" in the world we live in.

We don't seem to have a problem hearing the world just fine. The world's communication to us is crystal clear, no transmission problems there! Is the world making you happy? Are you happy with your place in it? Are you feeling peace and personal freedom? I wasn't, and I would argue you're probably not totally either. We are communicating with the wrong life-force. I had it backwards, we have it backwards. We need to learn to block out what the world is trying to tell us and at the same time learn to unblock what is keeping each of us from having an open line of communication and relationship with Christ.

So if you want to be different, and you know you do, then make the effort to change, to be different. Call on Jesus and He will transform your life. Pastor Craig Groeschel says, "We are not who others say we are, we are not even who we think we are, we are who God says we are, and God says that we are over-comers!" You are an over-comer, and if God can turn my disastrous life around, He can certainly turn yours around as well. But you have to be willing to get yourself into a position where Christ can make that happen.

You must start by realizing that you are powerless, and your life is unmanageable. You have to understand and believe that God can and will change you if you allow Him to. You have to let go of your life, be willing to lose your old life, give up trying to control the world around you, and turn it over to Christ. You have to dig deep into your past and identify all of your defects of character in order to generate an accurate self-appraisal of who you used to be and of how you've shown up in life and in relationships. You need to gain an understanding of who your Mr. Hyde is and of the person that you no longer want to be, and replace it with the unmistakable perception of exactly who you can become. You have to be willing to share your past with another, desperately want to be different, and then ask God to remove all of the things that have been blocking you from having a relationship with Him and the rest of His children. You must work toward cleaning up those past mistakes in life and the people you've hurt along the way in order to realize a freedom you never knew existed. You have to be willing to "keep your office clean and organized" as you go through life and not let the small daily messes we make grow and fester, only to become larger problems that render us ineffective and sick again. Take a page from Grandma Dorothy's playbook and stay as close to God as you can, making Him a part of your every waking moment. Most importantly, you've got to continually keep your thoughts on how you can help others. I'm not talking about volunteering at John 3:16 missions five days a week or moving to Africa to help starving children (although if God is calling you to do those things, you might consider it). I'm talking about helping others by using your life's experiences combined with your God-given talents to fulfill the purpose that God has outlined for your life. What did God give you? What paths has He led you down in life? Think about it. How would God draft your resume?

I have a close friend named Angela who's been in the consumer banking business for years. She understand budgets, loans, credit card debt, mortgages, car and student loans, bank fees, debt ratios, retirement plans, and basic investing in low-risk bonds and mutual funds. She sees people every day who are buried in debt and making decisions that continue to compound their problems instead of their savings accounts. She's watched good people lose their houses, their cars, and oftentimes their families by poorly managing their financial lives. God has given her those experiences in life, and He wants her to use those experiences to help others. At the same time, God created Angela with a compassionate heart, a gentle way about her, and with a gift for winning trust from others. God made her empathic and non-threatening, and without even trying she can disarm your defensiveness and open you up to a place where you're begging her for guidance. People listen to her and value her opinion when it comes to finances, and with her experience and personality, God has allowed her to help so many people with their financial lives. That's her purpose!

I know another woman who was raped many years ago. It had to have been an awful experience, and I can only imagine what a difficult obstacle that would be to overcome, but because of it, she can relate to others who have been victims of sexual abuse. God gave her a forgiving heart and showed her how to move past that hurt and live a happy and contented life. From that experience and her ability to open up her past to other scared and ashamed victims, she is fulfilling a purpose God has outlined for her life and changing lives by helping others. Maybe that's why she's so happy and content.

Then there's the guy I met at the gym several months ago who's been asked by God to help ex-cons put their lives back together after getting out of prison. He spent nine years in jail himself, knows how tough it was to assimilate back into society, but with God's help he overcame and is now a successful and productive part of our community. God gave him those experiences so he could relate to others in the same situation. God also made him a strong and firm individual who knows how to administer "tough love," which is exactly what many of these ex-cons need. His life is complete, and his joy comes from seeing once hopeless men begin new and rewarding lives.

I couldn't do any of those things. Although I do have experience in the financial world, God didn't give me a personality filled with patience and empathy. My response to someone in a financial mess would be, "You dummy, why would you buy a $50,000 truck when you're three months behind on your rent payment and in hock to the payday loan store at 90 percent interest?" God most likely didn't equip me to help those people. I may be a forgiving and open person, but I have no idea what a woman goes through after a rape, or what someone has suffered with through sexual abuse, so God is not asking me to help those women. I've never been to prison (OK, I have, but only for a night) and had to come out with nothing—no money, no family, no job prospects, and no hope. God did not give me the talent of being able to exhibit "tough love" either. So that's not my calling, and I'd be wasting my experiences and talents, not to mention probably hurting the people I was trying to assist, more than helping them.

I'm an alcoholic who's roared through a lot of innocent lives, done a lot of damage, and lost everything. God pulled me through that one, and I can intimately relate to others going through the same troubles. God gave me a solution and the personal skills to be able to communicate how others can overcome the same disease or any other addiction for that matter. That's my purpose. I've gone through a divorce, I've been unemployed for a long period of time, and I've lost relationships with my children. I'm qualified to help hurting people in those same situations and in many others.

Helping others, however, is not always easy. In fact, it rarely is. When we do take those risks, lose our fear, and decide to trust what God has asked us to do, we will often find ourselves uncomfortably inconvenienced, out a lot of time and sometimes a lot of money. I wouldn't trade away any of those frustrations today, because win, lose, or draw, I get to experience great joy in being able to serve God in the way He has chosen to use me.

In Matthew, chapter 25, verse 18, we hear the story about a master who calls in his three servants and entrusts them with his possessions before he leaves on a long voyage. To one he gives five talents, the next two talents, and the third servant, one talent. When he returns, the servant he had given five talents to has invested them and earned an additional five. The servant with two talents doubled what he was given as well, but the servant who was given one was afraid and buried the talent while his master was away. The master praises the first two servants saying, "Well done my good and faithful servants." They are rewarded, and He asks them to come and share in their master's joy! They earn happiness. The master condemns the third servant saying, "You wicked and lazy servant. [Ouch!] Take this useless servant and throw him out into the darkness where there will be wailing and grinding of teeth!" He earned unhappiness! What about you? What talents (life experiences and personality characteristics) has God given you? Are you burying them in the ground (and living in darkness filled with wailing and grinding of teeth) or using them for the benefit of your master (God) and earning yourself the joy God is promising you?

Take what you see as worthless in your life and make it valuable. God can take your weaknesses and make them your strengths. He can convert your pain into victory. Nothing is wasted; everything that has happened in your life can be used and needs to be used for the glory of God. Where is the worthlessness in your life? Where is the pain that is waiting to be transformed into triumph? Maybe you were abused as a child. Maybe you've lost a child, committed a heinous crime, or have struggled with depression. Maybe you've got a debilitating addiction, like me, or you're sick with loneliness and can show other lonely people that with Christ they will never have to be alone again. Maybe you've struggled with the weight of carrying around heavy secrets, and you've learned by exposing those secrets that they can no longer hurt you and instead can set you free. Maybe you're hopelessly single, have an eating disorder, are financially destroyed, or burdened caring for a terminally sick parent. Maybe your life hasn't turned out like you had hoped it would. Maybe it turned out exactly like God wanted it to and you just don't know it. Maybe His plan for your life was different than your plan. Maybe you should look at what God is trying to tell you! You can let all of these things destroy you, or you can use them to your advantage and turn trash into treasure with God's help. We can't change the past. We can't change who we've been, but we can learn from it. We can decide to be different people and to not repeat our mistakes. Even if we do, we have the power of choice to clean them up, use them to help others, and continually move forward. We can do that! You can do that!

My hope, my prayer is that somewhere in this book God has allowed me to touch a nerve, melt a heart, incite a passion, and generate a revelation in you. I want so much for you to have what was so freely given to me, and I am praying that God uses this book to draw you closer to Him so that He can begin to use you for His purpose like He is beginning to use me. I want you to feel some of the joy, the happiness, and the freedom that I feel today and that has escaped me for so many years. I want you to know the kind of Jesus that I know today, a Jesus that takes away my fears and my worries. A Jesus that shows me how to live this life on Earth in harmony with the rest of His children and at the same time is preparing me for the next life with Him. I pray that God fills you with a trust in Him and gives you a patience to wait while He works the miracle in your life, like he did in mine. I had to wait ten years, and I wish I could say I was trusting and patient during that whole period, but I wasn't. I wanted healing and I wanted it immediately, but that wasn't God's plan. My impatience, at times, made things worse, and most likely prolonged God's plan. I stepped in, far too often, tired of waiting, and exerted my own will and suffered the consequences. So if you can't see the light at the end of your tunnel of darkness, if it feels like the dawn will never arrive, pray for patience and trust your God. He will always come through.

I want to close this book with a journal entry of mine that I came across the other day. I had just been released from the Burning Tree long-term treatment facility and was spending a couple of months with my parents in Colorado before I planned to move back to Tulsa to begin my life again. This is what I wrote:

I woke up very early this morning and thought to myself, "I think I'll grab a cup of coffee, go outside and watch the sun rise above the Colorado Mountains." The cool morning air and rush of a nearby stream provided me with an overwhelming sense of serenity and peace.

As I waited for the dawning, a thought, a realization fills my mind with a vision of faith and promise. I realized that I had a complete, absolute, and certain faith that the sun would rise perfectly and majestically over the mountain silhouette before me, just like it does every morning. It wasn't the least bit difficult to have faith it would undoubtedly come true and that God would be giving me a brand new day in just a few short moments. A perfect, sinless, and pure snapshot of time would emerge and have all its glory before my humanness, and that of the world would begin to tarnish and doubt its promise.

"Is God not bigger than the sunrise?" I thought to myself. "Why isn't my faith in Him as certain as it is in my faith that the sun will surely rise this perfect morning, warm the earth, give life to the planet, and propel all of God's creation through another day?"

As I waited, I began to see signs that my faith in the sun's ascension were beginning to prove out, the horizon began to glow, the birds began to awaken and sing. What I was certain of was beginning to occur this beautiful morning. I had no doubts. Then out of nowhere, my impatience began to creep in. "What is taking so long? Would the sun hurry up and rise so I can go about my day!"

I considered giving up on it, heading back inside for a shower, and the thoughts of what was ahead that day began to crowd my mind. I began to get up, but stopped and was frozen by an insight that although the pre-dawn hour had been wonderful, if I left now, I'd miss out on what could be the greatest blessing of the day. I'd take and be satisfied with the good of what I'd experienced so far this morning, but would miss out on the greatness that God had in store for me today, just because I was impatient and allowed the world and my own "chatterbox" with all their demands guide me.

I began to wonder, how often do I do the same thing in life? Knowing, having faith that God has something perfect in store for me, like the sunrise, but I'm too impatient to wait for it and decide to take "good enough" off the table and forfeit "great."

There is always great darkness before the dawn in life, and I can choose to accept the dimly lit haze of the morning as "good enough" in this life or I can trust God, wait in patience, and receive the sunlight of the Spirit and the gift that God's perfect plan has waiting for me.

May God unfold the perfect plan He has for your life and give you the patience to wait for it.